SELF-CARE

A Theology of Personal Empowerment and Spiritual Healing

A BridgePoint Book

BridgePoint,
the academic
imprint of
Victor Books, is
your connection
for the best in
serious reading
that integrates
the passion of
the heart with
the scholarship
of the mind.

SELF-CARE

*A Theology of Personal Empowerment
and Spiritual Healing*

RAY S. ANDERSON

A
BRIDGEPOINT
BOOK

Copyediting: Robert N. Hosack
Cover Design: Joe DeLeon

Library of Congress Cataloging-in-Publication Data

Anderson, Ray Sherman.
   Self-care: a theology of personal empowerment and spiritual healing / by Ray S. Anderson.
      p.   cm.
   Includes bibliographical references.
   ISBN 1-56476-411-7
   1. Self-esteem—Religious aspects—Christianity. 2. Self-acceptance—Religious aspects—Christianity. 3. Spiritual healing.
   I. Title
   BV4647.S43A53   1995
   233'.5—dc20   94-36738
                                           CIP

BridgePoint is the academic imprint of Victor Books.

© 1995 by Victor Books/SP Publications, Inc.
All rights reserved. Printed in the United States of America.

1 2 3 4 5 6 7 8 9 10 Printing/Year 99 98 97 96 95

CONTENTS

❧

❧

INTRODUCTION

In a "Peanuts" comic strip created by Charles Schulz, Lucy looks critically at a drawing made by Charlie Brown. It is of a boy with his hands behind his back. "You drew this boy with his hands behind his back because you yourself are shy and immature," intones Lucy with devastating directness. "No," replies Charlie, "I drew him with his hands behind his back because I myself can't draw hands."

Charlie is practicing self-care. He acknowledges his limitations as an artist, but deflects the shaming attack on his person with deft and disarming logic. Actually, it seldom works that way in real life. We too often *feel* like we should be hiding some part of ourselves, and if someone points it out we all too quickly are ready to agree. Negative self-esteem, I will argue in this book, is a form of emotional self-abuse. When the core of the self is vulnerable to attack, we are often our own worst enemy.

Self-Care is not just another self-help book. This is a book about the self, first of all, and then how that self, endowed by God with a divine image, can experience self-worth, emotional health, and a strong and vital faith in the face of life's inevitable and irrational pain and suffering.

Self-care is not an individual project of self-help. Rather, it is care for the self as created in the image of God and valued by God for its own intrinsic worth. This care begins with the intentions and aspirations of our original caregivers, parents, and family members who undertake responsibility for the development of the self through personal and social interactions.

Sooner or later, each of us assumes the responsibility for our own self-care, which entails, among other things, making wise choices with regard to the persons with whom we live and to whom we look for support, love, and community.

Life is not user-friendly, to use a phrase current among those of us who are struggling to master the mysteries of computer technology. When we have finally learned to hit a fastball, to change the metaphor, life throws us a curve. When we have been "brushed back" a few times, and even hit in the head, it is no wonder that we flinch every time we think of getting in the batter's box.

Far too many of us struggle with negative self-esteem and deep wounds to the self which fester and erupt at the most inappropriate moments. I am convinced that this is as much a problem of an inadequate concept of the self as it is with so-called dysfunctional and distorted patterns of behavior.

The '80s might well have been called the decade of victim rights. Those who suffered from sexual harassment; emotional, physical, and sexual abuse; and from dysfunctional family relationships were encouraged to stand up for their rights and seek justice, if not also retribution. The "victim mentality," however, is not a transforming one. While persons who suffered were encouraged to "take care of themselves," they often were not provided models and means for empowerment and transformation. The removal of pain is not an end in itself. Nor does acknowledgment of violation and deprivation bring a deep sense of fulfillment without the restoration of positive self-esteem. Self-care, as I propose in this book, goes beyond recovery from abuse and dysfunction. It is the realization of God's gift of personal-empowerment and spiritual healing.

Christian psychologist Larry Crabb suggests that real change must take place from "the inside out." "More often than not," he suggests, "psychological efforts do not resolve the deepest issues, which are spiritual. . . . Dealing with our insides can be frustrating. Disciplined Christian living fails to resolve all the problems in our soul."[1] I agree. This is why I suggest that personal empowerment comes through a kind of spiritual healing that restores the self to its God-given capacity for faith, hope, and love in the context of human relationships. Offering assurance of pardon for sin without restoration of the self is religious malpractice. Spiritual healing, through personal empowerment as a work of God's grace at the deepest core of the self, restores in us what sin has destroyed and heals our relationship to God as well as others.

I write as a theologian and pastoral counselor. My own contribution is an attempt to provide a biblical and theological perspective on the nature of the self as a foundation for therapists, pastors, and all persons who seek to appropriate and apply spiritual healing in the midst of life's conflicts and contradictions. My approach is grounded in the Judeo-Christian tradition of humans created in the image and likeness of God.

The first few chapters of this book lay the foundation for understanding the nature of the human self as a many-faceted system of perceptions, feelings, and self-evaluation, all grounded in a network of social relations. Understanding the self as social provides the basis for understanding why dysfunctions in social relationships often have such a destructive and crippling effect upon the self. At the same time, this perspective on the self shows the importance of effective re-socializing experiences in the healing process. The lack of positive self-esteem is a strong contributor to both abusive relationships and the inability to recover.

Inevitably, for those with strong religious convictions, the experience of suffering, the pervading presence of evil, and the devastating and tragic losses in life produce a crisis of faith. These are ultimately theological issues, and I have attempted to deal with them, as I noted, from the perspective of *both* a theologian and a pastoral counselor. As a result, this is more of a textbook for further study and reflection than a "how-to" manual for those looking for quick solutions to life's most perplexing questions. The most difficult textbook is life itself, one that none of us can avoid reading and interpreting. My hope is that this book will serve as a guide to interpret the text of life given to each of us and lead to more effective and creative living.

For those readers who are not trained in either psychology or theology, I beg their indulgence where technical jargon and scholarly references may seem to intrude. I have attempted to touch the emotional and personal core of human life, both of mine and others, throughout the book. This is what we all share in common, regardless of our expertise in the academic disciplines and professional societies.

RAY S. ANDERSON

PART ONE

Becoming an Empowered Person

1

The Growth of the Self:
A Developmental Process

When I was a child, I spoke like a child, I thought like a child, I reasoned like a child; when I became an adult, I put an end to childish ways (1 Cor. 13:11).

Few of us remember the birth of self-consciousness in the days of our childhood. Surely there were moments of awareness that burst into our minds only to disappear as suddenly as they came. In retrospect, self-reflection can only go so far as memory of the self will take us. Some, like Annie Dillard, are able to capture those moments with stunning clarity.

> *Children ten years old wake up and find themselves here, discover themselves to have been here all along; is this so? They wake like sleepwalkers, in full stride; they wake like people brought back from cardiac arrest or from drowning: in medias res, surrounded by familiar people and objects, equipped with a hundred skills. They know the neighborhood, they can read and write English, they are old hands at the commonplace mysteries, and yet they feel themselves to have just stepped off the boat, just converged with their bodies, just flown down from a trance, to lodge in an eerily familiar life already well under way.*

> *I woke in bits, like all children, piecemeal over the years. I discov-*
> *ered myself and the world, and forgot them, and discovered them again.*
> *I woke at intervals until, by that September when Father went down the*
> *river, the intervals of waking tipped the scales, and I was more often*
> *awake than not. I noticed this process of waking, and predicted with*
> *terrifying logic that one of these years not far away I would be awake*
> *continuously and never slip back, and never be free of myself again.* [1]

Whatever it is, this mysterious capacity for self-consciousness is a gift that we cherish when we are healthy and happy, but
which we sometimes wish we could banish like a tormenting
demon when it only produces self-inflicted wounds. At the core
of self-consciousness lies our self-identity, a curious artifact of
adolescent urges and a kaleidoscope of sensual experiences and
mental images. The psychiatrist in Peter Shaffer's play, *Equus*,
ponders this mystery as he seeks to unravel the twisted threads
of a tormented young boy under his care.

> *A child is born into a world of phenomena all equal in their power to*
> *enslave. It sniffs — it sucks — it strokes its eyes over the whole uncomfort-*
> *able range. Suddenly one strikes. Why? Moments snap together like*
> *magnets, forging a chain of shackles. Why? I can trace them. I can even,*
> *with time, pull them apart again. But why at the start they were ever*
> *magnetized at all — just those particular moments of experience and no*
> *others — I don't know. And nor does anyone else. Yet, if I don't*
> *know — if I can never know that — then what am I doing here? And I*
> *don't mean clinically doing or socially doing — I mean fundamentally!*
> *These questions, these Whys, are fundamental — yet they have no place in*
> *a consulting room.* [2]

The purpose of this book is to explore the innate capacity of
the self for healing and growth through experiences of devastating and crippling failures, losses, and abuses. I will trace out the
developmental and integrative trajectory of the self from the
perspective of humans as bearers of the divine image. A theology
of emotion and self-esteem will be developed as a basis for
understanding how both feeling and thinking are integrated into
the core of the self. With this foundation, the book will then

consider aspects of self-care when the self has experienced abusive relationships, shame, broken promises, and tragic losses in life. The inherent worth of the self as a God-given capacity for health, happiness, and wisdom will be affirmed as a model of self-fulfillment through God's grace and love. First, we must look briefly at the various ways in which the concept of the self has been viewed in recent thought and contemporary psychology.

THE CONCEPT OF THE SELF
IN MODERN THOUGHT

The term "self" is difficult to define and subject to a wide range of interpretation by contemporary philosophers and psychologists. A brief history of the development of the concept will demonstrate the difficulty we have in using the term, as well as pointing to a clarification of the concept from the perspective of a biblical anthropology.[3]

The concept of the self in modern philosophy can be traced back as far as Descartes (1596–1650) who introduced the concept of the self as a spiritual substance. Locke (1632–1704) disputed the concept of Descartes and suggested that the existence of the self depends on consciousness of oneself continuing in the present the same as in the past. This self is the seat of personal identity as distinct from the soul or spiritual substance. Hume (1711–1776) found it impossible to intuit a permanent self by an analysis of consciousness. The self only had subjective validity as an inference drawn from experience, though he admitted that the self was always more than the experience of the self at any one time. Kant (1724–1804) restricted the status of the self to the phenomenal realm of experience. The self is something which persons are called upon to realize and bring into existence through response to duty and freedom. In this conscious ethical action, the true self comes to know itself. Fichte (1762–1814), followed by Hegel (1770–1831), developed an ideal concept of the self through a dialectical process by which an absolute subject emerges which guarantees the unity of the self in the face of the antithetical principles of existence. William James (1842–1910) suggested a psychological approach to the self as the functional center of the person who is known by others as this person, and thus who knows himself or herself through these many "social selves." Psychology, concluded James, has little use for a concept of the self as an entity.

From the philosophical perspective, the question of self-identity as one aspect of the life of persons may be assumed but not precisely located as a spiritual, ethical, or psychological *entity* within persons. While self-consciousness appears to be a common characteristic of personal life, it is not clear what the self is apart from that consciousness or whether, indeed, there is such an entity called the self.

Modern psychology at first tended to reject a concept of the self as inaccessible to empirical study and thus not formalizable in psychological theories. The banishment of the self was most pronounced in the work of Skinner (1953) and the development of behaviorism. At the same time, in the more recent work of the neo-Freudian analytic school of ego psychology represented by the British object relations psychology, there is renewed interest in the self (Guntrip, 1971). This is also true in the so-called third-force psychologies: humanistic psychology, existential psychology, and phenomenology. In these movements the self is considered not only as driven by urges or outside stimuli, but moved by meanings and values.

Social psychologists gave attention to self-conception variables in their theories about interpersonal attraction and conformity behaviors, but with little concern for the concept of a self lying behind the socially formed identity of the person. Theorists and researchers have thus far considered the self almost entirely as a phenomenon of self-consciousness. Rogers (1961) was one of the first clinicians to attempt extensive research on self-conceptions and described the self as an organized configuration of perceptions which are admissible to awareness. While there is continued interest in the phenomenon of the self in both philosophical and psychological literature, there is little agreement as to the existence of a self beyond the variables of self-perception.[4]

The concept of the self has intruded into contemporary issues where legal and moral capacity is assessed with regard to an individual's actions. Moral philosophers and ethicists are generally committed to the concept of a self that has continuity over time as a basis for attributing moral responsibility. Many assert that it is illogical to hold a person morally responsible for an act unless that act is freely performed by the person. In this respect, Kant at least provided a basis for considering the self as a moral agent accountable to the categorical imperative of willing the good as an ethical duty for all persons in all situations. Macmurray argued that selfhood is derivative of personal agency in positive interaction with other persons.[5]

As this is being written, the governor of California has refused to grant clemency to Robert Alton Harris, a convicted murderer sentenced to die in the gas chamber. Expert testimony from psychiatrists and social workers was submitted arguing that Harris was damaged in the womb by the use of alcohol on the part of his mother and that he was severely abused as a child. Consequently, those seeking clemency for him argued that his actions as an adult were not entirely his own and that he should not be executed as punishment for them. In issuing his statement refusing to grant clemency, Governor Wilson said: "As great as is my compassion for Robert Harris the child, I cannot excuse or forgive the choice made by Robert Harris the man. . . ." Wilson went on to cite "clear and chilling evidence of his [Harris'] capacity to think, to conceive a plan, to understand the consequence of his actions, to dissemble and deceive and destroy evidence."[5] Despite the mitigating circumstances of his childhood, the governor considered Harris' act of murder to be the act of an adult self and that he should now pay the penalty for that act.

THE BIBLICAL USE OF THE TERM "SELF"

The Christian faith requires the concept of the self in much the same way as does moral philosophy. God is viewed as the judge of all humankind who holds persons responsible for their actions. The continued identity of the self as originally created by God, fallen into sin, restored through divine forgiveness based on the atonement of Christ, and destined to inherit eternal life through resurrection is essential to Christian faith. Created in the image of God, who is considered to be the quintessence of personal being, humans are held to be inherently personal. Violation of this personal being unique to each individual carries with it severe consequences in the biblical literature (cf. Gen. 9:6; Matt. 18:6). Some Christian theorists adopt a functional view of the self and deny that the self is an internal organ of identity, but only a "theory which persons have about themselves."[7] This concept, however, appears to undercut the biblical emphasis on the self as an essential and not merely functional attribute of personal existence.

The Bible rarely uses the word self in the sense of self-life. In the New Testament, the major instance is the phrase "deny themselves" (Matt. 16:24; Mark 8:34; Luke 9:23). These three passages refer to the same incident in which Jesus reminds His disciples that, like His own devotion to the service of God, they too must be willing to turn away from the kind of self-preoccupation that leads to loss of life. Jesus teaches that to gain life requires investment in daily commitment to God's sovereign will. The "old self" (Rom. 6:6; sometimes called "flesh" by Paul, Rom. 7:18), is devoted to self-interest, while the "new self" (Eph. 4:24; Col. 3:10, sometimes spoken of as being "raised with Christ," cf. Eph. 2:5-6), is devoted to self-fulfillment and realization of one's deepest longings and eternal joy through the indwelling Holy Spirit. In the vocabulary of the New Testament, self can mean negatively the egocentric self-life, but it can also mean positively the person's soul or spirit which is of inestimable value both to God and therefore to oneself. We are to love God with all of our heart, soul, strength, and mind, and "our neighbor as ourselves" (cf. Matt. 22:39).

Without a sense of the value of the self as an intrinsic quality of personal life created by God and sustained by God, even through spiritual and moral defection on our part, there would be no basis for moral responsibility and spiritual freedom to love either God or the neighbor. While sin is viewed as vitiating the entire self so that all moral and religious motives and actions are corrupted (Rom. 3:9-20), each person is still considered responsible for immoral and unlawful actions. While psychological ambivalence is confessed by Paul, he can still claim a love for the law of God in the depths of his "inmost self" (Rom. 7:22). From this we can conclude that the self that God created within each person has been endowed with a capacity to love Him as well as oneself and that sin does not utterly destroy the self. It is not the annihilation of the self that makes it impossible for us to love God and others unless renewed by God's grace. Rather, the failure of the self to overcome the destructive and disabling consequences of sin leads to this inability. The "new self" which is renewed through Jesus Christ in the power of the Holy Spirit is not a replacement for the self, but a renewing of the self that God gave to each person and that God loves in each person.

THE SELF AS IMAGE OF GOD

In the biblical account of the creation of the first humans, we are presented with a story of creation that is told from the perspective of God's liberation of the Hebrew people after 400 years of slavery in Egypt. If we place ourselves in the time of the original writing of the first few chapters of Genesis, we are back in the fifteenth century B.C. with Moses who, having been designated as the leader of these freed slaves, faces an incredible task of molding them into a community and nation. One can assume that the self-identity of these people was seriously damaged through four centuries of slavery. Although they were children of Abraham, Isaac, and Jacob, and heirs of the covenant promise, they had been deprived of self-determination and freedom for many generations.

Men and women both suffer the indignity and shame of being a slave people, though each in their own way. For Moses, the patriarchal tradition grounded in Abraham, Isaac, and Jacob led him to restore male leadership as the building block of the new community of Israel. His immediate problem was that the male members of the community had, for 400 years, been treated as slaves. Their self-identity must have been severely eroded over the centuries as they had no role function in the community outside of their family structure. In a patriarchal tribal society, where the males were the designated carriers of the covenant promise, and the females the bearers of the covenant children, the reduction of the men to slaves would have seriously damaged their sense of dignity and self-worth. Like ants living on an ant hill, these men spent their days in the anonymous file of workers on Pharaoh's public work projects, probably building some of the pyramids.

The role and situation of the women under these same conditions was quite different. While they were restricted to the domestic tasks of caring for children and providing a semblance of family identity, they too would experience the shame which their men felt in having no identity as bearers of God's covenant promise. Nonetheless, the women had a sense of connectedness with the promise as bearers of the children of the covenant.

Assuming this perspective, the sudden liberation of the people from slavery would have exposed the deep wound to the self-identity of the people, with the males suffering their own particular brokenness and shame. If we were to place ourselves alongside Moses and ask him, "What is your immediate problem and how do you intend to solve it?" we might hear something like this:

"I have upwards of 500,000 men who came out of Egypt with a slave mentality and a deep sense of shame due to their isolation and disconnection from each other as a community. I need to instill in them a sense of their own worth and value as bearers of God's promise and to empower their healing from the accumulated shame of being no more than slaves. God has inspired me to tell them of the creation in which God's original intention is that both men and women bear the divine image and likeness equally and discover their true identity as derived out of the being of the other."

Moses, writing under divine inspiration, intended in the Creation story a radical reminder of the inherent dignity and worth of each person by revealing the divine image and likeness as the foundation of personhood. We read the account of the creation of the first humans as intended to heal contemporaries of Moses of the shame and fragmentation of the life of the self which centuries of slavery produced.

The first account in the opening chapter of Genesis grounds

humanity in the mutual differentiation and relation of male and female as expressive of the divine image (1:26-27). With the male and female split apart by the ravages of slavery which penetrated to the very core of their existence, the Hebrew people to whom the story was told needed to find healing, unity, and hope. The mutual empowering which God intended in the original relation was felt as a loss when the identity of the male was obscured. If it is true that the Hebrew women preserved a sense of identity through their connectedness with the children of the covenant, the males needed to discover their own being and connectedness to this "stream of consciousness" embodied by the women and children. The recovery of self-identity as both male and female is thus grounded in the divine image as a mutual and complementary empowering.

But there is more to the story. For the Hebrew male who has suffered loss to his communal identity through the isolation and fragmentation of being an anonymous slave, the pathetic figure of the first man (Adam) as alone and unfulfilled is a powerful reminder of that experience. Thus, in the second Creation account in Genesis 2, Moses depicts the solitary man (Adam) as having no partner to complement his own humanity and constitute true selfhood. "It is not good that the man should be alone," was God's verdict upon this situation (2:18). This is a replica of the male's situation as a slave in Egypt. It is not only one of absolute individuation, but carries the connotation of shame. For when the man attempts to complete what is lacking through relation with the earth and the animals God created, he ends in failure and frustration.

Only when God creates woman by differentiating and completing the man do we find the first expression of self-conscious personhood in the Creation account. "This at last is bone of my bones and flesh of my flesh; this one shall be called Woman, for out of Man this one was taken" (2:23) Up to this point in the narrative, there is not a single instance of self-reference and self-expression on the part of the human. Now, human selfhood is complete and the shame of estrangement is healed. "And the man and his wife were both naked, and were not ashamed" (2:25). If they now have the feeling of being "not ashamed," there must have been some understanding of what shame was. This, I believe, is the purpose of describing first of all, the solitary human in absolute isolation from any other. This is the root of shame: self-consciousness unmediated by the being of another.

Reading the narrative through the lens of the liberated slave people, we see that shame is not a feeling created by the presence of another, but shame is the loss of selfhood when broken off from the other. Shame attacks the very core of the self by isolating it and depriving it of relation. While the feeling of shame may be intensified by the presence of another, the core of shame is the sense of being exposed to the other, not in relation to the other. Because it was the male who experienced the devastating shame of the slave experience in Egypt as one of isolation and brokenness, it was the man who was presented in the Creation account as "alone" and broken off from the other. Rather than this giving some priority to the man as though being created first yields preeminence and status, it is the shame-based male who must first be healed before the divine image can be restored. The concept of shame will be discussed in greater depth later in chapter 7.[9]

Only when human selfhood is understood as a unity of personal being, with the self and others, is the divine image moving toward completion and wholeness. In this way, the psychological as well as the spiritual relevance of the Creation story can be understood as offering insight and hope to contemporary men and women.

THE SELF AS PERSONAL UNITY

1. Soul and body as a unity of experience[10]
The biblical depiction of the life of the self is hardly analytical and precise. The focus is primarily upon the phenomena of life. The descriptions of the self as related to various components of the person tend to locate the self as the composite function of these elements. What is clear is that the Hebrew view of the person is one of a functional unity rather than a hierarchical duality or even trinity.

The human person is both body and soul, embodied soul and besouled body. The person is not just a soul who has a body, but rather exists as a body/soul unity. The body is the soul in its outward form, while the soul is the body in its mode of personal experience. The theologian Karl Barth says: "I cannot express or represent myself without the participation of my body and without its co-responsibility for the manner and genuineness of my expression and manner."[11] While the Greeks viewed the individual as primarily a soul encased within a temporal body, the Hebrews viewed the body and the soul as the reality of the person. The only expression for the soul is its life in the body, and the body has no life except that of the soul.

The soul is the vitality of the body. While the body is necessary for the expression of the soul and is the soul in its outward form, the soul is the life of this particular body. That which affects the life of the body affects the life of the soul; in the same way, without the soul as its source of life, the body has no life of its own.

The life of the soul (nephesh) is its orientation toward God. All creatures have soul, but the human soul is qualitatively different in that it is given directly by God through the divine breath (Gen. 2:7). The human soul (nephesh) is not determined by the general principle of creaturely, natural life, but is life oriented toward God in a special sense.

Nephesh, as the human soul, denotes both the inner and outer life of the person. It denotes not only "animated" life, but also the place where the activity of life takes place. The particular "features" which characterize a person's soul are thus features which are expressed as an embodied soul.

Spirit (ruach) enlivens the soul/body unity. Like soul, spirit does not determine the difference between the human and the nonhuman. Even animals have spirit (ruach) (Ecc. 3:18-21). Yet, the human spirit is unique in its orientation of the body/soul unity toward God and in a special relationship determined by Him. The whole person is spirit since the spirit is the principle and power of life in its orientation toward God. The spirit of a person is the very life of the soul/body unity, and not a third factor in the human personality.[12] The simplest way to depict the relationship of soul, body, and spirit is to say that body represents the physical life of the self while soul represents the nonphysical *life* of that particular body.

The spirit then is the actual life of this body/soul duality. Schematically, it might look something like this. Figure 1.1 shows the interrelation between soul and body as a functional unity. The spirit is the "breath of life" necessary for the life of both soul and body. The spirit is the spirit/life of both body and soul. Without spirit, neither body nor soul has life.

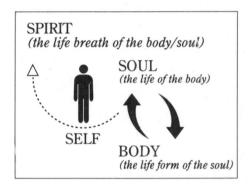

Figure 1.1

The Greek word which translates the Hebrew word for soul is *psyche*, from which we have the English word psychology—the study of the soul, or self. The difficulty of attempting to construct a theory of the self upon these terms, however, becomes apparent when we see that the biblical view of the self is a functional composite of both the physical and nonphysical life of the person with "spirit," or "breath of life," representing the life and orientation of both soul and body. If we explain the self *essentially*, we say that it is a duality of physical and nonphysical life. If we explain the self *functionally*, we say that it appears to have several spheres in which life is experienced and by which the self can be encountered. The soul, the body, and the spirit are spheres of the life of the self. Each of these spheres, however, are expressive of the single life of the self. Here we begin to see the functional unity of the psychological and spiritual spheres of the self as orientations of the life of the self toward the life of others (including God as Spirit) and the life of the self.

2. The heart *(leb)* as the center and unity of the self

Beyond the functional spheres of the self, rooted in the essential duality and unity of the physical and nonphysical expression of life, is what we might call the "agency" of the self. The self not only experiences life but actively creates and responds to life. The biblical term for the self as an agent with moral and spiritual capacity and responsibility is the heart.[13]

The heart is the totality of the soul/body unity as the character and operating power of the self. The heart is the direction of the person's activities and actions. It is the seat of the intellectual and volitional activity of the soul. The will is a function of the heart as an expression of the direction that the self takes in the manifestation of its life in the world and before God. Without this volition, the soul has no expression of its own. Yahweh wants a priest who shall "do according to what is in my heart and in my mind" (1 Sam. 2:35).

When Pharaoh resisted the will of God, his heart is said to have turned against the people (Ex. 14:5), meaning that his will was turned in a different direction than he originally expressed. When God "touches a heart," He determines its will (cf. 1 Sam. 10:26).

An intelligent person is said to have a wise heart (Prov. 2:10), while a foolish person lacks wisdom in the heart (Prov. 14:33). Because the heart is the seat of the intellectual and moral life of the person, it should be guarded with the greatest vigilance. "My child, be attentive to my words; incline your ear to my sayings. Do not let them escape from your sight; keep them within your heart. For they are life to those who find them, and healing to all their flesh. Keep your heart with all vigilance, for from it flow the springs of life" (Prov. 4:20-23).

In the Bible, persons are not seen as centers of self-consciousness apart from their relation to others and as represented in their actions. The concept of the heart, therefore, gathers up all that we mean by emotions, feelings, motives, and intentions as well as intellect, and connects them to one's actions. The self is viewed primarily as an agent that acts and is morally and spiritually responsible for these actions. Self-identity, then, is largely determined by one's relationships and actions.[14] In measuring the validity of another person's words and intentions, even those who claim to be prophets of God, Jesus offered this advice, "A good tree cannot bear bad fruit, nor can a bad tree bear good fruit. . . . You will know them by their fruits" (Matt. 7:18, 20).

THE SELF AS SOCIAL/SPIRITUAL UNITY

1. The openness of the self as personal being

Openness toward others is part of the fundamental nature of the human self. The self as the expression of the life of the body is an orientation toward the other; thus, the human soul, or self, is not a self-contained entity. The "individual" is only self-consciously defined in relation to others. Individualism as a philosophy of the human person is a restriction of the self and can become a distortion of the self.

Earlier I suggested that the devastating effects of the 400 years of slavery in Egypt fragmented the Hebrew people, especially the males who were dissolved into the anonymous work force in Pharaoh's building projects. They were denied opportunity for self-expression as bearers of the Abrahamic covenant promise. The pathetic figure of Adam as the solitary man in Genesis 2 depicts the incompleteness of the individual broken off from all social and human relationships. The core of the self is not grounded in individual self-consciousness but in openness of being toward the other. Only when Adam knows himself as differentiated from Eve and yet intrinsically bound to her as "bone of bone and flesh of flesh" does self-consciousness emerge as self-expression.

The self becomes "singular" in relation with other persons. In other words, our individuality is derived out of relationship. Rather than losing our identity in a relationship, we are meant to discover it and have it affirmed. This is a criterion for healthy relationships. Relationships that promote our own sense of selfhood and empower us to be individuals are not only necessary for us to develop a healthy sense of self-identity and self-worth, but a standard by which relationships are to be evaluated and supported. When a relationship becomes oppressive and destructive to the integrity and dignity of the self, the restoration of the individual self is not accomplished by moving out of relationship into sheer individuality, but through finding healing and self-identity in other relationships.

When the self comes into relation with another, a mutual will is formed which results in a psychic and spiritual unity. The word *nephesh* (soul) rarely occurs in the plural, because souls which are together are generally taken as a unity. When confronting Yahweh the Israelites invariably say, "*our soul* waits for the Lord" (Ps. 33:20). The community becomes a "collective person." The soul is partly complete in itself and partly forms an entirety with others. Thus, wisdom warns against being a companion with fools, for one's very soul is united with them leading to destruction (Prov. 13:20). Starting from its center as an integration of the self as a soul/body unity, the life of the self as an orientation of the spirit seeks its boundaries in others — parents, siblings, friends, and community.

The life of the person is thus fluid to some extent, as these boundaries of the self expand and shrink, going through changing and shifting commitments. At the same time, the center of the self as the *essential* person remains constant, even in its growth and change. This accounts for learned personality and behavioral changes with no loss of continuity of the core self.

The presence of one self to another can be experienced as "resistance," with the other forming an opportunity for relation or for opposition. The active will of the other in a relation is a form of resistance which we experience in others, either in a positive or negative form. This resistance provides an objective basis for our own subjectivity, so that our sense of self is based on a practical and not merely theoretical concept. Another way of saying it is that we cannot experience true subjectivity apart from the encounter and relation with other subjects. John Macmurray puts it as plainly as can be said.

I need you to be myself. This need is for a fully positive personal relation in which, because we trust one another, we can think and feel and act together. Only in such a relation can we really be ourselves. If we quarrel, each of us withdraws from the other into himself, and the trust is replaced by fear. We can no longer be ourselves in relation to one another. We are in conflict, and each of us loses his freedom and must act under constraint. There are two ways in which this situation can be met without actually breaking the relationship — which, we are assuming, is a necessary one. There may be a reconciliation which restores the original confidence; the negative motivation may be overcome and the positive relation reestablished. Or we may agree to cooperate on conditions which impose a restraint upon each of us, and which prevent the outbreak of active hostility. The negative motivation, the fear of the other, will remain, but will be suppressed. This will make possible cooperation for such ends as each of us has an interest in achieving. But we will remain isolated individuals, and the cooperation between us, though it may appear to satisfy our need of one another, will not really satisfy us. For what we really need is to care for one another, and we are only caring for ourselves. We have achieved society, but not community. We have become associates, but not friends.[15]

The resistance of the other in either a negative or positive form, grounds my own self-consciousness in an objective relation to the other person. The consciousness of the self, therefore, is not only an act of cognition; it is the self's reflection grounded in experience of the other. My self-consciousness is not only conscious reflection upon my self, but knowing and experiencing my self in relation with others. My relation to others involves feelings as well as ideas, intentions as well as actions. The demand which the other makes upon me is to "know my heart," not merely enjoy my company.

The achievement of community of persons is grounded in actions which embody intentionality to share a common "soul" or a common history and a common destiny. "The inherent ideal of the personal is a community of persons in which each cares for all the others, and no one cares for himself."[16]

2. The growth of the self as a developmental process

We are now ready to move toward the focal point of this chapter. The nature of the self has been shown to be inclusive of an embodied, personal, and spiritual identity which integrates feelings and perceptions through intentional actions with beneficial results which receive God's approval and blessing. In the biblical terminology, this is to have wisdom. The term "heart" is the biblical equivalent for what I have called the "self." To be a self in this sense, is to experience what the Bible calls the "image and likeness of God."

While the image of God as the total self must be acknowledged as fully present from the beginning of the human person, the *content* of this image is only realized through a development process. Self-identity, then, is acquired as the particular form of the image of God resulting from the growth and development of the self. The psychological literature on the stages of self and identity development is an expanding and varied field of study. Along with Erik Erikson's well-known stages of self-development, are Kohlberg's stages of moral development, Fowler's stages of faith development, Piaget's stages of cognitive development, Kohut's stages of identity formation, and Gilligan's theory of women's developmental stages.[12] It is not my intention to add to or interact with these developmental theories, but to suggest that from a theological perspective the image of God is developmentally related to the growth of the self as embodied, personal, and social being. It is my thesis that the integration of psychological and spiritual aspects of the self can best be seen as part of this developmental trajectory of growth. My focus is on the growth of self-identity based upon the nature of the self as described above.

The growth of the person into a self-identity takes place in a context of social and spiritual interaction, with intentionality of love as the motive force. The integration of the various components of the self into an I-Self reality, is part of the construct of an I-Thou experience. The mental and physical dimensions of the self are correlated through the openness of the self toward a transcending subject (self).

Romney Moseley, in his book, *Becoming a Self — Critical Transformations before God*, suggests that there are two factors which enter into self-development. "First, the self is formed as it interacts with the world. Second, there are stages of relative stability as the self progresses from egocentrism to higher levels of social perspective-taking. In the course of development, the self is liberated from its captivity in the egocentric perceptions of early childhood."[18]

My own formulation of the developmental process is slightly different. Rather than contrasting an egocentric stage with a social stage of self-identity, I see the development of the ego self as continuous with the development of the social self.

The newborn infant certainly possesses an ego self, though largely undeveloped. This ego self is the seat of feelings (emotions) and the core of what will become self-identity. The infant first of all experiences at a subconscious level a social relation with the primary caretaker(s) through which differentiation at the personal and sexual level gradually emerges. Through this process the full range of psychical feelings and responses are developed from their original, limited capacity. The core of the self as spiritual being, which from the beginning has been in place, now is opened up to response to God and to the other. The egocentrism of the self, present from the beginning, is thus developed simultaneously with the self's development of social identity. The process of development is not from egocentric to social perspectival as much as it is from immature self to mature self-identity, both as egocentric and social relating.

I have attempted to depict this in figure 1.2. The dotted line is the process of the growth of the self through each of the spheres, beginning with the social and moving toward the spiritual. The solid line moves from the self through each sphere toward God. This depicts the integration of the self as the self and in relation to the other. The physical and mental aspects of personal life impinge upon each of the spheres and the physical and mental health of each have an effect upon the spheres.

The growth of the self does not "add" stages as it develops, but the dimension of the self in each sphere is enlarged and becomes more functional. The psychical life of the infant, for example, is present from birth, and no doubt before. At the same time, the full range of the psychical range of feelings and experiences is quite limited. Children cry when they experience pain, both physically and mentally, but they do not weep out of the depth of sadness of which an adult is capable. Children experience joy and feelings of happiness, but have not yet developed a

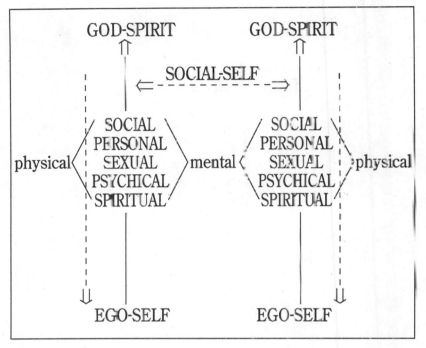

Figure 1.2

depth that is able to integrate pain and loss into that joy.

The developmental model depicted above has a twofold dimension. There is a vertical integration of the self as personal being through each of the spheres with an ego self identity which includes appropriate mental and physical self-reference. This developmental process requires constant adjustment to the ego self as changes occur both inwardly and with reference to the embodied life of the self.

At the same time, there is a developmental process where integration of the ego self with the social self must take place through the changes which are occurring in this dimension of personal experience. From the standpoint of the self, this integrative project and process is a single one provided that it takes place in a relatively healthy and wholistic way. The depiction of the ego self and the social self is schematic and not intended to suggest that the self actually has two centers.

Charles Gerkin suggests that the core of the self can be termed the "soul" in a theological sense incorporating the various psychological terms.

> *To use the designation self is to emphasize the line of experienced*
> *continuity and interpretive capacity which emerges from the self's object*
> *relations. To use the term ego is to emphasize the coming together of a*
> *nexus of forces demanding mediation and compromise. . . . The term*
> *soul is here used as a theological term that points to the self's central*
> *core subject to the ego's conflicting forces and to the ultimate origins of*
> *the self in God. The soul is the gift of God bestowed upon the individual*
> *with the breath of life. It is thus the self, including its ego conflicts, as*
> *seen from an ultimate perspective — the perspective of the self as nur-*
> *tured and sustained in the life of God.*[19]

My own use of the term "self" accords with Gerkin's attempt to speak of a central core of the self as grounded in social differentiation and also includes the ego dynamics subject to psychological assessment and therapeutic attention.

Inadequate integration through the developmental process, however, can lead to a splitting of the ego self from the social self to some degree resulting in some level of dysfunction. In extreme cases, the ego self may also suffer splitting, which may account for the phenomenon of multiple personality disorder.

From the perspective of a theology of the self as grounded in the image of God, this depiction of the self is intended to show both a developmental process as well as an integrative process as a foundation for further consideration of the healing process which needs to take place where disorder and dysfunction has occurred.

When we speak of the self as created in the image of God, we must remember that the biblical view of the self is one of relatedness. Humans were originally created to be persons in relation. The social structure of the self is the essential self, as we shall see in the chapter which follows.

SUMMARY

In summarizing what has been said about the self from the perspective of biblical anthropology, the following conclusions may be drawn:

- The life of the self is embodied life, with the physical

sphere as much a part of the self as the nonphysical (mental) sphere.

- The life of the self is personal life, experienced as openness of spirit to the life of others in a bond of mutual trust and support.
- The life of the self is spiritual life, oriented to God as Spirit and endowed with a value and destiny which has intrinsic worth to God and therefore to all others.
- The image of God represents the totality of the self, as embodied, personal, and spiritual life.
- The identity of the self is not so much determined by self-reflection as by intentions and actions through which the self is related to others.
- The development of the self is an integrative process through which the ego self and the social self maintain a differentiated and yet unified center of self-identity.

PRAXIS

"I do not come to church to hear about people's emotional and psychological problems," Norm told his pastor following the service. "I expect to learn more about the truths of God and the Bible in our sermons. After all, salvation has to do with our spiritual nature, and if we were truly spiritually minded we wouldn't have all those other problems." The pastor gently suggested that spirituality had to do with the whole person, but could tell that this only reinforced Norm's concerns. It was only six months later that Norm called from a pay telephone and said, "Pastor, I have just been arrested for indecent exposure, and I need your help."

- In what way does Norm's view of spirituality relate to the incident which caused his arrest?
- Referring to the diagram of the self used in this chapter, explain the relationship between the spiritual dimension of the self and issues related to sexual identity and behavior.
- What biblical basis can be established for the assertion that our spiritual life must be integrated with our sexual, personal, and social identity?
- What strategy should the pastor now take in providing pastoral care and assistance for Norm?

2

The Social Self:
A Relational Model

In the image of God he created them; male and female he created them. . . . and the two will become one flesh (Gen. 1:27; Eph. 5:31).

The initial utterance of Adam upon encountering Eve, so the Bible tells us, was, "This at last is bone of my bones and flesh of my flesh" (Gen. 2:23). Should we not be surprised at this? Were we not expecting something a bit more relational, if not romantic? Granted, Adam has a tender place in his side and a piece of rib cartilage missing. The prompting of physical sensation has a way of prioritizing our feelings!

But we may have missed the clue to the extraordinary discovery which lies behind the utterance. For the first time, Adam utters the personal pronoun, "my." "This" creature, as yet unnamed, is of "my bones and my flesh," Adam cries out. We forgive him this initial preoccupation with his own self-recognition and self-perception. Up to this time he has not only been "alone," but without a perception of his own self as differentiated and yet united to another. The dawning of self-perception appears in the encounter with another self. This is a healing encounter, for it is one which creates wholeness out of what had only been a part. We must not pass too quickly over this momentous moment. The emergence of the self does not occur by transcending the "flesh and bones" of our physical existence, but through the encounter by the self of the other through one's own embodied existence.

SELF-CONSCIOUSNESS AND THE SOCIAL SELF

In chapter 1 I described the self as a differentiated unity of soul and body with spirit constituting the life breath of the body/soul unity.

Schematically, the differentiation is represented by the interplay between the physical and nonphysical elements of the self, each having its own contribution to the life of the self, but both alike, essential to the life of the self in the form of spirit. This depiction of the self, however, does not constitute the true differentiation of the self for, apart from the encounter and relation with another self, the distinction between soul and body suffers a "splitting" when the self turns back upon itself.

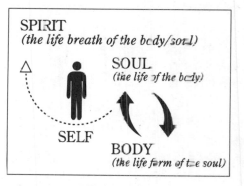

Figure 2.1

Self-consciousness, unmediated by the self of another, tends to divide rather than unite the self. The physical sphere of the self's existence acquires an impersonal nature as the spirit and soul merge in the moment of self-consciousness. The result is a form of existential anxiety rooted in the opposition of the physical sphere of the self to the life of the soul, with spirit hovering ambivalently over this abyss. When self-consciousness is intensified it leads to what Kierkegaard called dread (angst), whose only refuge is in a movement of self-transcendence through the dread toward an infinite Spirit (God).[1]

Ernest Becker, in his Pulitzer Prize-winning book *The Denial of Death*, drew heavily upon Kierkegaard's existential view of the self in arguing that this dualism within the self between the physical and nonphysical is the root of anxiety as the core of most mental and emotional illness. The unity of the self can then only be gained by the act of faith as self-transcendence toward a cosmic "god" entity. One's own mortality, then, can finally be accepted and not denied or repressed through this existential movement of self-transcendence.[2]

Kierkegaard's psychological analysis of the self as posited in a dialectic of self-consciousness, followed by Becker, falls short of the biblical concept of the self as constituted by differentiation through encounter with another self. The "not good" of Genesis 2 is a judgment against the concept of the self as a solitary existence whose project is to gain self-actualization through an existential decision.

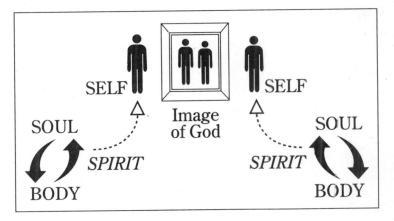

Figure 2.2

A more adequate depiction of the self must include the encounter and interchange between the self and another. In figure 2.2 the differentiation is depicted in the meeting of one self with another constituting a social matrix for the self. The frame at the center of the diagram represents this social matrix. The biblical concept of the image of God is grounded in the differentiation of the self with others. While each person is fully endowed with the image of God, this divine image is experienced in the self's differentiation through encounter with others.

Self-consciousness is mediated through the encounter with other selves rather than the self's reflection in isolation. One can withdraw from the other in self-reflection as a form of self-consciousness. The primary orientation of the self, however, is toward the other as an *act* of self-consciousness and intentionality.

The other person provides the necessary boundary, or resistance, for the self to be differentiated in a relation of mutual trust and acceptance. When we give priority to self-reflection and self-consciousness in abstraction from relation to the other, our movements toward others will be cautious and even mistrustful. "I need you to be myself," says John Macmurray.

> This need is for a fully positive personal relation in which, because we trust one another, we can think and feel and act together. Only in such a relation can we really be ourselves. If we quarrel, each of us withdraws from the other into himself, and the trust is replaced by fear. We can no longer be ourselves in relation to one another. We are in conflict, and each of us loses his freedom and must act under constraint. There are two ways in which this situation can be met without actually breaking the relationship — which, we are assuming, is a necessary one. There may be a reconciliation which restores the original confidence; the negative motivation may be overcome and the positive relation reestablished. Or we may agree to cooperate on conditions which impose a restraint upon each of us, and which prevent the outbreak of active hostility. The negative motivation, the fear of the other, will remain, but will be suppressed. This will make possible cooperation for such ends as each of us has an interest in achieving. But we will remain isolated individuals, and the cooperation between us, though it may appear to satisfy our need of one another, will not really satisfy us. For what we really need is to care for one another, and we are only caring for ourselves. We have achieved society but not community. We have become associates, but not friends. [3]

Martin Buber, the Jewish philosopher most remembered for his classic treatise on the nature of the self as personal and relational, wrote:

> *The You encounters me by grace—it cannot be found by seeking. But that I speak the basic word to it is a deed of my whole being, is my essential deed. . . . The basic word I-You can be spoken only with one's whole being. The concentration and fusion into a whole being can never be accomplished by me, can never be accomplished without me. I require a You to become: being I, I say You.*[4]

The priority of the social relation in the differentiation of the self is a direct implication of the image of God as grounded in co-humanity rather than in individuality. The awakening of the infant to selfhood, and the beginning of the development of the image of God as a possibility and personal history of fulfillment, is linked to the encounter with others. This begins at the earliest point of the infant's life, and the "face" that shines upon the infant in love reflects and mediates the love of God, a point articulated eloquently by Hans Urs von Balthasar.

> *Through the interdependence of the generations, the social element embraces the individual and influences him. . . . God, who inclined toward his new-born creature with infinite personal love, in order to inspire him with it and to awaken the response to it in him, does in the divine supernatural order something similar to a mother. Out of the strength of her own heart she awakens love in her child in true creative activity. . . . The essential thing is that the child, awakened thus to love, and already endowed by another's power of love, awakens also to himself and to his true freedom, which is in fact the freedom of loving transcendence of his narrow individuality. No man reaches the core and ground of his own being, becoming free to himself and to all beings, unless love shines on him.*[5]

Kierkegaard took self-consciousness as the critical point for his analysis of the self and posited a dialectic between embodied and disembodied existence. The self only emerged in relation to an infinite and transcendent Spirit through a decision that he called faith. Kierkegaard regarded anxiety as the fundamental problem to be resolved through faith as a supreme act of the individual, as opposed to either group consciousness or universal ideals. If there was one epitaph to be put on his gravestone, Kierkegaard is reported to have said, let it be *The Individual.* While social relations were considered to be an ethical choice and responsibility, the self is grounded ontologically in its own act of self-conscious "willing to be the self" before God as infinite Spirit [6]

I have shown that this depiction of the self is inadequate to satisfy the biblical account of the self as inherently social, with self-relatedness an ontological construct of the self prior to an existential act of self-reflection. Rather than self-consciousness being the critical point by which the self "becomes the self," I suggest that self-fulfillment is a more accurate indicator of the inherent motivation of the self. When self-fulfillment is viewed as the fundamental drive of the self, frustration to this drive is experienced long before self-consciousness enters to produce anxiety. It is frustration to this need for self-fulfillment, rather than existentia anxiety, which is both the source of personal pain and social disorder.

SELF-FULFILLMENT AND THE SOCIAL SELF

Self-fulfillment is an intrinsic need and a positive good for every person. It is when self-fulfillment becomes a craving for indulging the self that the craziness and the chaos begins. As Paul warned the Roman Christians, when we turn away from our spiritual origin and destiny in God and become obsessed with our created human nature, we become "foolish, faithless, heartless, ruthless" (Rom. 1:31). This kind of self-indulgence leads to the dehumanization of others and the deterioration of our own spiritual existence.

The positive direction of self-fulfillment moves toward the spirit of the other with openness, trust, and a commitment to uphold the humanity and spiritual life of the other. When we find the spirit of another person matching and meeting our own spirit, then we have discovered true fulfillment.

The move toward self-fulfillment, however, meets with resistance when the self encounters the will of the other self. While the social construct of human personhood is essential for there to be authentic selfhood, it is also in this social relation that the self encounters resistance.

The encounter of the self with other selves is experienced as resistance to what I called the "ego self" in the previous chapter. This resistance is encountered early in the infant's development and experienced as a threat to self-gratification and also as a loss of power to fulfill one's own needs and desires.

At the age of twenty months, my grandson Brandon had what I considered to be his fair share of toys. As I observed him playing outside with the neighbor children, there appeared to be a fair ecological balance within that general age group. But as I watched them happily playing, it soon became apparent that happiness is a fragile experience in the toyland of childhood.

It was the yellow car in which his playmate Thomas sat that captured the imagination of Brandon. Walking right up to it, he attempted to push Thomas out and crawl in himself. The consternation in the face of Thomas was only exceeded by the bright-eyed zeal in the eyes of Brandon who, despite being outpointed in months and size, sought to take physical ownership of what had already become his by desire. The result? Two unhappy little boys. One denied access to a toy he truly needed to be happy, the other desperately gripping the steering wheel of a car that was now secured with fear and trembling.

The fun had gone out of the toy. It was now a possession to be defended against the unprovoked terrorism of his little friend. Would he ever again be able to play happily with his little yellow car without a sense of fear that he could lose it in a moment to his closest playmate? And how about Brandon? Will his collection of toys be sufficient now that he has been denied the one thing on which his heart was set?

The fact that a few hours later both boys were happily playing together (the yellow car had been confiscated by parental discretion), reminds us of how quickly happiness can be restored when the attention span is short! And yet, one suspects that a lesson had been learned — someone else always has more toys!

This is the first lesson of childhood unhappiness. Life is not fair. What your heart desires your hands cannot acquire. What is rightfully yours can be lost to another.

When that which is deemed necessary for one's pleasure is denied, either by confiscation or negation, it is not experienced as delayed gratification of pleasure but as a violation of one's right of ownership. When the yellow car is confiscated, both Brandon and Thomas are offended, each in his own way. No compromise can be accepted and no promise of future pleasure will suffice, for the immediate sensation is outrage over a violation of what each feels is rightfully his, not only loss of pleasure.

In some cases, children can be coaxed out of their temper tantrums by an immediate offer of an even greater gratification — a double-dip ice cream cone, for instance. This, however, only compounds the problem. The use of pleasure to alleviate a sense of moral outrage is a "quick fix" of happiness, leaving the underlying unhappiness unhealed and untouched. There is a deeper longing which remains unfulfilled. Later, I will show how this "primitive moral" instinct, when frustrated, can lead to abusive relationships and even to violence.

SELF-FULFILLMENT AS THE GIFT OF LOVE

"When I was a child," the Apostle Paul wrote, "I thought like a child, I reasoned like a child" (1 Cor. 13.11). From our own experience we can gain some insight into what he meant. In a "childish" way of thinking and reasoning, a 'bird in the hand is worth two in a bush," as proverbial wisdom put it. Promise a two-year-old boy a new toy as compensation for giving up his immediate possession of the TV remote control, and you have added nothing to balance the scales of justice in his mind! The child's sense of values is weighted heavily in favor of that which provides immediate gratification.

This is rooted in what I have called "infantile narcissism," the self-love of the child. The intrinsic longing for self-fulfillment comes to expression first as a feeling of gratification when immediate needs are met. The capacity for delayed gratification of these needs for the sake of a more lasting and cherished form of self-fulfillment is one mark of growth and maturity. "When I became an adult," Paul testified, "I put an end to childish ways." As a result, he concluded, "faith, hope, and love abide, these three; and the greatest of these is love" (1 Cor. 13:11, 13).

These three—faith, hope, and love—when realized as deeply held feelings of self-worth and value, serve as positive balances in "keeping accounts" so as not to end up in the deficit column of personal happiness. Despite grievous losses and searing disappointment, Paul had learned to balance his own accounts. He suffered real losses, personal injury, attacks on his character, and most of all, failure to realize his plans to go to Spain to preach the Gospel. He chose to balance these losses with gains which could only be grasped by faith, hope, and love. To be sure, there were occasional tokens and gifts which met immediate needs, but these were received by a heart already satisfied that the balance has been tipped in his favor.

Writing from a Roman prison where he was languishing after being arrested in Jerusalem three years earlier, Paul could say to the Christians in Philippi, "Whatever gains I had, these I have come to regard as loss because of Christ. More than that, I regard everything as loss because of the surpassing value of knowing Christ Jesus my Lord" (Phil. 3:7-8). In responding to their gift of money to meet his physical needs in prison, he added, "I have been paid in full and have more than enough, now that I have received from Epaphroditus the gifts you sent, a fragrant offering, a sacrifice acceptable and pleasing to God" (Phil. 4:18). Their sacrificial gift was only a token of what Paul actually needed to sustain his daily life in terms of material things. His own faith, hope, and love were revived via this tangible gift. Moreover, he added immediately as assurance to them, "And my God will fully satisfy every need of yours according to his riches in glory in Christ Jesus" (Phil. 4:19).

"Whatever gains I had, these I have come to regard as loss because of Christ." We want to know how Paul came to actually feel that the value of faith in Christ balanced the real losses he experienced in his life. How do we give up our childish ways in order to discover the self-fulfillment we are searching for? If there is a way, we must find it.

1. Learning the value of faith

"Faith, hope, and love abide, these three." By Paul's reckoning, these are the values which make it possible for an adult to let go of childish ways. Let us take faith, for example. I have learned that the most powerful drive for humans is the need for self-fulfillment as the expression of a deep longing for life to have meaning and purpose. As children, we experience this longing through gratification and pleasure. This is not wrong, in and of itself. We encourage children to respond at the level of feelings of pleasure and self-gratification. This is the beginning of one's sense of value in life. At this level, there is little tolerance for delayed gratification. Indeed, withholding or denial of pleasure is met with a feeling of panic and outrage, combined with a resistance that borders on supernatural power! Just try to wrest a muscular three-year-old away from the candy dispenser in the store!

The search for self-fulfillment during adolescence and early adulthood is derailed when a belief system is added on rather than being developed with regard to personal values. Religious truths can become indoctrination when commitment is required on the basis of them without recognition of personal values. There is a dichotomy between faith (what one believes) and values (fulfillment of needs) which can go undetected for years and cause an imbalance. This is true, especially when accommodations are made by the religious belief system so as to make belief more satisfying and gratifying to the individuals who become adherents. Faith thus becomes more narcissistic by catering to the felt needs to be successful, prosperous, and affirmed. Without realizing it, one's faith has become "value driven" and the concessions made are all demanded from the side of faith. One can preserve faith if necessary by abandoning the institutional and formal structures of faith in favor of a "personal" belief system that is not subject to judgment and control by others.

This is only one side of the coin. Where the faith system remains rigid and demanding of adherence to its tenets without regard to felt needs, faith may be viewed as dispensable. Faced with this demand, many have chosen to abandon all pretense of faith itself and base their commitments and decisions on the values of self-fulfillment. This is deplored by those who link faith with commitment to absolute moral principles and doctrinal truths that transcend such subjective values. The charge of relativism, subjectivism, and humanism is leveled against those who choose the values of self-fulfillment over objective beliefs.

It is not hard to find texts of Scripture which support the dichotomy of faith and personal values. One has only to remember the biblical injunctions to "deny oneself" (cf. Matt. 16:24), to "hate our own lives" (cf. Luke 14:26), to "put to death the deeds of the body" (Rom. 8:13), "not to please ourselves" (Rom. 15:1), and that "our old self was crucified with him" (Rom. 6:6). Paul admonishes, "Do nothing from selfish ambition or conceit, but in humility regard others as better than yourselves" (Phil. 2:3). Paul can even say, "For I know that nothing good dwells within me, that is, in my flesh" (Rom. 7:18).

There is a strong theological tradition which teaches that the human self is hopelessly sinful and without merit, except that it is transformed and renewed by the grace of God. Even then, echoing Paul, the grace by which one lives is not one's own life, but "Christ who lives in me" (Gal. 2:20). Under the influence of this tradition, self-fulfillment is considered to be rooted in sinful pride, not in authentic human selfhood.

At the same time, it should be noted that in the very same context in which Paul says that "nothing good" dwells within him, he can say, "I delight in the law of God in my inmost self" (Rom. 7:22). And the command of Jesus to love one's neighbor is grounded in the assumed reality of "love of oneself" (cf. Matt. 22:37-40; Lev. 19:18; Rom. 13:9; Gal. 5:14). Here we have an admission of the core value of self-fulfillment expressed as inward "delight" and "love of oneself." Rather than the self being "annihilated" by the grace of God, it is renewed in its capacity to value for itself the gifts of God and affirmed as a fundamental value in human love.

In his perceptive book, *Life and Faith*, William Meissner suggests that a theology of faith and grace must be accompanied by a psychology of faith and grace. "Grace," says Meissner, "not only alters our theological condition, changing us in reference to the supernatural, but it delves into our very nature and makes contact with the depths of our psychic reality."[7] The psychological aspect of faith is the value of faith to the self as a reality of self-fulfillment; this is both a present experience and future promise.

When the Apostle Paul came to the end of his life, he said that he had done all things so as to "gain Christ" (Phil. 3:8). He wrote that he was "straining forward to what lies ahead," and pressing on "toward the goal for the prize of the heavenly call" (Phil. 3:13-14). In a final letter to Timothy he wrote, "I have fought the good fight, I have finished the race, I have kept the faith. From now on there is reserved *for me* the crown of righteousness" (2 Tim. 4:7-8, emphasis mine).

I am now convinced that the abiding power of faith is gained when *what* we believe to be true is received into the self as a gift of God which meets the deepest longing for self-fulfilment. Faith does not create its own value over and against the value of the self. Rather, faith transforms the value of self-fulfillment from its "childish" grasp on what is immediately at hand to the abiding value of what is achieved through the giving over of self to longer range personal goals.

The "gift of faith" is the power of God's grace empowering the self to truly desire what He promised in fulfillment of a personal life venture. The child does not venture life, but grasps life. The child does not yet have goals which lie beyond what can be gained in the moment. Faith is what connects the hunger of the self to the hope of the self that greater fulfillment lies ahead. Without the hunger, there is no fuel to fire up faith. Without the hope, there is no mark on which faith can set its sight. This is why the author of Hebrews could write, "Faith is the assurance of things hoped for, the conviction of things not seen" (Heb. 11:1). The writer goes on to say that faith brought benefits and rewards to those who possessed it. By faith, the ancestors "received approval" (Heb. 11:2). By faith Abel's sacrifice was "more acceptable," and he "received approval" (Heb. 11:4). By faith Abraham "received an inheritance" (Heb. 11:8).

Faith is rooted in the hunger of the self for recognition,

7

relationship of,
purpose, fulfillment
(future, now)

approval, and those values for which the greatest sacrifice is not too much. We learn to have faith when we discover this hunger and dare to hope for fulfillment.

2. Learning the value of hope

Psychologist Mary Vander Goot accurately identifies the source of much unhappiness in contemporary society when she writes: "Today many people are longing for what now seems like an old-fashioned value, a cause, a goal, or an ideal that could be the lodestar of their lives. The emotional evidence of their predicament is their feeling of fragmentation. Their emotions seem to be like echoes without original sounds. They lack a center: they have no direction."[8] There is a hunger which is necessary for there to be faith. We have all felt it, this longing for fulfillment which lies beyond the horizon of our daily life.

The theologian, Emil Brunner, speaks of a "sorrow-of-heart" which experiences the disharmony of existence without a center which lies outside of the self. To attempt to organize the self around its own center, warns Brunner, produces what might be called spiritual or psychological health, but without a center which gives the self a place of hope in God, this "health" is itself a form of madness, or insanity. "To place the central point of existence outside God, who is the true Centre, in the 'I' and the world, is madness; for it cannot be a real centre; the world cannot provide any resting-place for the Self; it only makes it oscillate hither and thither."[9]

We expect theologians to speak of hope and some have even become known for their "Theology of Hope" (e.g., Jürgen Moltmann). But theologians themselves have been known to have despair and to fall into the "sorrow-of-heart" of which Brunner speaks. I am speaking here of hope not only as objectively grounded in God, but as a deeply felt value of the self. I call hope the vision which is seen with the eyes of faith and which is the balance to satisfy the deepest longing of the heart.

While hope must have its center in God, as Brunner suggests, its value must be realized and felt in the heart. When we have discovered the longing which fuels faith and inspires hope, we have learned its value. For a faith which does not arise from this unquenchable hunger for life is not faith, but fantasy There is a cosmic disposal for beliefs which have lost their value and been discarded. Without the value of hope, faith can lose its own value and turn back into despair. We are not born with the value of hope, but it can be learned.

Consider Jesus. In His conversation with the Samaritan woman at the well, He said, "If you knew the gift of God, and who it is that is saying to you, 'Give me a drink,' you would have asked him, and he would have given you living water." The woman protested, "Sir, you have no bucket, and the well is deep. Where do you get that living water?" Jesus responded, "Everyone who drinks of this water will be thirsty again, but those who drink of the water that I give them will never be thirsty. The water that I will give will become in them a spring of water gushing up to eternal life" (John 4:11-14). He thus touched the core of this woman's passion, which hitherto, had been indiscriminately poured out in a series of unfulfilling relationships. What others may have seen as promiscuous sexual passion, Jesus diagnosed as an unfulfilled thirst for a love that gave back as much as it took. She cried out, "Sir, give me this water, so that I may never be thirsty or have to keep coming here to draw water" (John 4:15). Practical she was, though a thirst had been opened up in her which would soon become faith.

In His own life, Jesus revealed a consuming hunger for fulfillment which drove Him ever deeper into His mission, to go to Jerusalem and present Himself as Israel's Messiah. When it became clear that this was leading directly to danger, Jesus cried out: "I have come to bring fire to the earth, and how I wish it were already kindled! I have a baptism with which to be baptized, and what stress I am under until it is completed" (Luke 12:49-50). What we would not give for this single-minded passion of faith!

The author of Hebrews recognized both the hunger and the hope which Jesus had when he summoned us to look to Jesus, "the pioneer and perfecter of our faith, who for the sake of the joy that was set before him endured the cross, disregarding its shame, and has taken his seat at the right hand of the throne of

God" (Heb. 12:2). Jesus learned the value of hope as an anchor for His own soul when exposed to the assaults against Him. Without the hunger for an ultimate joy, He would have chosen a more accessible goal and settled for some form of immediate success. He had plenty of invitations and a score of opportunities to do just that. Without hope as the "lodestar" of His faith, He would have fallen into the shame of despair and been consumed by the very faith that drove Him beyond more attainable goals.

Mark this well. Faith is a dangerous and destructive drive without hope to sustain its passion. Temptation's power seems to be in ratio to the power of faith. One can hardly be tempted if one does not have faith. But having faith as a deeply felt longing for fulfillment in life beyond one's own immediate circumstances means that one can be led astray by the "fool's gold" which glitters but does not abide. False hope can be the destruction of real faith, as many have discovered to their dismay.

The author of Hebrews writes with pastoral concern, so that those who are awakened to the value of faith may have it grounded in a hope that will abide. "We have this hope, a sure and steadfast anchor of the soul, a hope that enters the inner shrine behind the curtain, where Jesus, a forerunner on our behalf, has entered, having become a high priest forever" (Heb. 6:19-20).

If faith has its value lodged in the self's hunger and longing for life's deepest joy, where do we locate hope? For hope to have value it must also be resident in the feeling self, not merely held in the mind as an abstract concept. If hope is to be a "steadfast anchor of the soul," as the writer of Hebrews put it, it must be experienced in the self alongside of faith. For hope to have value it must be more than a statement of what one believes. It must be a resident hope, not an alien one.

To be sure, the *content* of hope lies outside of the self, in God as Brunner has said, and more specifically in Jesus Christ, as the author of Hebrews has testified. It is the content of hope upon which faith finally rests. Without this content, assured by the very reality of God and made manifest through the life, death, and resurrection of Jesus Christ, hope shatters like glass under the impact of the "slings and arrows of outrageous fortune," as Shakespeare so eloquently put it. But this hope is alien to many people because it does not *abide* in the soul as the counterpart of faith. I feel concern for the value of hope as well as for its truthfulness and objective grounding in Jesus Christ

I believe that the answer is to be found in what we call spirit. Faith arises in the passion of the soul as a longing and hunger for meaning and purpose. This is the value of faith, and it is a driving force that is willing to sacrifice most other values in order to fulfill its need. But along with passion in the human soul, is spirit. Spirit is more elusive than passion, for it exists in the self more as a gift than as a ground of being. In the story of the original creation of the human, we are told that God formed the human from the dust of the ground and, "breathed into his nostrils the breath of life" (Gen. 2:7). The Hebrew word for breath is the same as for spirit.

The author of the Book of Ecclesiastes writes, "Just as you do not know how the spirit [breath] comes to the bones in the mother's womb, so you do not know the work of God, who makes everything" (11:5). In the time of death, the author concludes, "the dust returns to the earth as it was and the spirit [breath] to God who gave it" (12:7). The human self has a unique spiritual capacity which is directly related to the spirit of God. It is spirit in the human soul along with feelings that give rise to hope as a value of the self.

When Jesus appeared to His disciples following His resurrection, we are told that He "breathed on them and said to them, 'Receive the Holy Spirit' " (John 20:22). He thus prepared them to have the assurance of their own shared destiny with Him as an indwelling spirit of hope. Peter begins his first epistle by reminding us that God, through His great mercy, "has given us a new birth into a living hope through the resurrection of Jesus Christ from the dead" (1 Peter 1:3). Paul writes that "hope does not disappoint us. because God's love has been poured into our hearts through the Holy Spirit that has been given to us" (Rom. 5:5).

From this we can conclude that hope, which is anchored in Jesus Christ as the one who lives and by whom we can have assurance of eternal life, arises in the human self as His Spirit moves within us. There is a created human spirit which is given by God through the mystery and miracle of birth, but there is also the Spirit of God, or the Spirit of Christ, which is communicated to the self and experienced as the power of spirit within the self.

The Hebrew scholar Abraham Heschel suggests that, while our passions move us (what I have called the value of faith), it is spirit which gives the direction and goal to the self (what I have called hope).

> *Emotion is inseparable from being filled with the spirit, which is above all a state of being moved. Often the spirit releases passion, an excessive discharge of nervous energy, enhanced vitality, increased inner strength, increased motor activity, a drive. While spirit includes passion or emotion, it must not be reduced to either. Spirit implies the sense of sharing a supreme super individual power, will or wisdom. In emotion, we are conscious of its being our emotion; in the state of being filled with spirit, we are conscious of joining, sharing or receiving 'spirit from above' (Isa. 32:15).*
>
> *Passion is a movement; spirit is a goal.* [10]

The value of hope is thus the "filling of spirit" which empowers the self to release the passion of faith toward the goal which hope sets forth. This is why I define hope as the vision which is seen with the eyes of faith and which satisfies the deepest longing of the heart. This is why genuine feeling, as for instance sorrow or joy, is not possible without spirit. "For such feelings arise only out of or in spiritual connections. A good meal does not arouse joy; it merely gives pleasure; if I eat with joy it is because my spirit is turned in a certain direction, to that which is true, or good, or beautiful, which is connected with the act of eating, as indeed the Apostle is able to say: 'whether ye eat or drink, do all to the glory of God.' Through joy pleasure is lifted to a higher plane since its subject is understood in a larger context."[11]

3. Learning the value of love

When faith and hope become disengaged from our childish grasp on our own immediate pleasure and become values which motivate and empower us to pay the highest price for the greatest good, we call that love. And where love abides, as the apostle has written, we have what is greatest (1 Cor. 13).

"We no longer love each other," married couples sometimes confess to me as we begin pastoral counseling. "It is probable that you never did." I quickly respond. I meet their protests with agreement. "Yes, I know that you once felt the irresistible passion, expressed in the language of love with words and touch, and sealed with a solemn vow to love until death's last breath. But love cannot be lost until it is learned. And what feels like the loss of love may actually be the costly separation of self-gratification from self-fulfillment."

Let me explain. The apostle's hymn of love begins with the assertion that "if I have all faith, so as to remove mountains, but do not have love. I am nothing. If I give away all my possessions, and if I hand over my body so that I may boast, but do not have love, I gain nothing" (1 Cor. 13:2-3). The value of love is so great that without it even the passion of faith and the most supreme sacrifice of life comes to nothing. Lest we assume that love is a mysterious force that borders on the divine, Paul describes it in terms of the most difficult and painful context, where our skin and temper rub together in the narrow confines of a human relationship.

"Love is patient; love is kind; love is not envious or boastful or arrogant or rude. It does not insist on its own way; it is not irritable or resentful; it does not rejoice in wrongdoing, but rejoices in the truth. It bears all things, believes all things, hopes all things, endures all things" (1 Cor. 13:4-7).

These are beautiful words, often read at weddings. The value of patience, kindness, and giving way to the other must be learned. The practice of love in this range is off the scale for a child's repertoire of response. The learning of love is not the acquiring of skills, such as can be learned through instruction and repetition. What Paul describes has to do with values, not affections or feelings alone. When I learn the value of patience and kindness, I receive the rarest gift of all, the trust and companionship of another human person. When I learn the value of self-forgetfulness for the sake of enlarging and empowering the life of another, I experience an intimacy and union which deeply touches my own soul to its very core.

There are occasions, however, when the pain is so unbearable and the wound so deep that before the learning can begin there must be healing. But then let the healing begin at least, and let faith and hope be restored so that love can be produced out of empowerment rather than impoverishment.

The value of love can only be measured by what it costs, what we are willing to trade away for the sake of the transparency and vulnerability of looking another person in the eye and saying, "My soul is bound on this earth to our common destiny, I desire above all else to gain my soul. And I give you your freedom from my deepest needs in order to have my greatest desire." The value of love is freedom. Not freedom from the tyranny of the demands of others, but freedom to make others free.

Love probes the depths of the heart and arouses feelings. These feelings lead to emotions which control, to a large extent, our behavior. In the chapter which follows, we will look at the role of emotions in our relation to God as well as others. While feelings do not lie, our emotions can often lead us astray. The Bible has much to say about our emotions, as we will see.

SUMMARY

In this chapter the life of the self was developed as self-conscious existence in relation, formed in the image and likeness of God:

- Self-consciousness arises through authentic encounter and interchange with another person: the self is intrinsically social.

- The self is differentiated from other selves in such a way that personal existence involves a spiritual interchange with God and others: spirituality is grounded in sociality.

- The infantile self possesses the positive value of pleasure, which seeks fulfillment through gratification of the senses: self-gratification is a twisted form of self-fulfillment.

- True self-fulfillment comes through the social interchange of love where the infantile drive toward pleasure is shaped by the perceived benefits to the self resulting from being loved and valued by others: self-love is an intrinsic drive toward self-fulfillment.

● Faith, hope, and love are expressions of the self which lead to self-fulfillment when they are valued by the self: self-fulfillment is finally a greater value to the self than self-gratification.

PRAXIS

When Norm, who had been arrested for indecent exposure, was placed on probation, one of the conditions was that he meet regularly with his pastor for counseling. "What gives you the greatest fulfillment in life?" the pastor asked Norm. "My work and my relation to God," Norm responded quickly. "What about your wife and daughter?" "Well, of course," Norm replied, "they are important to me, but I thought that you meant for me as a person." The pastor paused and then asked, "What gives you the greatest pleasure?" Norm was silent for a long while and then replied, "You don't want to know."

● What significance do you see in the distinction made by Norm between his own personal life and the importance he attaches to his wife and daughter?

● Why was Norm reluctant to talk about what gave him pleasure as compared to what gave him fulfillment?

● From what was said in this chapter about the relation of the pleasure instinct to self-fulfillment, what insight do you gain into Norm's problem?

● The pastor has decided to explore the level of intimacy and communication which Norm has with his parents and his wife, rather than pursue the apparent problem with his sexual life. Why do you think he chose this approach?

3

The Subjective Self:
A Theology of Emotion

How long must I bear pain in my soul, and have sorrow in my heart all day long?" (Ps. 13:2) "I was silent and still; I held my peace to no avail; my distress grew worse, my heart became hot within me. While I mused, the fire burned; then I spoke with my tongue (Ps. 39:2-3).

One looks in vain through the standard textbooks in systematic theology for a discussion of the emotional life of the self. In the literature on the nature of persons, under the heading of theological anthropology, there is virtually no mention of the subjective aspect of humans as image bearers of God. When one turns to the subject of faith, where the role of emotion might well be expected to contribute to an understanding of the experience of salvation, the focus is on the object of faith rather than the subjective response of the believer. Where faith is taken to be a subjective element of human response, it is treated as a "gift," produced by the inward working of the grace of God.

Theologians appear to have an innate disregard for the theological significance of emotion, except to treat it as a relic of the "old self" and to use it in doctrinal disputes with other theologians!

WHY IS EMOTION NEGLECTED
IN THEOLOGICAL LITERATURE?

The lack of a theology of emotion in theological literature may be explained by the view of Thomas Oden. Theology, says Oden, has no interest in feelings and emotional responses. The affective life of the self, with its emotions, is better left to the psychologists.

> *Christian teaching is not primarily focused upon an analysis of human feelings. However important our emotional responses may be to us, they are not essentially or finally the subject matter of Christian theology, which is a logos, a series of reasonings not about one's private feelings but about nothing less than theos as known in the faith of the Christian community. . . . Understandably, our dialogue with this incomparable One powerfully affects our feelings. . . but Christian teaching is less focused on the aftereffects than on the One who elicits and grounds these effects (Calvin, Inst. 1:13; 3:20).*[1]

This dichotomy between faith as an intellectual grasp of *logos,* or the objective Word of God, and the affective elements of faith as experience of self and God, has led to a distortion in our understanding of God as well as to a repression of the subjective life of the self in the faith experience. From the first Christian theologians up to the present time, the doctrine of the impassability of God has been held with various degrees of emphasis as orthodox theology. That God should have passions and be affected by anything outside of His own being, was intolerable to the theologians who wanted to preserve the unchangeable and eternally serene character of God. Only recently have Christian theologians begun to question this doctrine and to argue that God indeed experiences pain and suffering as well as pleasure and joy.[2]

At the same time, this dichotomy forced Christians to repress their feelings for the sake of conformity to the objective "rule of faith" where right thinking took precedence over contrary feelings. If the affective life of the self is to be studied at all, it was assigned to the growing discipline of psychology with the assumption that emotions needed to be understood only to be made conformable to the life of faith, but added nothing to the quality of that life itself. This breach between the disciplines of theology and psychology has its roots in the failure of theology to have a biblical view of God and to construct an integrative model of the human self.[3]

Self-recovery begins with a restoration of the full range of human emotion as an integral part of God's image, in which each person is created. Restoration of that image entails the recovery of the self as God intended it to be and as revealed in His own person.

Wolfhart Pannenberg, a contemporary German theologian, has made an important step in this direction. Contrary to the Stoic tradition in Greek philosophy with its disdain for the emotions, Christian theology must be fully cognizant of the affective life of faith.

> *Christian thinkers could not accept the Stoic condemnation of the affects for the simple reason that Scripture repeatedly speaks of the sorrows and joys of the devout. Referring to Paul, Augustine explained that even the good could experience sadness. The Gospel reports that even the Lord himself became angry, felt joy, wept over Lazarus, "desired" to celebrate the Passover with his disciples, and was troubled in the face of his own death. The question therefore is not so much whether the devout mind can feel anger, but rather why it feels anger; not whether it grows sad, but at what it feels sadness; not whether, but why it is afraid. The impassiveness (apathia) which is part of the Stoic ideal of the sage may be good and desirable in itself (provided it does not degenerate into insensibility of spirit, stupor), but not in this present life which is ensnared in sin. . . . According to Augustine, on our journey to God the affects are the feet that either lead us closer to God or carry us farther from him; but without them we cannot travel the way at all.[4]*

A theology of emotion is first of all a theology of emotional health, not an analysis of emotional sickness. Because theology begins with the revelation of God, a theology of emotion must first make clear the nature of God as one in whose image and likeness we are formed.

THE EMOTION OF GOD

Abraham Heschel, the Old Testament theologian, locates the source of divine feelings in the depths of God's pathos. Therefore, to comprehend God one must have a "depth-theology" which does not relegate the affective life o psychology.

> In order to conceive of God not as an onlooker but as a participant, to conceive of man not as an idea in the mind of God but as a concern, the category of divine pathos is an indispensable implication. To the biblical mind the conception of God as detached and unemotional is totally alien. . . . The essential meaning of pathos is . . . not to be seen in its psychological denotation, as standing for a state of the soul, but in its theological connotation, signifying God as involved in history. . . . It is of extreme importance that theology should endeavor to operate with categories indigenous to the insights of depth-theology instead of borrowing its categories from speculative philosophy or science. . . . To theology, the ultimate theme is that which man is unable to objectify, which he refuses to conceptualize. [5]

In contrast to the Greek concept of the divine, the Hebrew's knowledge of God was experiential and relational. Contrary to the concepts of God held by their contemporaries, their God, Yahweh, was a God who expressed pleasure, responded to the feelings of His people, and demonstrated anger at their disobedience and unfaithfulness. They had no difficulty in ascribing to their God both wrath and love, because they understood that behind both was a passion, a pathos, to which they could appeal in their own distress. Heschel points to this aspect of God when he says:

> God does not reveal himself in an abstract absoluteness, but in a personal and intimate relation to the world. He does not simply command and expect obedience; He is also moved and affected by what happens in the world, and reacts accordingly. Events and human actions arouse in Him joy or sorrow, pleasure or wrath. He is not conceived as judging the world in detachment. He reacts in an intimate and subjective manner, and thus determines the value of events. Quite obviously in the

biblical view, man's deeds may move Him, affect Him, grieve Him or, on the other hand, gladden and please Him. . . . Pathos denotes, not an idea of goodness, but a living care; not an immutable example, but an outgoing challenge, a dynamic relation between God and man; not mere feeling or passive affection, but an act or attitude composed of various spiritual elements; no mere contemplative survey of the world, but a passionate summons. [6]

Rom/2:15
?
No
Rom 5:10

Humans, created in the image of God, relate to each other and to God through pathos (emotion) which is the root of true knowledge and the source of intention and action. The worst condition of the soul <u>was apathy</u>, having no feeling or passion with regard to God and others. The prophets repeatedly attempted to stir up the emotion of the people so that they might respond to the outpouring of God's divine passion, whether expressed as anger or love. The recovery of the self did not result in the denial or abandonment of the emotions, but in the transformation of apathy into passion and of negative emotion into positive. God was viewed as effecting new and healthy emotions in the self.

Far from insisting upon their effacement, the biblical writers frequently regard some emotions or passions as having been inspired, as reflections of a higher power. There is no disparagement of emotion, no celebration of apathy. Pathos, emotional involvement, passionate participation, is a part of religious existence. The utterances of the psalmist are charged with emotion; they are outpourings of emotion. Reading the prophets, we are stirred by their passion and enlivened imagination. Their primary aim is to move the soul, to engage the attention by bold and striking images, and therefore, it is to the imagination and the passions that the prophets speak, rather than aiming at the cold approbation of the mind. [7]

Because love is attributed to God as the essence of divine motivation and action, it is also the core expression of the image of God in human beings. Love is not only an act of volition, says the Swiss neo-orthodox theologian Emil Brunner, but it is an expression of *feeling*. To the Western mind, with its European bent toward the abstract, the contrast between feeling and intellect is an assumed dichotomy in the self. Feelings, and therefore, experience, are discounted as subjective and unreliable. In the biblical perspective, however, feelings are something located at the core of the self in its orientation toward God and the other.

> *Feeling therefore has its rightful place in man's "experience" of his relation with God, because this "experience" is something which man has received, and not something which he has created. To be apprehended by the love of God, means to be smitten in the very centre of one's being, to suffer it, not as pain, but as the supreme joy, as happiness and peace; that is, the Self knows that it is "at home" in God, and that the "I" and the "Self" have become one.*[8]

With the fall into sin, the original unity of feeling with love and knowledge was severed, resulting in the psychological separation of feeling from the spirit. The severance of pleasure from relation to God means that the self is abandoned to the world of the senses.

> *In his feeling he is completely passive; he has no power over his feeling, the disharmony of his existence comes out in his feeling, against his will, while in thought and will, to some extent at least, he is able to go beyond himself. His feeling as a whole is the total balance of his existence which is drawn up and presented to him without his will . . . . This unstilled longing for life, this negative balance of life, is therefore in the Bible everywhere the most important point of contact for the Gospel message. "If any man thirst let him come unto Me and drink" (John 7:37).*[9]

While feelings lie at the core of the self, it is the human spirit which directs these feelings toward God and others. Without the sharing of spirit, the self is left with only sensations and feelings. Pleasure becomes joy when life is shared with another and, particularly, when shared pleasure has a common spiritual bond, as the apostle wrote: "So whether you eat or drink, or whatever you do, do everything for the glory of God" (1 Cor. 10:31).

SOME BIBLICAL CASE STUDIES
OF EMOTION

When we understand that God is experienced as having strong emotions, we should not be surprised to discover that humans, created in the divine image and likeness, are addressed by God at the level of feelings and emotions.

For example, we might look at the incident recorded in Genesis 4, where Abel receives God's approval for his offering while Cain's was rejected. "So Cain was very angry, and his countenance fell. The Lord said to Cain, 'Why are you angry, and why has your countenance fallen? If you do well, will you not be accepted? And if you do not do well, sin is lurking at the door; its desire is for you, but you must master it' " (Gen. 4:5-7). God goes directly to the heart of the matter in addressing Cain's anger. The emotion of anger is not a sin. Cain is given a chance to deal with it by reconsidering what he has done. Sin may overtake him (it "is lurking at the door"), but he can still recover if he deals with the emotion of anger by revealing his deeper feelings of rejection. The reason for his anger—after all, God did ask him for a reason—is clearly to be found in his feelings. The emotion of anger cannot be dealt with until the deeper feelings of rejection and possibly shame, are disclosed. God was probing for these feelings, not blaming him for his actions nor his attitude.

Perhaps we can also see here a distinction between the feelings of rejection which Cain experienced ("his countenance fell"), and the emotion of anger. Anger is more than a feeling, it is an emotion which carries some attribution, usually against someone else, but also against oneself. The immediate shock of having the offering rejected is felt at the core of his being. Anger is the emotional response based on this feeling which causes his disposition and behavior to change. As it turns out, this emotion of anger was not dealt with by Cain and, fueled by other emotions of jealousy and revenge, he soon found opportunity to kill his brother, Abel (4:8).

A second example of the role of emotion can be found in the case of Elijah. Following Elijah's successful contest with the prophets of Baal, he received word that Jezebel, the notorious and powerful wife of King Ahab, was seeking to kill him. "Then he was afraid; he got up and fled for his life, and came to Beer-sheba . . . [and] he left his servant there. But he himself went a day's journey into the wilderness, and came and sat down under a solitary broom tree. He asked that he might die: 'It is enough; now, O Lord, take away my life, for I am no better than my ancestors' " (1 Kings 19:3-4).

The threat from Jezebel produced an immediate feeling of fear, leading to an emotional state of panic, depression, unworthiness, and finally a death wish. Awakened from a deep sleep by an angel, he found food and drink. This happened a second time, and on the basis of that nourishment, he went forty days and nights to Mount Horeb, where he took refuge in a cave. It was then that the Lord appeared to him. "What are you doing here, Elijah?" (19:9) His response was to complain that, despite his zeal for God's cause, everyone else has failed and he alone is left. It was then that he experienced a wind so fierce that it split mountains and rocks, followed by an earthquake, and finally a fire. Then there was silence, within which came the sound of a voice, that of God, who asked him again what he was doing there. When Elijah once more began to complain and to express his despair, God interrupted and gave him a commission and task to perform, undergirded by a promise. As he began his journey back, he encountered Elisha, who became his servant, and eventually his successor (cf. 19:5-20).

What is notable in this account is the role of Elijah's feelings and emotions in the context of his service to God. Despite having experienced the triumph of the contest with the prophets of Baal, Elijah was plunged into an emotional abyss by the threats of Jezebel. His feelings of fear and panic led him into an emotional state of self-pity, bitterness at the failure of others, and even to a desire to die. These are the classic signs of depression. At the same time, he is given physical nourishment by an angel of God and receives a word from God that begins with a question rather than with blame. "What are you doing here, Elijah?" Twice this question is asked (9:9, 13), permitting Elijah to express his emotions, after which there is a strange and eerie

silence, in which he finds self-recovery through God's empowerment and a new mission to perform.

Jonah is another example of one who experiences a similar
process of self-recovery. Jonah, who had earlier fled from the
mission God had sent him on, is rescued from the stomach of
the whale and finally goes to Nineveh to preach God's judgment
upon the city. When the people of the city repented, Jonah
became angry. "He prayed to the Lord and said, 'O Lord! Is not
this what I said while I was still in my own country? That is why
I fled to Tarshish at the beginning; for I knew that you are a
gracious God and merciful, slow to anger, and abounding in
steadfast love, and ready to relent from punishing. And now, O
Lord, please take my life from me for it is better for me to die
than to live.' " And the Lord said, "Is it right for you to be
angry?" (Jonah 4:2-5)

The pattern is clear. With feelings of rejection, humiliation,
and shame, came the emotional state of self-pity, anger, and a
death wish. Jonah went outside of the city and sat in a sulking
manner, demanding by this petulant act, that God go ahead and
destroy the city, thus exonerating Jonah in His own eyes! As a
therapeutic intervention, God caused a bush to grow up to provide him shade from the heat, causing Jonah to have feelings of
happiness (4:6). But then God suddenly destroyed the bush,
with the result that Jonah was once again plunged into his de-
pressive state. "Is it right for you to be angry about the bush?"
asked God. "Yes, angry enough to die," replied Jonah! (4:9) God
then used the bush as a device to access the deeper feelings of
Jonah, behind his anger. "You are concerned about the bush, for
which you did not labor and which you did not grow. . . . And
should I not be concerned about Nineveh, that great city?"
(4:10-11)

Once more we discover the importance of emotion in the
recovery of Jonah's self-identity and in his restoration to functional life. The anger of Jonah was the point of entry for God's
intervention. Yet, the anger was not addressed as something for
which Jonah was to be blamed. Rather, behind the emotion of
anger was the deeper feeling of care for himself. When that care
was projected upon the bush, God used that as a basis for the

inner healing which Jonah experienced, leading (we hope!) to a reframing of that anger and a reentry on Jonah's part to the joy of God over Nineveh's repentance.

Finally, we turn to Jesus Himself, who was never shy about revealing His strong feelings and depth of emotion. Near the end of His life, one incident stands out. As John tells it, Jesus was suddenly overcome emotionally by the impending threat of death, and cried out: "Now my soul is troubled. And what should I say — 'Father, save me from this hour'? No, it is for this reason that I have come to this hour. Father, glorify your name" (John 12:27). The Greek word for soul is *psyche*, from which we derive our word psychology. It is not mental confusion that Jesus is experiencing, but a deep psychological upheaval. The author of Hebrews points to the same emotional state when he says: "In the days of his flesh, Jesus offered up prayers and supplications, with loud cries and tears, to the one who was able to save him from death, and he was heard because of his reverent submission" (Heb. 5:7).

We shall never know nor be able to comprehend the depth of feelings which raged through the soul of Jesus during those last days. What is clear is that He expressed Himself to God through these feelings and thereby seemed to have touched the inner core of that divine pathos of which the ancient Hebrews knew well. Not only that, but the core identity of Jesus was not merely "logos" as a principle of eternal reason, but that of "son." It was the intimate relation of a son to a father that Jesus reached for in His times of greatest stress. It was from Jesus that the disciples first heard that all too intimate and familiar word, "Abba" (father), and could only guess at the depth of feelings that were aroused by that expression (Mark 14:36).

"Be angry but do not sin," counseled the Apostle Paul (Eph. 4:26). "Rejoice in the Lord always; again I will say, Rejoice. . . . Do not worry about anything, but in everything by prayer and supplication with thanksgiving let your requests be made to God. And the peace of God, which surpasses all understanding, will guard your hearts and your minds in Christ Jesus" (Phil. 4:4-7).

Feelings are not only permitted, they are essential to our

personal and spiritual well-being! The core of the self is only approached through the emotions, be they negative or positive. Behind these emotions lie the feelings which expose the self to pain as well as to healing. Self-recovery begins with acknowledgment of those feelings which our emotions make visible.

FEELINGS TOUCH THE CORE OF THE SELF

When called names as children, we learned to respond with the taunt, "Sticks and stones may break my bones, but words can never hurt me!" Wrong! We *felt* the blow of unkind words at the very core of our being and even now carry above or below consciousness, the anger, shame, and humiliation caused by words intended to hurt us.

Feelings are more than sensations produced by external stimuli. Feelings are more than emotions which flood the terrain of the inner self. Feelings *are* the self as a living and experiencing being. Where the self exists feelings are present, even if unrecognized or unexpressed.

Feelings may be the most critical indicators of well-being that we possess. The feelings that we acquire as infants and children form the matrix of the self for our adult years. Feelings need care and nurture as much, if not more, than the physical parts of the self. When our feelings are sick, there is no health in us. Without feelings, we have no contact with the world and no relationship with others.

Feelings are an essential and accurate expression of the self, says Archibald Hart, professor of psychology at Fuller Theological Seminary. While our emotions may be distorted by making incorrect interpretations of what we experience, feelings are connected directly to the self and serve as a guide to restoring the unity and health of the self.[10]

The earliest responses of the infant to the attention of another do not always require touch. Through all of its senses, the infant experiences itself under the stimulation of smells, sounds, and visual images as well as touch. The core of the self in the infant actively responds to the self of another and is experienced as feelings. Infants can actually *feel* the presence of another without being touched. These feelings are not merely sensations which the self has, as though there is an unfeeling self hidden behind the responsive self. The feelings *are* the self, and the capacity to respond to the presence of another is the capacity to feel. This response means growth for the self when the presence is love and care.

When feelings as the response capacity of the self are nurtured and encouraged, touch can also produce the feeling of happiness and pleasure. This is the infantile ' narcissism" I referred to in the first chapter. It is the intrinsic longing of the self for fulfillment which underlies the pleasure-seeking instinct. By reinforcing this sense of pleasure, infants begin to develop a sense of the self and a capacity to interpret the sense experience phenomena of life as either pleasant or unpleasant, a lifelong process.

Who knows what the feelings of pain and pleasure are like for the child too young to remember and tell us? The infant cries when hungry, hurt, and apparently when fearful. At least we associate the tears with the circumstances that seem to cause them. In his book *Persons in Relation*, John Macmurray said that there are body sensations for pain, but not for pleasure.' Feelings of pleasure, he suggested, are not the result of sensation alone, but originate in the capacity of the self to interpret sensation as feelings of pleasure. The same touch that produces a feeling of pleasure, if continued, will soon become uncomfortable and begin to feel painful.

EMOTION INCLUDES FEELINGS WITH COGNITIVE CONTENT

We are now ready to clarify the subtle but important distinction between sensation, feeling, and emotion. Sensations are largely physiological responses to external stimuli with little, if any, cognitive content. My muscles may tighter or my "skin crawl." When I become aware of a sensation it is experienced as a feeling. The subjective element is now involved. This emergence of self-consciousness with regard to a feeling does involve some level of cognition to the degree that it registers with the self as "my feeling." I may feel irritated, apprehensive, or become more attentive to the thing which caused the sensation.

With the entrance of cognition, the feeling tends to become an emotion. I become more aware of the context and experience a response to the sensation, such as anger, fear, or judgment. Emotion involves a higher level of cognition than does feeling, though the two tend to blur, so that we often use the words, feelings, and emotions interchangeably. Warren Shibles associates cognition primarily with emotion and not with feeling.

> *Feelings may be a part of what we mean by emotion. They may precede, coexist with or follow cognition. By feeling is largely meant sensation or bodily state. Cognition can usually affect or alter feeling only slightly. Feeling may depend on interest and attention. One may attend to the back of his neck or how his foot feels.* [12]

From this it is clear that we can only articulate a feeling by expressing it as a thought. When we are unable to bring a feeling into a cognitive form, we are thus unable to communicate it. We are then dependent upon someone else to intuit what the feeling is, but even then, if it is to be actually verified, it must be recognized as having the form of a concept. "We ask for reasons, for emotions, but not for feelings," says Shibles. "Because emotions involve cognitions they can be shared, whereas, feelings cannot be shared. . . . Feelings do not have objects as emotions do."[13]

Suppose someone swings a piece of lumber and strikes me on the back of the head. If I do not see the action, my first response is a sensation of extreme pain. Subjectively, I immediately acknowledge this as a feeling of distress, even though the sensation is almost entirely physiological. As I turn around to discover another person in the room with the board in his hand, I experience anger. Anger is a strong emotion which is directed toward an object. If I assume that this injury was inflicted upon me intentionally, my anger becomes outrage and I add moral indignation to the feeling of pain. As an emotion, anger carries an attribution made by the cognitive function of the mind. The attribution is a judgment made that the injury was inflicted upon me by this person and my anger is directed toward him, not toward the point of the pain.

At this point, the person who struck me offers deep apologies and convinces me that it was an accident. He did not know that I was standing behind him. On being persuaded that the blow was not intentional on his part, and with the moral judgment resolved by his taking responsibility for it and offering to do what is necessary to restore me to health, I alter the original attribution which led to the emotion of anger, and allow the anger to dissipate. I am still left with the feeling of pain, however, and will make some new attribution with regard to the feeling of pain resulting in a different emotion. Now, my emotion may be one of self-pity due to the fact that I have no one to blame but myself for not being more aware of my surroundings! Or, I may adopt a stoical attitude and attribute the accident to one of those things which cannot be prevented. "Accidents happen," I assure the person who struck me, "and I will be okay when the swelling goes down."

In this way, we see that emotions may be caused by an attribution which has no basis in fact. I felt anger as long as I assumed that I was intentionally hit. The emotion of anger can be changed with a new attribution which corresponds more nearly to the reality of the situation. Feelings, however, are deeper levels of the self than emotion and are not so susceptible to "reframing" because they are not primarily the result of a cognitive attribution. This is why feelings are a more accurate indication of the state of the self than emotions. At the same time, feelings must be interpreted to be integrated into the subjective state of the self, even though there will always be some aspect of feeling which defies such transfer to thought. Pannenberg puts it nicely when he says:

> ... every understanding, including every understanding of the self, must move beyond feeling into the medium of thought. ... The fact remains, however, that in its reaching out to the totality of life, feeling anticipates the distinction and correlation effected by the intellect, even though because of its vagueness feeling depends on thinking for definition. Thought, on the other hand, can never exhaustively transfer to its own sphere what is present in feeling. [16]

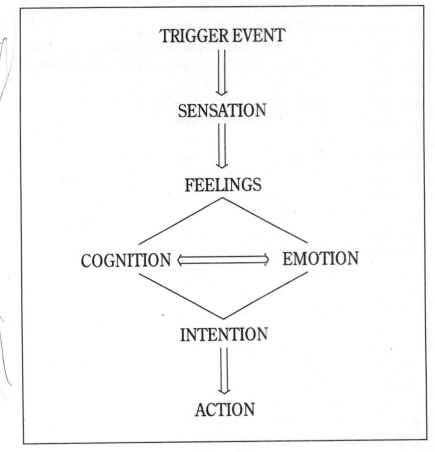

Figure 3.1

The sequence of sensation, feeling, and emotion can be il-
lustrated by a diagram in which the feelings produced by a sensation are captured as an emotion by the act of cognition. This
then leads to an intention and finally an action. If the action
taken results from an intention which is grounded in an emotion
formed by an incorrect or unrealistic cognition, there is liability
for serious error leading to great wrong. In the case of Cain, for
example, as described above, his anger seemed to be directed
against his brother Abel, as though Abel had intentionally cheat-
ed him out of God's approval. Following through with an intention based upon this erroneous emotion, he took the desperate
act of killing his brother. If he could have expressed his real
feelings to God, the emotion of anger could have been trans-

formed into one of sorrow for displeasing God, and then gratitude for being given a second chance. Far from being a deterministic factor of the human personality, emotions are capable of transformation and change. We should never feel that we are the victims of our emotions. Emotion represents the creative possibility of growth and change in the recovery of self.

EMOTION IS CREATIVE

Emotions are flexible and fluid. We can move from an emotional high to a low as quickly as the sun moves behind a cloud or a thought passes through our minds. Even where emotions have become habitual ways of perceiving the self, it is emotion that is most susceptible to change. Warren Shibles agrees and suggests that the key to such change is to understand the relation of cognition to emotion.

> The view that emotions cannot be changed, or can be changed only slightly, is false. It is now known that emotions, to a large extent, involve thought. Therefore, we can change our emotions by changing our thought. We can even learn how to change from being an angry person to hardly ever being angry. We can change our entire personalities in this way. We can eliminate negative emotions (jealousy, anger, envy, etc.) and develop positive emotions such as warmth, love, being happy, enjoying humor, etc.[15]

Emotions are functional and stimulating. Emotion is not a "state of being" outside of our control. Emotional patterns were formed through cognitively conditioned experience and are subject to modification through "re-cognition.' So-called "crimes of passion" are thought to be explained by uncontrollable emotions. But this view of emotion places it outside of the control of the self, and "passion" thus acquires a kind of fatalistic character. Shibles will have none of that.

> The view that "passion" is self-justificatory is unacceptable. It will not do to say one did an irresponsible act "out of passion." Emotion was once called passion. "Passion" derives from the Latin passio meaning:

"suffering, affection, being affected." Pathos derives from the Greek word meaning, "suffering, passion, misfortune." Affection derives from the Latin affectus *meaning "to do something to," and from* affectionem *"a permanent state of feeling." This commits the fallacy of thinking that emotion is passive like a feeling.* [16]

Feelings, of course, being related to sensations, are less amenable to change through cognition. We are not expected to change our feelings by altering our cognitive patterns, but we are able to direct those feelings through the emotions, which are susceptible to cognition.

"Re-cognition" might take the form of shifting from left brain to right brain mode of awareness. Many of our emotional patterns were first formed through awareness prior to the development of language skills. Right brain functions tend to process sensory data through imaging and visualizing. These forms of cognitive awareness stimulate emotions as much or more than logical and verbal cues. In this case, we acquire emotional patterns long before we create cognitive "maps" of our experience through left brain activity.

"Re-cognition" as a way of changing emotional patterns does not only mean forming new mental concepts (left brain), but experiencing new awareness of self and one's environment (others) through creative imaging and visualization techniques (right brain). Prior to much of the left/right brain research, William James suggested forms of consciousness which lie outside of the normal thought process.

Our normal waking consciousness, rational consciousness, as we call it, is but one special type of consciousness, whilst all about it, parted from it by the filmiest [sic] of screens, there lie potential forms of consciousness entirely different. We may go through life without suspecting their existence; but apply the requisite stimulus, and at a touch they are there in all their completeness, definite types of mentality which probably somewhere have their field of application and adaptation. [17]

If cognition is considered to be a function of the entire brain function, then imaging functions may be as useful in working with the emotions as conceptual functions. This would be particularly the case where the formation of the emotion took place through a visual rather than conceptual process. The self's experience through visualization and imagination opens up the emotional life to a creative cognitive function which works along with the conceptual function. This was a very important part of the function of memory and imagination for the Hebrew people, as John Pedersen makes clear.

> New and large experiences make one forget the lesser; they are displaced from the soul and exercise no influence. When the new heavens and the new earth are created, then the Israelites shall no more remember the former, and it shall not rise in their heart (Isa. 65:17; Jer. 3:16). It means that the new order of things shall fill their soul, so that the old no more stirs any emotion in it.[18]

The intentions of the heart, which express the same thing as we mean by the term "will," are connected to the concepts of the mind through the emotions. This is why attempts to change behavior by appealing directly to the mind through concepts usually fails. The creative dimension of the self is not isolated in mental activity, but is a process of cognition which includes emotion as well as intellect. Imagination, for example, as the power of visualizing something new, receives its stimulation through the emotions. John Macmurray reminds us that reason is essentially an affair of emotion.

> It is not that our feelings have a secondary and subordinate capacity for being rational or irrational. It is that reason is primarily an affair of emotion, and that the rationality of thought is the derivative and secondary one. For if reason is the capacity to act in terms of the nature of the object, it is emotion which stands directly behind activity determining its substance and direction, while thought is related to action indirectly and through emotion, determining only its form, and that only partially.[19]

Reason receives its direction through emotion, and emotion receives its stimulation through feelings, for the self *is* its feelings. And feelings are generated by the stimulation of contact with the self's environment and context. The stimulation of other selves, therefore, affects one's emotions in a different way from any other encounter. It is through social interaction that the emotions of the self come to rest beyond the feelings that produce them.

Psychologist Mary Vander Goot suggests that emotions are intended to signal some action with regard to persons and objects.

> *The signaling function that emotions serve is tied in with actions. It is as though our emotions turn us toward certain actions and away from others. Those emotions that we experience as being undesirable tend to turn us away from their objects. For example, we try to move away from those things that we fear. In contrast, those emotions that we experience as being desirable tend to draw us toward their objects. For example, we try to be with persons whom we like.*[20]

EMOTION IS SOCIALLY CONDITIONED

The human self as created in the image of God is essentially social in nature and makeup.[21] It follows, then, that the self's encounter with other selves has an effect in shaping the emotions that is quite unique and unparalleled by any other encounter in human experience.

> *In human beings, who are in a special way social beings, the self-transcendence of the affective life is largely oriented to the social environment. The positive affects, in which individuals open themselves to their world, are ecstatically inserted into interhuman relations.*[22]

The self has its own emotions, to be sure. But these emotions were conditioned from the beginning by the stimulation of feelings in the self by contact with other selves. As I have suggested above, the cognitive power of the brain includes non-conceptual as well as conceptual functions. Long before concepts are shared, there is clearly a sharing of self with self at the emotional level.

Hans Urs von Balthasar expresses this thought beautifully when he says:

No man reaches the core and ground of his own being, becoming free to himself and to all beings, unless love shines on him. . . . God, who inclined toward his new-born creature with infinite personal love, in order to inspire him with it and to awaken the response to it in him, does in the divine supernatural order something similar to a mother. Out of the strength of her own heart she awakens love in her child in true creative activity. . . . The essential thing is, that the child, awakened thus to love, and already endowed by another's power of love, awakens also to himself and to his true freedom, which is in fact the freedom of loving transcendence of his narrow individuality.[23]

This first experience of love is obviously experienced as a depth of feeling before it comes to expression as an intention. If the self should be impoverished of these feelings, its emotional life will be narrow and rigid. The "narrow individuality" of which von Balthasar speaks describes all too well the isolation of the self which has failed to integrate feelings with intentions. The emotions remain trapped within a pattern of self-attribution so that attempts to form effective and lasting relationships, despite the best of intentions undergirded with sacred vows, continually fail. Pannenberg explains why this is so.

The orientation of human beings to a fullness of life that transcends them and manifests itself especially in the community of their fellow human beings finds expression in the positive affect and passions, especially in feelings of sympathy but also in joy and hope. These draw individuals out of their isolation and therefore may not be simply condemned as expressions of human egocentricity. On the other hand, it is characteristic of such affects, moods, and passions as are negatively related to the environment and other people (fear, anxiety, arrogance, sadness, envy, and hate) that they isolate individuals within themselves. The positive affects and passions, on the contrary, must be understood as expressions of an "anticipatory expectation" in which the human being is aware of the "positive or negative termination into which the value of his being necessarily flows."[24]

EMOTIONAL WISDOM LEADS TO
EMOTIONAL HEALTH

1. Listening to what our emotions tell us

The first question asked of Cain by God was, "Why are you angry, and why has your countenance fallen?" (Gen. 4:6) God prodded Cain to listen to his emotions, to hear what his anger was saying about the inner disposition of his soul. As long as Cain allowed his anger to be directed toward an object outside of himself, he was not listening to what his anger was telling him about himself.

"Why am I angry?" he might have responded. "I am angry because I feel devastated and miserable at the core of my very being. You have no idea what it feels like to have something you have carefully prepared rejected by the one to whom it is offered!"

"Tell me about it," God might have replied. And if Cain continues to express those deep feelings of rejection, hurt, and shame, he will find a reason for his anger and discover the place to begin the process of healing.

"Emotions signal something about the state of our well-being," says Mary Vander Goot. "Those which we experience as being desirable are those which signal that we are in a state that contributes to our good. Those which we experience as unpleasant are those which signal the need for a corrective. The signaling effect of emotion applies not only to our own well-being but also to the well-being of others."[25]

There is a wisdom hidden in our emotions, if we will but listen. Some of the messages which our emotions can reveal to us take us back to feelings which have long since been repressed or denied. We need to recover those feelings and reattach them to the living and growing self, making use of the emotional creativity at our disposal.

Self-recovery begins by seeking emotional health through emotional wisdom. Listening to what our emotions are telling us about our feelings is the beginning of wisdom.

2. Taking responsibility for emotional habits

"Be angry but do not sin," counseled the Apostle Paul, "do not let the sun go down on your anger" (Eph. 4:26). Anger can become an emotional habit. Because it permits the self to project negative feelings on another, it serves well to protect us from deeper feelings of shame, hurt, and rejection. Taking responsibility for anger does not mean denying this emotion, nor repressing the feeling which gave rise to it. Rather, it means doing something about the anger instead of letting it do something to you—and to others.

Paul, apparently, felt that such emotions, which often led to hurtful intentions and actions, were susceptible to the management of the self, if not transformation into more positive emotions. "Put away from you all bitterness and wrath and anger and wrangling and slander, together with all malice, and be kind to one another, tenderhearted, forgiving one another, as God in Christ has forgiven you" (Eph. 4:31-32).

I don't think that the Apostle Paul meant that we should "ventilate" our emotions as a form of releasing them. Rather, the emotions which controlled such attitudes and behavior were to be "put away." Unfortunately, Paul does not tell us how this is to be done! But it surely involves a letting go of the negative emotions by the creative process of forming new and more positive ones. The practice of "venting" one's emotions so as to gain freedom from them is judged by writer Warren Shibles not to be helpful.

> We are told we must release our emotions or tell what we really feel inside us. The picture of "release" and of emotions as things "inside us," is damaging and unhelpful. It creates the view that we are irrational and that there are evil forces within us at work which we can do little about except to let these "forces" be released now and again as water is released from a dam. . . . To "release" emotions is not to effect a cure, but in fact is to create a harmful pattern of behavior. One may find himself constantly "releasing" his emotions, thereby often becoming angry and violent. The therapist who encourages the patient, "Look at your emotions," "Tell what you really feel," or "Be honest about your emotions," is misleading the patient. . . . Instead, it would be more sound to ask the patient not about his emotions but what he thinks, what he has said to himself and to others, what his beliefs are about himself and others, what images recur, and what he has done.[28]

As I read Shibles, I sense that he does not appreciate the role of feelings in the formation of the emotions and the importance of accessing those feelings to release the emotion from its habitual pattern. Emotions, such as anger, jealousy, and fear, may rest on incorrect cognitive attribution. To this extent Shibles is correct in suggesting that a cognitive approach be taken in order to re-frame the cognitive attribution behind the emotion. Vander Goot offers a similar approach when she points to the fact that emotions may be either true or false.

> *There is a sense in which emotions may be true or false. Just as the truth of a statement depends, in part, on how well it corresponds to an event, so the truth of an emotion depends on how appropriate it is to an event. . . . Emotions may be spoken of as true or false because emotions are a form of knowledge. . . . They are triggered by the way we have perceived or know past events in our lives, and then they become part of our store of feelings that signal to us what needs to be done.* [27]

When we have listened to what our emotions tell us, we have moved out of the "blind rage of feelings" into an understanding of why we feel and act this way. We then can begin to take responsibility for emotional habits by tracing them down to their roots. "Either make the tree good, and its fruit good; or make the tree bad, and its fruit bad; for the tree is known by its fruit" (Matt. 12:33).

3. Locating our emotional center
In chapter 2 I said that, while our passions move us, it is spirit that gives the self direction and hope.[28] The human self has a spiritual core that is created in the image and likeness of God, who is Spirit and life. While feelings are the core of emotions, spirit is the core and center of self. As we noted earlier, genuine feeling, according to Brunner, is not possible without spirit.[29]

The emotional center of the self is neither located in the determinative events of the past nor in the capricious events of the present. The self has its source in Spirit and therefore has a destiny which is also its center. This is a center which cannot be molested nor violated.

Do not store up for yourselves treasures on earth, where moth and rust consume and where thieves break in and steal; but store up for yourselves treasures in heaven, where neither moth nor rust consumes and where thieves do not break in and steal. For where your treasure is, there your heart will be also (Matt. 6:19-21).

Note that we are to lay up "for ourselves" treasures in heaven; the desire for self-fulfillment is not itself an unworthy emotion. The self needs a center which reaches back into its origins within personal history and, at the same time, orients the contemporary self to a guiding star of future hope which shines its brightness into the darkest of days. As Vander Goot reminds us, "people are longing for . . . an ideal that could be the lodestar of their lives."[30]

How could we discover and claim that center for ourselves without being stimulated by the emotion which it summons forth within us? Our emotion is the touchstone of that star, and as Augustine said so many years ago, "The affects are the feet that either lead us closer to God or carry us further from Him; but without them we cannot travel the way at all."

What our feelings cannot tell us and our emotions cannot teach us, is what the Bible calls wisdom. In the biblical view of the self, wisdom comes from the heart and from the heart issues the intentions and actions which receive God's blessings. In the next chapter we will explore further the nature of the self as "heart-felt response" to the Word of God and the practical realities of life.

SUMMARY

● The absence of a theology of emotion in textbook theology reflects an abstract concept of God. The Bible reveals to us a God who expresses strong feelings and who cares deeply about the objects of his love: pathos is at the very core of the being of God.

● God confronts persons at the level of emotions and uses emotion to motivate response and to bring healing and hope: emotion is at the core of faith and love.

Rom 10:17

● Emotion differs from feeling in that emotion has the add-ed factor of some attribution at the thought level: when we think about our feelings, we stir up emotions.

● Because emotions arise through perceptions based on feel-ings, emotions can be changed with new perceptions: this makes emotions susceptible to change.

● We begin to take responsibility for our emotions when we listen to what they tell us and allow them to be guided by the spiritual interchange with God and others: emotional health has its source in emotional wisdom.

PRAXIS

As the pastor met with Norm and his wife, he found them composed and outwardly cordial to each other. After a few minutes of casual conversa-tion, the pastor asked, "Have you talked about the incident when Norm was arrested for indecent exposure?" "That's between him and God," Ella quickly responded. "He said that he confessed his sin to God and that he had been forgiven. So I have forgiven him too." The pastor waited for a few moments before speaking. He noted that Norm and Ella were sitting close together on the couch holding hands, but they did not look at each other. Then he asked quietly, "How do you feel about Norm now?" Letting go of his hand, Ella began to weep. "I feel humiliated and angry at what he put our family through. But I know that I'm not supposed to feel that way. I have told him that I forgive him, but he doesn't believe me."

● Why did the pastor ask Ella about her feelings rather than attempt to reinforce the spiritual value of forgiveness?

● From what was discussed in this chapter about feelings and emotions, how do you account for the anger which Ella feels toward Norm?

● As long as Ella feels humiliated, how can she deal with her anger?

● What emotion do you suppose lies behind Norm's inabil-ity to believe that Ella has forgiven him?

● What next step should the pastor take in giving pastoral counsel to Norm and Ella?

4

The Responsible Self:
The Wisdom of the Heart

Keep your heart with all vigilance, for from it flow the springs of life (Prov. 4:23).

When body parts become metaphors, language goes on a holiday! I have often "put my foot in my mouth" when giving a talk and have even been known to "cut off my nose to spite my face." When theologians wax eloquent over some arcane doctrinal subtlety, they are accused of going on a "head trip." At the same time, psychotherapists are known affectionately within their trade as "head shrinkers"! If I let my "heart rule over my head" when buying a new car, it can "cost me an arm and a leg"!

Let's take the heart and head metaphors as a case in point. In our North American culture, the head has become synonymous for the intellect and for rationality, while the heart is considered the seat of the emotions and feelings. This can be the cause of considerable confusion when we read the Bible, where the intestines are considered to be the seat of emotions and the heart the center of wisdom and rationality! A paradigm shift is obviously in order. In this chapter, the Hebrew metaphor will prevail and the heart will be considered to be the core of the self as a thinking, feeling, and willing person.

A BIBLICAL CONCEPT OF THE HEART

In the Old Testament, the heart is the center of the subjective self. What a person is in his or her heart is who that person is "body and soul." "With all my heart" necessarily means with all my soul, and therefore, "with all my might" (cf. Deut. 6:5). The heart is the unity of the body and soul in their true order as the person who lives and exists in the image of God.

We can make a distinction between feelings as the irrational aspect of the self which "stirs up" the heart, and emotion which is the attitude of the heart as oriented toward the promises of God. The psalmist prays: "Relieve the troubles of my heart, and bring me out of my distress" (Ps. 25:17). The first sentence literally reads, "Expand the narrow places of my heart." H.W. Wolff comments: "Here the pains of angina and its anxiety coincide. But in Ps. 119:32, talk about the 'enlarging' of the heart, that is to say the relieving of its cramp, has already left the idea of physical recovery far behind:"[1] "I run the way of your commandments, for you enlarge my understanding [heart]" (Ps. 119:32).

The tranquil heart which is "enlarged" contributes to the health of the person's whole life: "A tranquil mind [heart] gives life to the flesh, but passion makes the bones rot" (Prov. 14:30). The word "heart" as used here refers to an attitude of the mind, a mood or temperament. This is what Proverbs 23:17 means when it admonishes: "Do not let your heart envy sinners, but always continue in the fear of the Lord." Wolff says: "The heart that is stirred up is a man who reacts emotionally, or gets excited. The cultivation of obedience is contrasted with unbalanced feelings."[2]

The biblical view of the self is not so concerned with the self's inner workings, in what we would call a psychology of the self, as it is with the agency of the self. While the affective content of the emotions are recognized and valued, they are not broken off from the central purpose of the self as expressed through intentionality. In the same way, the intellectual or rational aspect of the self is not viewed as a capacity for abstract thought but as fully integrated with the affective power of the emotions.

As a matter of fact, there was no Hebrew equivalent to our infinitive, "to think." Rather, the function of the heart is "to remember," "to reflect upon," and "have true knowledge."

> *For the Israelite* thinking *was not the solving of abstract problems. He does not add link to link, nor does he set up major and minor premises from which conclusions are drawn. To him thinking is to grasp a totality. He directs his soul towards the principel matter, that which determines the totality, and receives it into his soul, the soul thus being immediately stirred and led in a certain direction. In the Hebrew dictionary we look in vain for a word which quite corresponds to our "to think." There are words which mean "to remember," "make present," and thus to act upon the soul. There are words expressing that the soul seeks and investigates; but by that is not meant an investigation which analyses and arranges according to abstract views. To investigate is a practical activity; it consists in directing the soul towards something which it can receive into itself, and by which it can be determined. One investigates wisdom, i.e. makes it one's own.* [3]

Emotion as well as reason are located in the heart. The heart is the center of knowledge expressed through both thought and emotion, leading to intentions and actions. The self is always judged by its intentions which come to expression in actions. The intention of the self as personal agent is rooted in the heart and completed in action. When the action receives the approval of God, this contributes to the wisdom of the heart. Further intentions can be informed by the knowledge of anticipated blessing, and so the heart "grows in the knowledge of God" while, at the same time, bringing both emotion and thought under the discipline of the wisdom of obedience.

In figure 4.1, the heart is shown to be the core of the self. Both emotion and thought enter into the intentions of the heart which are directed toward actions, with accompanying motives, leading to a result. When this result is approved by God it is experienced as a blessing of God upon the self. Anticipating this blessing gives wisdom to the heart in its intentions, motives, and actions. Through this process the heart is "instructed" by God.

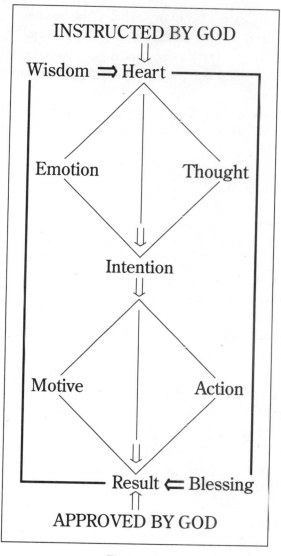

Figure 4.1

in its intentions and actions. The concept of "will" is expressed in the diagram through the intentions of the heart. Thus, both emotion and thought enter into the intention of the heart in the form of what one wills to do or not do. Motives are ambiguous unless clarified by intentions.

One may have more than one motive in an action, but only one intention, as John Macmurray points out.

No action can have contradictory intentions. We cannot aim in different directions at the same time. It can, however, have contradictory motives, one of which is suppressed, and therefore "unconscious". . . . In our relations with other persons this ambiguity of motivation is felt as a tension and a constraint between us, and therefore in each of us.[4]

Motives are always to some degree hidden from us as well as others. Motives are difficult to analyze and bring under judgment as to whether they are worthy or unworthy. Intentions, however, while driven by motives, can and should be subject to scrutiny and evaluation. Too often we question the motives hidden within some action when we should actually seek out the intention.

While it may be my intention to discipline a child so as to produce positive behavior for the child's well-being and the good of others, I may also carry conflicting motives into that action. As a result, my discipline may be driven by anger as well as by love or by a need to reestablish my power and control over one who defies my will. Some of these motives may be hidden from me, and I may even have contradictory motives. I cannot, however, as Macmurray has said, have more than one intention in my action. And that intention is subject to examination by others, who have a right to question my intentions if the discipline becomes abusive rather than corrective. I cannot repent over my motives for they do not lie within my will. I must acknowledge and repent over my intentions, however, if they are not directed toward the good of others.

In years gone by, when a young man came courting a young woman, the father was known to have confronted the suitor by saying, "Young man, what is your intention concerning my daughter?" It is worth noting that he does not inquire about the motives of the young man, but of his intentions. He may know all too well what some of the motives may be, or prefer not to know! But it is the young man's intention that must be stated and to which he can be held accountable.

The Hebrews did not disdain the use of the mind, nor prefer experience to the intellect. On the contrary there is consistent appeal to the mind that it reflect upon the benefits of God's actions, as well as contemplate the wisdom of actions which bring God's approval and blessing. The Israelite meditates (reflects) upon the result of God's action, not the action itself.

Intentions are not first of all formed out of a mental process in abstraction from action, but are derived out of the anticipated action and its results. John Pedersen contrasts the Hebrew view of intention and action with that of our modern European concept.

> *All mental activity points in the direction of action. But what is the place that action occupies in the psychological process? According to European psychology, action first originates in the region of ideas; then it is penetrated by feeling, which in its turn makes it to be determined by volition; this again leads to resolution, which is followed by action. Thus the activity of the soul is completed; the result of the action lies entirely outside its sphere, being added as a new element.* [5]

For the Israelite, however, it was quite different. The soul perceives the result of the action as a good, so that the intention rises in the heart to produce the action. Rather than creating abstract concepts of God through the mind alone, the Israelite was invited to contemplate the benefits of God's actions so as to love, honor, and worship Him as the source of the benefits. Consider the vivid images of Psalm 23, where David calls to mind the Lord as the shepherd, with green pastures, still water, an overflowing cup, and a banquet table, all consummated by a life lived in the house of the Lord forever!

The Israelites were continually exhorted to remember and recite the great events in their history by which God fulfilled promises and acted on their behalf so as to produce blessing and bounty. Psalm 78, for example, opens by promising the "dark sayings" (v. 2) from of old which contain the wisdom of their relationship with and knowledge of God. What then follows is simply a recitation of the great events in their history which contained God's actions, beginning with Jacob, the formation of the twelve tribes, the exodus from Egypt, the entrance into the Promised Land, and the glorious reign of King David. The recitation of these mighty deeds of God were expected to evoke strong emotion as well as instruct the mind.

THE RESPONSIBLE SELF ~ 55

We recall the wisdom of Joseph who, after being rejected by his brothers and left for dead, did not think about their actions, nor their motives, but contemplated the results of their actions as good despite their evil intentions. "You intended to do harm to me, God intended it for good. . . . So have no fear" (Gen. 50:20-21). When we contemplate the benefits of God's actions, as well as the actions of others, there is a "healing of memory," and a reframing of our emotional reactions.

THE ROLE OF EMOTION
IN THE RATIONAL PROCESS

To think about an object is to be moved emotionally by the object. For the Hebrews, the mind was moved by contemplation of an object.[6] The intentions of the heart were not abstract and empty concepts broken free from objective reality. Rather, the heart was understood to be connected at its source to the law of God from which it received its instruction and directed by intentions toward those actions which would be approved by Him. This is why wisdom was esteemed so highly and to be valued above all other goals.

> *Happy are those who find wisdom, and those who get understanding, for her income is better than silver, and her revenue better than gold. She is more precious than jewels, and nothing you desire can compare with her. Long life is in her right hand; in her left hand are riches and honor. Her ways are ways of pleasantness, and all her paths are peace. She is a tree of life to those who lay hold of her; those who hold her fast are called happy" (Prov. 3:13-18).*

As we have seen above, the wisdom of the heart directs the intentions and actions in such a way that God's approval and blessing result. The antithesis of rationality is not irrationality, but folly. To be a fool is to use reason in such a way that one does not gain wisdom. "The discerning person looks to wisdom, but the eyes of a fool to the ends of the earth" (Prov. 17:24).

A brief, but perceptive essay on folly was written by Dietrich Bonhoeffer and published after his death in *Letters and Papers from Prison.* "Folly is a more dangerous enemy to the good than evil," wrote Bonhoeffer. "Against folly we have no defense. Neither protests nor force can touch it; reasoning is no use; facts that contradict personal prejudices can simply be disbelieved. . . . So the fool, as distinct from the scoundrel, is completely self-satisfied."[7]

When the mind has become captive to the power of an ideology, it becomes blind to the consequences of its actions and insensitive to the pleadings of the emotions. The most dangerous of all folly is not created by following one's emotions, but giving over one's mind to a way of thinking that is impenetrable by the logic of feeling. This kind of thinking produces folly at the sociological, political, and religious level. Racism, sexism, demagoguery, and persecution in the name of God all reflect a kind of folly that is grounded in a "truth" that has become inhuman and unfeeling.

We often account for a foolish action by saying that the heart ruled over the head. By that we mean that our emotions caused us to do something rather than thinking clearly and objectively. The implication is that we cannot really trust our emotions and that so-called objective thinking or rationality is more reliable.

To counter this, some have repeated the saying attributed to the philosopher Pascal: "The heart has its reasons which reason knows nothing of." One wonders how many people have called themselves fools because they did not follow the leading of their emotions and missed an opportunity for fulfillment because it was judged to be "impractical." But if we cannot trust our reason, how can we reasonably trust our emotions?

Wisdom, as contrasted with folly, is neither pure intellect nor unthinking emotion. The good, as the object of wisdom, stirs up the emotions of the heart and leads to reflection on how best to direct one's life so as to attain what is ultimately good. "The emotional life is not simply a part or an aspect of life," says John Macmurray.

> *It is not, as we so often think, subordinate, or subsidiary to the mind. It is the core and essence of human life. The intellect arises out of it, is rooted in it, draws its nourishment and sustenance from it, and is the*

subordinate partner in the human economy. This is because the intellect is essentially instrumental. Thinking is not living. At its worst it is a substitute for living; at its best a means of living better. As we have seen, the emotional life is our life, both as awareness of the world and as action in the world, so far as it is lived for its own sake. Its value lies in itself, not in anything beyond it which it is a means of achieving.[8]

The contrast does not seem to be between emotion and reason, but between feeling and intellect. But even here this contrast represents the dissociation of feeling from intellect, not a necessary separation. When feeling becomes separate from intellect, and intellect from feeling, a split has occurred within the self which must be overcome for reason to be restored. This splitting is the result of a falling away from the unity of the experience of the self as the object of God's love. Brunner depicts the contrast as part of the original apostasy, or falling away from God.

The contrast between feeling and intellect which characterizes European thought about the higher life of the mind is not part of man's origin, but it is a product of his apostasy. Feeling therefore has its rightful place in man's "experience" of his relation with God, because this "experience" is something which man has received, and not something which he has himself created. To be apprehended by the love of God, means to be smitten in the very centre of one's being, to suffer it, not as a pain, but as the supreme joy, as happiness and peace.[9]

The role of emotion with regard to reason thus is to ground reason in the good as created and willed by God. All that God created was said to be good (Gen. 1). "Everything created by God is good, and nothing is to be rejected, provided it is received with thanksgiving; for it is sanctified by God's word and by prayer" (1 Tim. 4:4-5). Paul wrote this as a reminder that the good which seeks the human heart lies within the created world as well as beyond it.

What we call reason is not merely an intellectual capacity. Some who are exceptionally gifted intellectually still act irrationally at times! True rationality is grounded in the self's response to its encounter with the real world, including a capacity or ability to respond to the actions and feelings of other persons. This response-ability is grounded in the self's capacity for sensation coupled with an intellectual power of discrimination between the sensations, leading to a motive and intention directed toward action. It was Aristotle who first said, "There is nothing in the intellect that is not first of all in the senses." Reason is the distinctive quality of the self that makes us human, that reflects the image and likeness of God. John Macmurray links reason to emotion in the same way that actions are linked to motives.

> *Reason—the capacity in us which makes us human—is not in any special sense a capacity of the intellect. It is not our power of thinking, though it expresses itself in our thinking as well as in other ways. It must also express itself in our emotional life, if that is to be human. Emotion is not the Cinderella of our inner life, to be kept in her place among the cinders in the kitchen. Our emotional life is us in a way our intellectual life cannot be; in that it alone contains the motives from which our conduct springs. Reason reveals itself in emotion by its objectivity, by the way it corresponds to and apprehends reality. Reason in the emotional life determines our behavior in terms of the real values of the world in which we live. It discovers and reveals goodness and badness, right and wrong, beauty and ugliness and all the infinite variety of values of which these are only the rough, general, intellectual abstractions. The development of human nature in its concrete livingness is, in fact, the development of emotional reason.* [10]

The core of reason is the correspondence of the self with reality. Our emotions, because they are stimulated by feelings and sense perception, provide the primary link with reality external to the self. The intellect is an instrumental factor in rationality through its power of discrimination, reflection, and intentionality. The thoughts of the heart are therefore linked with the intentions of the heart as carried out in actions. This makes emotion as well as thought the rational act of the person, instructed by true knowledge of God and related to actions which are approved by Him.

THE MORAL STATUS
OF EMOTIONAL REASON

Heschel has reminded us that the pathos of God is grounded in His sense of justice and ethical concern for the objects of His care. The "inner law" of pathos is the moral law. "Indeed, this is the essence of God's moral nature; His willingness to be intimately involved in the history of man."[11] Moral reason is grounded in emotional reason. God does not operate out of abstract moral laws which are needed to inform His feelings so as to produce wrath or love. The divine moral sense is located in what Heschel calls the pathos of God.

John 17:21

> *God does not reveal himself in an abstract absoluteness, but in a personal and intimate relation to the world. He does not simply command and expect obedience; He is also moved and affected by what happens in the world, and reacts accordingly. Events and human actions arouse in Him joy or sorrow, pleasure or wrath. He is not conceived as judging the world in detachment. He reacts in an intimate and subjective manner, and thus determines the value of events. . . . Pathos denotes, not an idea of goodness, but a living care; not an immutable example, but an outgoing challenge, a dynamic relation between God and man; not mere feeling or passive affection, but an act or attitude composed of various spiritual elements; no mere contemplative survey of the world, but a passionate summons.*[12]

When emotions operate as indiscriminate motives apart from intentionality, they lack both cognitive and moral content, for they are not oriented toward the other person. Mixed motives, or hidden motives, break the unity between thought and action and create dysfunctional interpersonal relations.

When intellect operates in abstraction from the motives and intentions of the self, it lacks emotional and moral content, for it is no longer held accountable for its effect upon others. The moral status of the self is grounded in its emotional reason, that is, in both the thoughts and intents of the heart.

Jesus linked the inner emotion of anger with the outward act of murder through an implied intentionality when He said: "But

I say to you that if you are angry with a brother or sister, you will be liable to judgment; and if you insult a brother or sister, you will be liable to the council; and if you say, 'You fool!' you will be liable to the hell of fire" (Matt. 5:22). In the same way, Jesus linked the inner emotion of lust with the act of adultery: "But I say unto you that every one who looks at a woman with lust has already committed adultery with her in his heart" (Matt. 5:28).

In both cases, the emotion is produced by the experience of the other. Where Jesus assumed that an emotion had already become an intention of the heart, the emotion is under the same moral judgment as would be an action produced by the intention. Both lust and anger are emotions because each has an element of cognition fused with a feeling. The moral factor is not linked with the emotion but with the intention which arises out of the emotion. Between emotion and action lies intention, as indicated earlier in figure 4.1. There it was shown that emotion and thought combine to produce intention. Motives and intention combine to produce an action. The moral status of the self is determined from the side of action, reaching back through intention into emotion and thought.

The biblical view of the self permits no evasion of the moral responsibility of the self, even where an act has not been committed. There is no room in a biblical psychology for emotions disconnected from intentions. We are not judged for having emotions, but we are held accountable for what is intended by them. The moral conscience relates to emotion through the intentionality which links feeling to faith. Faith is grounded in reason, not mere intellect. Reason provides the moral content of faith by including conscience as the "thorn in the flesh" of feelings.[13]

Emotion is neither "good" nor "bad" apart from intention. We cannot be held morally responsible for having an emotional reaction, such as anger, jealousy, lust, or fear. But we can be held accountable for what we intend by this emotion.

As Macmurray has reminded us, we can have mixed motives and conflicting emotions, but we cannot have contradictory intentions.[14] To conceal an intention when asked to reveal it is already an act of deception. To misrepresent an intention is already a lie. To nurture an emotion which does not intend another's good is already an offense against the other. The moral concern is not that we have a particular emotion, but what we intend to do with it. We cannot harbor an emotion and keep it alive except through intention. Therefore, emotion tends to become intentionality whether or not action is taken.

The moral content of emotion is therefore related to the social context of emotion as response to an intention toward the other. Failure to follow through with an intention which is for the good of another can result in the emotion of guilt, inferiority, or humiliation. We may fail to carry through with a good intention due to a variety of factors, but this failure is not itself a moral failure. The emotions produced through such failures are only resolved through the "emotional reason" which binds us in relationship to others. Where confession of failure is made, this constitutes a moral demand upon the community to deal with the failure and seek restoration through forgiveness and healing. The emotion of gratitude becomes the basis for the generation of new intentions and the restoration of relationship. The expression of new intentions can take the form of repentance. This is not the same as confession. Confession is acknowledgment of failure. Repentance is the positive offer of a new intentionality based upon the emotion of gratitude. It is hard to see that true repentance can take place where there has not been first of all confession, confrontation, moral judgment, forgiveness, and the intention of others to participate in the recovery. More will be said about the role of forgiveness in recovery in chapter 6 when we deal with abusive relationships.

"Be angry but do not sin," counseled Paul (Eph. 4:26). In the verse immediately preceding he exhorted: "So then, putting away falsehood, let all of us speak the truth to your neighbors, for we are members of one another" (4:25). Paul allowed for the emotion of anger arising within the self. From his general rule of speaking the truth to those with whom we are bound in common life, one might conclude that his answer to "How do I handle anger so as not to sin?" might go something like this: "Tell your neighbor of your anger but assure him or her that your intention is not to do any harm." In this case, one assumes that the anger is directed toward a person who has intentionally or unintentionally done something to provoke the emotion. The emotion of anger is thus bound to the rationality of that relation and can be, hopefully, negotiated and resolved through the expression of intentionality.

Are we bound to share all of our emotions in order to be truthful with others? I don't think so. The moral basis for community is in the intentionality of each to uphold the good and welfare of the other. Where we have emotions which arise solely due to our own feelings and not provoked by actions of another, the sharing of that emotion may produce confusion rather than healing.

I remember a class discussion of this point in which a woman student told of having a male friend confess to her that he had feelings of lust toward her and felt obligated to share this so that their friendship would not be hindered by these feelings. Her response was a very strong one. Because she felt she had done nothing to provoke these feelings in him, she felt violated and "dirty," as she put it, by the knowledge of his lustful feelings toward her. In this case, though his intentions were good, his action precipitated an emotional response in her that destroyed the relationship. If she should now ask, "How do I deal with my feelings of revulsion and anger toward him?" perhaps she should speak the truth with him by telling him of the effect of his actions in her. In this case, her emotions were caused by his actions. Whereas, in the case of his lust, this was not caused by her actions, but through his own feelings and thoughts.

She was morally offended by his telling her of his lustful thoughts. His lustful thoughts were not in and of themselves immoral as emotions, but only as secretly harbored intentions. In this case, the better route for him would have been to confide in a pastor or therapist with the goal of recovering an inner moral health, one that would allow good intentions to produce good thoughts and thereby positive and healthy emotions.

When good intentions are communicated regularly and authentically between persons in relationship, the motives and emotions of each tend to be brought into alignment with these intentions. Merely stating to oneself "good intentions" does not work in the same way. The alcoholic, or the offender in an abusive relationship, for example, performs an inner ritual of confession, absolution, sometimes even penance, followed by a reiteration of good intentions, only to fail consistently. Some have "hit bottom," so to speak. and in desperation sought help from a "twelve-step recovery program."

Program participants are not encouraged to make promises or to state intentions as a way of gaining self-acceptance or social approval. Rather, they begin with the admission of powerlessness to overcome their own problem and a commitment to "work the steps" of recovery under the guidance and support of a sponsor. An unexpressed intentionality to become responsible for one's own emotional life is present in "walking the talk." Intentionality is reborn by participating in relationships where honesty is the only virtue and recovery the only value.

By whatever form, successful twelve-step programs seem to have two things in common. The power of self-deception and denial is broken by the admission of the need for a "higher power" as a source of healing and hope. And, secondly. the unconditional acceptance coupled with a demand for honesty provided by others who are making the same journey toward recovery.

Recovery must empower one toward becoming a responsible self. This is not achieved by overriding emotion with reason—for the lack of emotion in reason leads to folly. Nor can recovery take place by cutting off reason and following our feelings—for the lack of reason in emotion leads to despair. The responsible self is a recovering self, open to the reason of love and joy; stimulated by the emotion of reflecting on the good and the true.

When the self finds true self-fulfillment in being valued and esteemed by others, self-worth arises in the place of self-condemnation and despair. Authentic self-worth arises out of relationships which value the self for its own sake, leading to positive self-esteem. In the chapter which follows we will examine the difference between negative and positive self-esteem, laying the groundwork for a theology of self-esteem.

SUMMARY

- The biblical concept of the heart includes both emotion

and thought. The heart is the center of knowledge leading to intentions and actions.

● The heart acquires wisdom by hearing the Word of God and by receiving (anticipating) the blessing of God upon the intentions which become actions.

● Emotion stirs up the heart even as instruction informs it. Both emotion and thought contribute to reason, and what is good and reasonable is determined by the blessing of God upon the action taken.

● Intention is the result of both emotion and thought and provides the moral basis for accountability. We are not morally accountable for having an emotion, but for the intention which proceeds from it.

● Responsibility for our intentions in a relationship provides the basis for accountability for both our thoughts and emotions.

PRAXIS

When the pastor met with Norm and Ella for the next counseling session, Norm spoke up first. "I can't believe how foolish my behavior was. It was really stupid of me to display myself in public. I'll never understand what came over me, but believe me, I have really learned my lesson. I know better than to do something like that again." Ella appeared more at peace and nodded. "I think that getting caught may be the best thing that happened to Norm," she said. "It was painful for all of us, but he has promised not to do anything like that again, and I believe him."

● Ella appears relieved that Norm has taken responsibility for his actions. Why may her confidence be premature?

● What clue do you find in what Norm said that he still has not integrated his emotional life with his rational self?

● From what was said in this chapter about the relation of both emotion and reason to intentions, in what way do you suspect that Norm will continue to have problems?

● The pastor has decided to work more closely with Norm on taking responsibility for his feelings rather than his actions. Why do you think that this therapeutic strategy might be more effective? What alternative would you suggest?

5

The Worth of the Self:
Positive Self-Esteem

Consider the ravens: they neither sow nor reap, they have neither storehouse nor barn, and yet God feeds them. Of how much more value are you than the birds!
(Luke 12:24)

There is no self so secure but that a bit of Willy Loman doesn't rise up like a ghost in the night to haunt our dreams with the specter of failure and futility. In his classic play, *The Death of a Salesman*, Arthur Miller traces the desperate unraveling of the dream for Willy Loman with unerring insight. Loman is a salesman whose self-image is unrealistically pinned to his dreams of success while denying the reality of his failures. The quiet desperation of Willy to succeed is projected upon his two sons, Biff and Happy, who, at first, are captivated by the dream and then are forced to become accomplices in the charade. At the end, unable to maintain the pretense, Willy precipitates an accident in which he is killed in the midst of a delusion that he will be viewed as a hero when the $20,000 insurance check arrives for his family. Following the funeral service, a postmortem on his life is conducted by Biff, one of his sons who could no longer sustain the pretense, while his brother, Happy, and Willy's friend, Charley, continue to defend Willy's self-image.

> BIFF: He had the wrong dreams, all, all, wrong.
> HAPPY: Don't say that!
> BIFF: He never knew who he was.
> CHARLEY: Nobody dast blame this man. You don't understand; Willy was a salesman. And for a salesman, there is no rock bottom to the life. He don't put a bolt to a nut, he don't tell you the law or give you medicine. He's a man way out there in the blue, riding on a smile and a shoeshine. And when they start not smiling back—that's an earthquake. And then you get yourself a couple of spots on your hat, and you're finished. Nobody dast blame this man. A salesman is got to dream, boy. It comes with the territory.
> BIFF: Charley, the man didn't know who he was.[1]

There is little agreement among psychologists as to just what constitutes self-esteem and less agreement as to what role it plays in a person's achievement of success and social adaptation. The Final Report of the California Task Force to Promote Self-Esteem, issued in 1990, found only anecdotal evidence that low self-esteem contributes to poor performance in school and leads to antisocial behavior. No direct causal connection could be established although there was a consensus that some correlation did in fact exist.[2] Despite this ambivalence, raising self-esteem, the task force concluded, was one way to develop increased responsibility on the part of individuals for the general good of society.[3]

DEFINING SELF-ESTEEM

In a book that emerged out of the research conducted by the California Task Force, self-esteem was defined as containing three elements.

> There is first a cognitive element; self-esteem means characterizing some parts of the self in descriptive terms: power, confidence, agency. It

means asking what kind of person one is. Second, there is an affective element, a valence or degree of positiveness or negativeness attached to those facets identified; we call this high or low self-esteem. Third, and related to the second, there is an evaluative element, an attribution of some level of worthiness according to some ideally held standard.[4]

When self-esteem is used in this way, it seems to include self-concept, self-worth, self-respect, and even self-confidence. Others attempt to distinguish between self-esteem and self-confidence by asserting that one may have self-confidence in the sense of succeeding in a task while, at the same time, have low respect and low esteem for the self.

Self-confidence is closely related to Bandura's (1977) concept of self-efficacy — the expectation of successfully meeting challenges and overcoming obstacles, and a general sense of control of self and the environment. Self-esteem is more an affective sense of accepting one's self and feeling self-worth. Thus, self-confidence may contribute to self-esteem, but the two are not synonymous. A person may expect to succeed at any task and still not accept such accomplishments as counting, of being worthy of self-respect.[5]

Some psychologists feel that high self-esteem indicates the capacity to cope with situations rather than avoiding them. In this view, self-esteem is largely a means of preserving one's identity in the face of psychological threats caused by events and factors external to the self.

We maintain that high levels of self-esteem are the product of a response style that favors coping over avoidance. When this is the case, conflicts are faced, understood, and resolved, resulting in self-confidence, personal approval, and feelings of personal well-being. Patterns of excessive avoidance, breed just the opposite results. The very act of avoidance, by denial and distortion, precludes any feeling of adequacy. Therefore, the tendency to cope or avoid virtually dictates the positive or negative nature of personal psychological experience.[6]

The capacity to cope successfully, however, may not include feelings of self-worth which appear to be indispensable to any concept of self-esteem. Coping may lead to self-confidence, but not always to positive self-worth. While self-confidence may result from positive self-esteem, I do not include it as a component of it.

I consider self-esteem to be the valuing aspect of self-concept. Rather than referring to high or low self-esteem, I prefer the terms positive and negative self-esteem. A positive self-perception indicates a high degree of congruence between one's self-perception and the "ideal" self. A negative self-perception suggests that the self fails to measure up to its own standard regardless of how that standard is set.[7]

Archibald Hart suggests that both low and high self-esteem may be unhealthy. "It is sufficient to stop hating yourself," he concludes. "For me a healthy attitude of the self toward the self is the absence of self-hate."[8] Self-hate may result from an unrealistic concept of the ideal or normative self as perceived by the self or derived from the assessment of others. Regardless of how "high" a level of self-esteem is held by the self, if it falls short of a perception of what one "ought" to be it will result in negative self-worth.

"The man didn't know who he was," said Biff Loman of his father. Willy Loman's self-perception was negative. For whatever reason, he despised himself and sought redemption in the only way left to his tormented mind. He concluded that he was worth more to his family dead than alive, and in his grandiosity, fed by despair, sought nobility through self-sacrifice.

The pathology of negative self-esteem often is concealed in heroic efforts to compensate for self-hatred. This may be one reason why it is so difficult to establish a direct causality between self-esteem and social behavior. When society rewards success and associates self-image with role status and product identification, conformity to these ideals becomes a powerful aphrodisiac. Self-esteem is gained at the price of self-authenticity. The spiral of negative self-esteem is accentuated by two images, that of success and that of power.

Where success is not attainable as self-image through conformity to societal and cultural norms, deviancy from those norms gives a feeling of power. While the world looked on with horror at what were perceived as outrageous and lawless actions in the televised riots in central Los Angeles in April of 1992, some of those who looted and burned buildings may have been compensating for feelings of powerlessness and nonidentity through desperate and dramatic actions of antisocial behavior.

Those who attribute such actions to "low self-esteem" are missing the mark. Many of those who participated in these lawless and violent actions found "high self-esteem" through this behavior, even as the executives who "looted" the savings and loan institutions of $50 billion found "high self-esteem" through their illegal and immoral actions. Actions which display power or success seek to give the self a perception of self-esteem. But deeper within, the self can judge and discredit its own actions, leading to greater fragmentation of the self. Where self-esteem is negative, success and power become tools with which to exploit others, yet insufficient to fill the gap between a negative and an idealized self-perception.

My concern in this chapter is to provide a critical theological analysis of self-esteem rather than a psychological one. There is an assumption common to certain traditions of Christian spirituality that feelings of self-worth and concern for self-esteem are inappropriate at best and unspiritual at worst. For many believers in this tradition, the self is to be viewed as hopelessly enslaved to sin. They like to quote the Apostle Paul (out of context!) who said, "For I know that nothing good dwells within me" (Rom. 7:18).

Don Matzat, a Lutheran pastor, in his book entitled *Christ Esteem — Where the Search for Self-Esteem Ends*, says:

> *Embracing a positive image of self will not, in the long run, make any difference, because I am still wrapped up in myself. Even if I feel bad about myself and do not like myself, I am still focusing upon myself and "myself" is the problem. The corrupted condition of my human "self" is not a mere figment of imagination which can be adjusted by thinking differently. . . The call of the gospel is away from self and unto Jesus, because* self *is the problem and Jesus is the solution.*[9]

Later in this chapter I will examine more closely the crucial theological issues behind such criticism of the contemporary self-esteem movement.

Is the core of the human self really so corrupt that it must be valued as worthless and replaced by a "Christ-self"? Or, is the self's deepest longing for fulfillment and value an intrinsic aspect of the image of God which has become disempowered and cast back upon itself in a backlash of negative and self-defeating perceptions and actions? I believe that it is the latter and will undertake an analysis of the process by which the positive self-esteem originally given and intended by God can be restored and empowered through His love and grace.

NARCISSISM, SELF-ESTEEM, AND THE EMPOWERED SELF

When Jesus said, "Truly I tell you, unless you change and become like children, you will never enter the kingdom of heaven" (Matt. 18:3), He implied that there is some essential goodness which the child possesses and which needs to be recovered. This childlike joy and happiness may be the motivating source for self-fulfillment that is indispensable to faith, hope, and love. The "self-love" which is typical of the child is a form of narcissism at its most elemental level.

When Jesus exhorts us to "receive the kingdom of God as a little child," it means that we rediscover the longing which opens us up to God's love and the fulfillment of the self in another. It may well be that Jesus was reminding adults that they carry within them a childlike longing which has become a "childish" bent toward controlling their own destiny and securing their own gratification through exercising power over the lives of others.

The love of Jesus is an empowering love, aimed at evoking in each person the desire for the kingdom of God and everything else added to it (cf. Matt. 6:33). God's desire is to give us all things that pertain to life and godliness.

Psychotherapist William Meissner suggests that there is a "childhood narcissism" which is essential to personal well-being in the adult. Experienced losses to this narcissistic core play a critical role in psychic development.

*The sense of loss and diminished self-esteem attack the fundamental
narcissism at the root of our emotional lives. This narcissism is essential
to our psychological well-being and any threat to it must be resisted.
And so loss sets in motion restorative efforts by which the ego strives to
recover the loss and reconstitute the sense of self-esteem. Self-esteem is a
fragile but indispensable vessel, whose preservation requires care and
constant effort in the fact of the onslaughts of deprivation and loss."*

This "fundamental narcissism" is what I have called "infantile narcissism." because it appears in its most delightful and
healthy form in infants. We do not scold infants for this innate
pleasure instinct, but encourage and reward it. It is only when
the infant grows into a child and then into an adult that this
instinct for self-pleasure becomes a source of irritation and dis-
approval by others. I use the phrase "infantile narcissism" intentionally so as to suggest that narcissism itself is not a negative
attribute of the self and, secondly, to trace out the growth process by which this fundamental narcissism can be empowered to
become the positive basis for self-esteem.

A serious mistake can be made in a theology of the self by
equating the sinful self with the narcissistic self. Theologians
who claim that all children are born with an inherited sin nature,
called original sin, are often tempted to view the self as totally
without value with every instinct of the self corrupted and dis-
posed toward wrongdoing. The redemption of the self, then,
entails a replacement of this sinful self with a new self, ground
in the grace of God. Don Matzat, previously cited, follows this
line of thought and suggests that the self with which we are born
is to be replaced by what he calls a "Christ self."

I too affirm the orthodox belief that every person is born
with a disposition toward sin; however, I view this bent as not
located in the instinct for self-fulfillment and pleasure, but in
the instinct to use power over others and one's own life to gain
that fulfillment. The image of God with which each person is
endowed is the source for positive self-worth and self-fulfillment. This is the infant's capacity to love itself—infantile narcissism. Original sin, however one defines it theologically, is the
condition of every human person by which the infantile narcis-

sism is fused with an instinct to control and gain power so as to provide one's own self with pleasure and fulfillment. Original sin may be posited as a sense of omnipotence which is fused with the narcissistic instinct giving the infant a sense of absolute power over others who cater to the infant's every need. Self-fulfillment is quite different from self-gratification.

For the infant, gratification and fulfillment are fused and undifferentiated. When resistance is encountered to self-gratification the infantile self feels powerless and threatened. When the infant's expressed need for self-gratification is resisted by the caretaker, it is experienced not only as denial of pleasure, but also as loss of power. This feeling of powerlessness at not being able to find immediate gratification of the pleasure instinct causes a variety of compensatory mechanisms to kick in. The goal of these mechanisms is to manipulate the source of gratification and produce a response. A new set of behavior patterns are quickly learned and reinforced by the caregiver's adaptation to the demands. The infant is soon back in control of its environment and the core narcissistic needs are being fulfilled. Unfortunately, however, the instinct for self-fulfillment and self-worth has become confused with the instinct for power and control as the provider of self-gratification. This is the point at which many identify original sin with the self, so that all attempts to speak of the intrinsic worth of the self in terms of the longing for pleasure and self-fulfillment are labeled sinful. Here too is the point where narcissism becomes associated with self-gratification rather than with self-fulfillment.

This confusion between self-fulfillment and self-gratification is subtle and yet so important that it is often overlooked by both parties in the conflict over self-esteem. Those who judge any attempt to speak of self-esteem as humanistic and unbiblical, fail to see the intrinsic worth of the image of God as the very core of the self. Those who encourage the development of positive self-esteem as the way to emotional health and a successful life may fail to see the need to liberate self-esteem from self-gratification and its power mechanisms.

The image of God and original sin must be differentiated clearly so that the core of the self is not *essentially* destroyed by sin. This is important for psychological reasons as well as theological. The psychology of self-identity requires a thread of continuity through even the most severe forms of mental illness and emotional disorder. The theology of self-identity likewise requires continuity through the radical experience of new birth and spiritual renewal. Theology has tended to be more con-

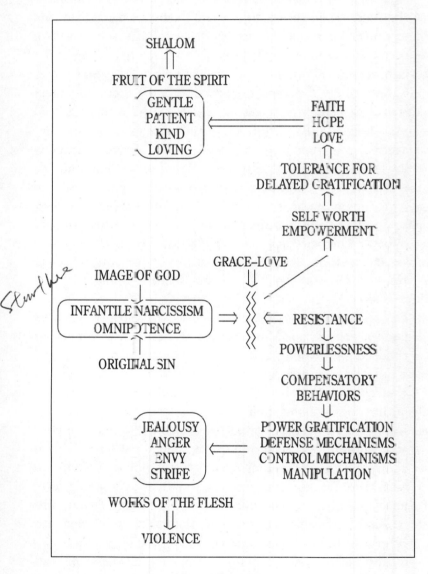

Figure 5.1

cerned with the eradication of sin and the implanting of a "new nature" than of preserving the self. Psychology has tended to be more concerned with restoring the self than with providing a "new nature" through spiritual conversion. Both theologians and psychologists need to discover a common pathway to the healing of persons.

Figure 5.1 on page 103 suggests such a pathway. Begin reading the diagram at the center where infantile narcissism and omnipotence are bracketed together. Note that the image of God is the source of infantile narcissism while original sin is the source of feelings of omnipotence. When resistance is met to the needs for self-gratification it is experienced as powerlessness with resulting behaviors which are antisocial and which can lead to violence. With the intervention of the grace of God the infantile narcissism is freed from the need to control and is empowered by love to experience self-worth. The intervention of divine grace may be seen as providing empowerment for the self to retain the infantile narcissism in the form of self-worth, or self-esteem, with delayed gratification the evidence of this "fruit of the Spirit." Tolerance for delayed gratification is the mark of growth and maturity resulting in qualities of life which lead to *Shalom* — the Hebrew word for peace, health, wholeness, and reconciliation.

The recovery of the image of God as the intrinsic value of the original self, resulting in positive self-esteem as empowerment for feelings of self-worth, has its source in divine love and grace. The empowering reality of divine grace does not annihilate the self, but liberates it from the sinful compulsion to find self-fulfillment through self-gratification. The "fundamental narcissism" of which Meissner speaks is thus preserved as the positive motivation of the self toward love, hope, and faith. This is *spiritual* fruit because it is empowered by the Spirit of God. It is a spiritual *fruit* because it is the result of the health and growth of the self as a human self grounded in the image of God. The integration of psychological concerns for health and wholeness coincide with theological concerns for a spirituality which is also the recovery of the true humanity of the self. In the same way, theological concerns for the effects of sin arising out of the self merge with psychological concerns for dysfunctional and disruptive behavior at the personal and social level.

Negative self-esteem is characterized in this model by a self-perception of powerlessness which drives the self toward behaviors which are exploitative and manipulative of others. These actions may prove successful and even lead to self-confidence and self-reliance while, at the same time, resulting in loss of self-worth due to the rejection of others and failures in establishing healthy interpersonal relationships. This results in the apparent paradox that some may achieve a sense of high self-esteem through these control mechanisms but also experience negative self-esteem in terms of self-worth.

Earlier in this chapter I referred to a theological tradition which labels the contemporary emphasis on self-esteem as unchristian and unbiblical. The critical issue with regard to this criticism seems to be that of a focus on the human self as having potential and possibilities for good apart from radical renewal by the grace of God or even replacement by a new spiritual self. Before we can proceed further with our analysis of self-esteem, we need to examine this concern on biblical and theological grounds.

THEOLOGICAL ISSUES
WITH SELF-ESTEEM

1. Self-esteem vs. self-denial

The theological issue raised at this point is with regard to several biblical injunctions and statements: to "deny oneself" (cf. Matt. 16:24), to "hate our own lives" (cf. Luke 14:26), "to put to death the deeds of the body" (Rom. 8:13), "not to please ourselves" (Rom. 15:1), "our old self was crucified with him" (Rom. 6:6). Paul admonishes, "do nothing from selfishness or conceit, but in humility count others better than yourselves" (Phil. 2:3). In Romans 7, Paul can even say, "For I know that nothing good dwells within me, that is, in my flesh" (v. 18).

Based on such biblical texts, there is a theological tradition which teaches that the human self is hopelessly sinful and without merit. To have regard for the self as a positive basis for self-esteem is considered to be sinful pride, not authentic human selfhood.

What has escaped the attention of those who use such texts to denigrate the self is that in the very same context Paul can say, "I delight in the law of God, in my inmost self" (Rom. 7:22). The command of Jesus to love one's neighbor is grounded in the assumed reality of "love of oneself" (cf. Matt. 22:37-40; Lev. 19:18; Rom. 13:9; Gal. 5:14).

While there is no explicit command to "love oneself," it appears to be assumed as the basis for the motive power to love others. The self is not a "third object" to love, alongside of God and the neighbor. The construct of "self and neighbor," with God as the middle term, does not create an antithesis between self and the other (God), but can be understood as the very construct of love itself. In other words, love of self and neighbor, as grounded in God's love of both, is not two separate commands to love, nor two kinds of love. Rather, this command to love includes three aspects: God, the neighbor, and the self. One cannot despise oneself and truly love God or the neighbor.

From this we could say that esteem of the neighbor is simultaneously esteem of the self. True esteem of the self, consequently, cannot be held without also esteeming God and the neighbor as of ultimate and essential value to the self. This seems to lie behind Paul's admonition in Ephesians, "In the same way, husbands should love their wives as they do their own bodies. He who loves his wife loves himself. For no one ever hates his own body, but he nourishes and tenderly cares for it, just as Christ does for the church, because we are members of his body" (5:28-30).

Instead of self-esteem being the root of sin, lack of self-esteem in this sense is sinful, because it violates the single construct of love as including God, neighbor, and self. The problem with the more Augustinian concept of a totally depraved and sinful humanity is not its view of sin as vitiating and devastating every aspect of human life, but in its individualistic view of human selfhood. The premise of this negative view of the self is that it stands in abstraction and isolation from others. A biblical anthropology which views human personhood as intrinsically social as being in the divine image, will have no problem with self-esteem as a positive integrative factor of the self as well as a motive power for non-abusive relationships.[11]

The Hebrew concept of personhood is bound up in the corporate sense of life. Therefore, as Pedersen says, "The command to love . . . means that the individual acts for the whole, and the whole for the individual."[12]

The command to love one's neighbor is not invalid because of the sinfulness of the neighbor; human selfhood is *essentially* good as grounded in the image of God, and is to be loved, our own as well as our neighbor's. The negative aspect of self-love is described consistently in terms of its violation of the construct of love as social. So Paul can warn Timothy that in the last days there will be times of stress.

> *For people will be lovers of themselves, lovers of money, boasters, arrogant, abusive, disobedient to their parents, ungrateful, unholy, inhuman, implacable, slanderers, profligates, brutes, haters of good, treacherous, reckless, swollen with conceit, lovers of pleasure rather than lovers of God, holding to the outward form of godliness but denying its power. Avoid them! (2 Tim. 3:1-5)*

This is as much a description of a person incapable of loving oneself, and without self-esteem, as it is of antisocial behavior. The command of Jesus to "deny oneself" (cf. Matt. 16:24) may well be understood as a challenge to move out of negative self-esteem to positive self-esteem. For, as I have shown in the model in figure 5.1, negative self-esteem is a self-perception of powerlessness which resorts to manipulation and exploitation of others for one's own self-gratification. Positive self-esteem results in true self-worth and produces the "fruit of the Spirit."

The psychological as well as spiritual effects of grace are thus related to the recovery of the self's positive regard for itself as an object of the love of others, as well as a contributor to the good of others, and thus a person of worth and value. Meissner says:

> *Grace, therefore, operates to increase the ego's capacity to mobilize its inner resources and to perform effectively the ego functions that underlie*

the regulation of instinctive forces, reinforce the orientation to reality,
organize and direct the executive functions, and most significantly, carry
on the dynamic processes of synthesis and integration within the ego
itself — specifically contributing to the consolidation of the self and to its
capacity for mature and meaningful relationships.[13]

2. Self-assertion vs. submission

If negative self-esteem can be attributed as a factor behind the
problem of the use of power mechanisms to gain self-gratification, the theological concept of submission to authority as represented by familial and marital role relationships is equally a
problem. Parents who have been influenced by a theology which
reinforces the authority of a parent — and particularly that of the
male parent — over children will find ample biblical texts to support the use of force, if not violence in carrying out that divine
mandate.[14]

"Wives, be subject to your husbands, as is fitting in the
Lord" (Col. 3:18); "Children, obey your parents in everything,
for this is your acceptable duty in the Lord" (Col. 3:20). These
Pauline injunctions upon familial relations are prefaced in the
Ephesian parallel passage by the exhortation, "Be subject to one
another out of reverence for Christ" (Eph. 5:21). Yet, this tends
to be overshadowed by the repeated use of submission as primarily from the younger to the older, from the learner to the teach-
er, from the weaker to the stronger, and from the woman to the
man (cf. Heb. 13:17; 1 Peter 3:1).

If, indeed, such submission produces suffering and injustice,
some find biblical warrant for enduring such indignity patiently,
placing one's confidence and hope in God. "But if you endure
when you do right and suffer for it, you have God's approval"
(1 Peter 2:20).

Nonresistance to evil seems to consign the one suffering
abuse to "turning the other cheek," or to patiently endure the
evil with a good conscience. "But even if you do suffer for doing what is right," urges the Apostle Peter, "you are blessed"
(1 Peter 3:14).

Some may interpret protecting oneself from abuse as rebel-
lion against the divine order which in matters of authority has

placed children under parents and wives under husbands As a result, the church is tarnished by horror stories of pastors who have counseled abused women to remain with their husbands as a sign of spiritual obedience and with the promise that this kind of godly submission will eventually cause the husband to repent. Similarly, we have all too well become aware of the unreported cases of child abuse within church families where abuse is sanctified as "discipline."[15]

Over and against this theological tradition and practice, we must say two things:

First, the essential value of personhood as created in the image of God is related to the relative value and purpose of role relationships. The ethical intent of the biblical teaching is that the integrity and value of human personhood is primary to role relationship and function. Even in situations where a cultural role tradition which places some as slaves and some as masters is assumed, the value of persons is clearly affirmed as a higher value.

Paul has no hesitancy in counseling slaves that to remain in the state in which they were called is no infringement upon their fundamental value as persons in the sight of God. Yet, at the same time, he says, "You were bought with a price; do not become slaves of human masters," and "Even if you can gain your freedom, make use of your present condition more than ever" (1 Cor. 7:23, 21).

Likewise, though he urges that husbands and wives should honor their marriage vows, at the same time he says that "if the unbelieving partner separates, let it be so; in such a case the brother or sister is not bound. It is to peace *[Shalom]* that God has called you" (1 Cor. 7:15).

Second, we must understand fully the radical effect of redemption through Jesus Christ as applying to all structures and orders of human life, even those which are so-called "orders of creation."

For God has called us to peace and, I might add, to health and not sickness, to safety in relationships and not to terror, to self-respect and not to self-condemnation and to well-being emotionally, spiritually, and physically, not to being hurt. Self-assertion as a claim upon the mandate of God that each person be treated fairly and humanly in a relationship is honored by Him and blessed by Jesus. He recognizes and responds positively to the blind and sick who press through the crowds, even over the protests of the disciples, to be healed. Paul asserts himself in demanding that he be treated with dignity and respect as a Roman citizen when treated wrongly by the magistrates in Philippi (Acts 16:35-39). Paul encourages self-assertion when he advises slaves to avail themselves of the opportunity to "gain your freedom" (1 Cor. 7:21).

Self-assertion, like self-respect, is bound up with the single construct of love as inclusive of self and the other, with God as the middle term. Each person in a family relationship is to uphold the peace and health of the relationship as an active participant, not a passive partner or victim. "And whoever does not provide for relatives, and especially for family members, has denied the faith and is worse than an unbeliever" (1 Tim. 5:8). Without proper self-respect, self-assertion will be without love for the other, and consequently a cloak for use of power to meet one's own need at the expense of the other.

Providing is more than supplying material or physical resources; it is contributing to the health and wholeness of the family system. Each person is not only entitled, but is commanded to assert oneself to make this provision. And if it be resisted or denied, one must make this provision for oneself as part of the larger family of God. This then calls the church, as the family of families, to intervene where violence and abuse is occurring and to empower both the abuser and the abused to move toward healing, moral and spiritual development, and responsibility toward self and others.

3. Sinful self vs. spiritual self

Can one who is a sinner have a "healthy self concept"?

Martin and Diedre Bobgan attack the concept of self-esteem and the concept of a "healthy self" as contrary to biblical teaching.

Jesus taught truth, not what psychologists might call a "healthy self-concept."... What a person does in relationship with Christ is what counts, not what he might think about himself or even who he is in himself. . . . While believers have an identity in Christ, it is a relationship-concept rather than the kind of self-concept that would focus on who I am.[16]

The Bobgans argue that each of us is in a state of self-deception and that the only truth concerning our self is what the Bible teaches—that we are sinners and unworthy of God's love and grace.

If the positive illusionists cannot or will not face the truth about themselves, it is unlikely that they will face the truth about their deceitful hearts and thus they will be most unlikely to see a need for God. Such individuals are hiding beneath their positive illusions and will generally see no need for a Savior. Why should they? Exaggerated positive illusions that sustain self-esteem, a false sense of personal control and an unrealistic optimism about the future leave little room for the cross. . . . As Jesus said, only those who think they are sick go to the physician. And professing Christians who continue in their creative self-deception are less likely to walk with him.[17]

The Bobgans cite such Scriptures as John 8:31-34, 44, in support of their claim that only the truth which God teaches about the self can be trusted. To John 8:44: "You are from your father the devil, and you choose to do your father's desires," the Bobgans respond, "Was that a 'healthy self-concept' or was it the truth?"[18] They support their negative concept of the self by such Scriptures as:

Jeremiah 17:9: "The heart is deceitful above all things, and desperately wicked: Who can know it?"
Isaiah 64:6: "But we are all as an unclean thing."
Romans 7:18: "For I know that in me (that is, in my flesh) dwelleth no good thing."
Ephesians 2:3: ". . . by nature we are the children of wrath" (KJV).

Based on such texts, the Bobgans go on to assert: "The Bible teaches that the sinful self is initially dealt with by the cross of

Christ and that believers are thereafter enabled to put off the old self by denying it, by not letting self rule."[19]

Don Matzat, whom I cited earlier in this chapter, carries out this theology of death to the self with a vengeance.

> *The Holy Spirit calls us to separate from ourselves as separating from that which is dead. Regarding yourself as dead is the ultimate act of self-rejection. It is one thing to feel bad about yourself; it is something far more intense to consider yourself a "dead thing." . . . Jesus calls us to separate from the "dead thing," to lose our lives, to deny ourselves and cling in faith to him.[20]*

Does our spiritual identity depend entirely upon rejection of our psychological identity as unworthy and the source of evil? The German Lutheran theologian Wolfhart Pannenberg does not think so. Pannenberg argues that the Reformation produced a type of piety, or spirituality, which was based on a perpetual "repentance for sin" which he calls "penitential piety."

> *Guilt consciousness is not, as such, a type of Christian piety. It has been pervasive in human experience and became an important element of many religious traditions. It was prominent in Judaism and rose to particular importance in Christianity because the Christian message is so closely connected with forgiveness of sins and redemption from the power of sin by the death of Jesus Christ. . . . Although for the Reformers the message of the gospel was liberation from sin, anxiety, and guilt consciousness, yet it was addressed to precisely that mentality. . . . the glorious freedom of the Christian in Protestant piety could not rid itself of guilt consciousness. On the contrary, Protestant piety would focus increasingly on the awareness of sin and guilt as a condition for genuine faith.[21]*

Pannenberg suggests that such a negative and pervasive view of self-identity as always incapable of authentic spiritual life makes the contemporary Christian vulnerable to the criticisms of Nietzsche and Freud. This is so, asserts Pannenberg,

> *because pietism, especially in its late revivalistic forms, made meditation on guilt and sinfulness the basic and permanent condition for commu-*

nion with God. But if consciousness of guilt is equivalent to nonidentity, this type of piety traps the individual in alienation. There is no escape from such alienation because there is combined with it a fantastic conception of self-identity in the name of salvation. Such a self-conception is doomed to remain fantastic because the permanent self-consciousness of personal sinfulness does not allow the individual to establish a new identity.[22]

Pannenberg insightfully suggests that a type of piety by which one attempts to gain a spiritual identity implies an interpretation of the world of human experience, a historical system of life. From this perspective one could fruitfully examine the concept of piety implicit in the various Christian views of the self underlying the approach to therapy and counseling.

Robert Schuller, for example, argues much like Pannenberg that the Reformation bequeathed to us a concept of the self as essentially sinful and negative. "Negative-thinking theologians looked at the doctrine of sin, salvation, and repentance (yes, even the Incarnation, Crucifixion, and, to a degree, the Resurrection) through distorted glasses tinted with a mortification mentality."[23] Too many prayers of confession of sin and repentance have been destructive to the emotional health of Christians, says Schuller, by "feeding their sense of nonworth." The "original sin" which we seem to inherit, says Schuller, is not an overly pronounced sense of pride and self-worth, but an "ugly loss of self-esteem."[24]

Contrary to the Bobgans, Schuller holds that the Bible teaches the "truth" concerning ourselves as "worth saving" because of the intrinsic value which we possess as created in the divine image. The "self-deception," then, is not an illusion that we are worth more than we actually are, but that we deceive ourselves by attributing less value to our selves! At the same time, one can question whether Schuller has really grasped the true nature of sin as the instinct for self-gratification driven by the need to fulfill one's own needs through manipulation and power mechanisms.

How can we resolve this tension between negative and positive self-worth in light of the Scriptures? Consider some of the teachings of Jesus:

Unless a grain of wheat falls into the earth and dies, it remains just a single grain; but if it dies, it bears much fruit (John 12:24).

Those who try to make their life secure will lose it, but those who lose their life will keep it (Luke 17:33).

Likewise, consider the view of Paul:

What is sown is perishable, what is raised is imperishable. It is sown in dishonor, it is raised in glory. It is sown in weakness, it is raised in power. It is sown a physical body, it is raised a spiritual body (1 Cor. 15:42-44).

The metaphor of sowing and reaping suggests that the self which does not express itself by thrusting itself into life, is already dead, and will not "bear fruit." The infertility of the self as unexpressed and the life "not lived" is clearly drawn out of the metaphor of sowing and reaping.

The "remaining alone" is suggestive of the alienation which Pannenberg says results from a kind of piety which continually exists in a state of penitence and guilt consciousness.

Jürgen Moltmann offers a cogent commentary on this theme when he says:

The secret of human life is easy to understand: anyone who wants to keep his life, and therefore holds on to it and keeps it back, will lose it; he already loses it by becoming incapable of living. But anyone who lives his life and commits it and surrenders it, will gain that life; he already gains it by becoming alive. Keeping his life means withdrawing his soul from the body, withdrawing his interest from life in the body, "keeping himself to himself" and, out of the sheer remembrance that he has to die, not daring to live at all. Anyone who holds himself back like this does not become immortal. He remains dead. Surrendering one's life means going out of oneself, exposing oneself, committing oneself and loving. In this affirmation life becomes alive in the truly human sense. Anyone who lives like this will be mortal, but he dies meaningfully. Life that is never lived cannot die. But life that is truly and fully affirmed can die. Dying belongs to the lived life and is part of it. [25]

Only a positive concept of the self can take responsibility for being guilty of sin in a healthy way. The self is good before it can become bad. Even in becoming bad, the self remains in the "image" of God and retains its self-identity through God's grace and love. The recovery of this self is what is promised in the Gospel, not the crucifixion and annihilation of the self.

Self-identity is grounded in relationship, both social and spiritual. Thus, we cannot have a positive and healthy spiritual relationship with God (such as the Boogans desire) without positive and healthy relations with others. Adam apparently could have had some kind of spiritual identity prior to the creation of woman, as God was in relationship and communication with him. But it was God who made the diagnosis, this is "not good" (Gen. 2:18). Adam's personal self-identity was to be grounded in cohumanity, not in sheer individuality.

As a biblical alternative to "penitential piety," which alienates and distorts the self, Pannenberg argues for "eucharistic piety" which "liberates the Christian from individualism on the one hand and from an overemphasis on the legal authority of ecclesiastical institutions on the other. . . . Only a broad conception of eucharistic symbolism as relating to the destiny of all humanity can achieve this, because nothing that is not relevant to all humanity can constitute the human identity of the individual."[26] In the body of Christ gathered as a eucharistic community, positively grounded in mutual love and belonging, is found the basis for self-identity, concludes Pannenberg.

Arthur Miller's Willy Loman is a fictional character. Yet, his pathetic attempts to rescue his self-identity from the abyss of failure touches a chord in all of us. Those closest to him perpetuated the fraud that was his life. Only his son, Biff, far too late, seemed to gain the insight that might have saved him "The man didn't know who he was."

The lack of positive self-esteem may be a contributing factor in relationships where a pattern of abuse is found. One of the keys to understanding why a loving relationship can become abusive is in the failure of persons to develop positive self-esteem. In the next chapter, this relationship between negative self-esteem and abuse will be explored.

SUMMARY

- Positive self-esteem is the absence of self-hate, as well as a strong sense of personal worth as the object of God's love and the affirmation of others.

- A theology of self-esteem is based on the self as originally created in the divine image and as the object of God's love and concern.

- The self as originally created by God includes a drive toward self-pleasure which has its goal in self-fulfillment. This drive is not in itself sinful. Sin emerges in the claim to power by which self-gratification becomes an end in itself, leading to behaviors which are destructive and even violent.

- Negative self-esteem results from a sense of powerlessness and lack of positive self-worth. The grace of God does not cancel out the intrinsic drive for self-fulfillment, but frees and empowers the self by developing self-worth.

- The concept of self-esteem may be criticized as having an exaggerated and presumptuous estimate of the self if it is understood as merely a projection of a self in defiance of the self's dependence upon God. At the same time, however, the self has intrinsic value to God and, therefore, in acknowledging Him, can freely acknowledge its own worth and value to God and others.

- Only one who has a positive self-esteem can take responsibility for sin and wrongdoing in a healthy way. This gives us a clue as to preventing abusive and violent behavior in domestic and social relations.

PRAXIS

Norm had been meeting with the pastor for several weeks following his arrest for indecent exposure. His attempt at taking responsibility for his actions by admitting that they were "stupid," to use his own words, and stating his intention never to do it again, did not give him the inward peace he sought. Nor was his wife, Ella, able to sustain her confidence in him. "I don't really think that he will ever change," Ella confided to the pastor. "He has withdrawn more into himself than ever." The pastor continued to explore Norm's feelings about himself. "I think that God has forgiven me," he said, "but I cannot forgive myself. I really hate myself for having sexual desires and thoughts that I cannot control." The pastor appeared to have ignored this last remark and asked, "Did your parents ever catch you doing something wrong, and how did that make you feel?" Norm responded quickly, "More often than I want to remember. One time especially, my mother walked into my room when I was masturbating and told me that I was violating my own body and that I ought to be ashamed of myself. She said that if I kept that up I would end up just like my father, always thinking about sex. I guess that she was right. Maybe I am just a demented person."

- The pastor's first impulse is to reassure him by suggesting ways in which he has proved to be a person of integrity and value. Why should the pastor not follow this impulse?

- From what was said in this chapter about self-esteem, what are some of the theological teachings that actually reinforce Norm's negative feelings about himself?

- What is your own view of the biblical teaching about self-worth?

- Now that the pastor has opened up this area of Norm's life, what spiritual counsel can be given and what approach should the pastor take in developing a more positive self-esteem in Norm?

PART TWO

Healing the Wounded Person

6

Abuse:
Why People Who Hate Themselves Often Hurt Others

You are more likely to be physically assaulted, beaten, and killed in your own home at the hands of a loved one than any place else, or by anyone else in our society. (Richard Gelles and Murray Straus)

You always hurt the one you love," is an adage that may have had its origin in a country and western song, but it is a painful reality for many abused children and spouses in our contemporary homes.

Sociologists Richard Gelles and Murray Straus state it as plainly as can be said.

> *You are more likely to be physically assaulted, beaten, and killed in your own home at the hands of a loved one than any place else, or by any one else in our society. . . . In our society, a person's earliest experiences with violence comes in the home—spankings and physical punishment from parents. We learn that there is always going to be a certain amount of violence that accompanies intimacy.[1]*

The incidence of abusive behavior is shocking and sobering.

We can account for violence in the streets by attributing such actions to persons who have no concern for the rights of others. I do not feel betrayed if a stranger assaults me. I may suffer injury and experience emotional trauma, but I am not hurt nearly so much as I would be if one that claims to love me causes the injury and the trauma. The fact that intimate social relationships are high risk situations for abuse demands closer analysis. If there is some correlation between intimacy and family violence, we need to discover the inner dynamics of such a correlation and attempt to develop preventative methods of intervention.

INTIMACY AND FAMILY VIOLENCE

Abusive behavior within the family is different from all other forms of violence in that it has its highest potential for injury where there is the greatest potential for intimacy and love. The most dangerous place for a child in our society is in the home, according to child molestation and abuse statistics. The most dangerous place for a woman is not on the streets, but in some form of intimate relationship with a man. In a published report by the American Medical Association, it was revealed that one out of every four women in the United States experiences some form of abuse from a man she lives with or to whom she is related. One-third of all women who arrive at doctors' offices or hospitals seeking emergency treatment, and up to one-quarter of all those seeking prenatal care, are victims of domestic violence. Each year, 4 million women are severely assaulted by their current or former partner. More than half of female murder victims are slain by their husband or boyfriend.[2]

Our first thought on hearing these statistics is to suppose that the absence of love in the context of domestic and family intimacy accounts for such abuse. If adults really loved their children, we protest, as well as each other, it would be impossible for such abuse to occur. Wrong. Family violence is not due to the absence of love, for love and violence can coexist as systemic components of primary relationships where persons are the most vulnerable. Gelles and Straus insist that love and violence can actually both be present in the same relationship.

> *That violence and love can actually coexist in families is perhaps the most insidious aspect of intimate violence because it means that, unlike violence in the streets, we are tied to abusers by the bonds of love, attachment, and affection. . . . Perhaps the greatest challenge to understanding intimate violence and devising adequate social polity is to see violence and love as coexisting in the same relationship.*[3]

Nor can we attribute acts of violence between persons who live together to some form of mental derangement, as though "normal" persons would never resort to such actions. The fact is, as Gelles and Straus report, "only about 10 percent of abusive incidents are caused by mental illness. The remaining 90 percent are not amenable to psychological explanation."[4] The majority of persons who commit family violence are "normal" persons measured by accepted societal standards. This means that psychiatric treatment will not ordinarily prove effective in reducing the incidence of this kind of abusive behavior.

Does this suggest, then, that there is a range of "normal" violence that should be expected and tolerated in these domestic settings? Is it not normal for parents to use force in disciplining a child? Do not people who love each other often express their anger through even "pushing and shoving"? Should we make allowance for the "normal" but not "abusive"?

The distinction between "normal" and "abusive" violence, once used to distinguish between the force used in attempts to discipline as against violence which causes injury no longer has credibility among many sociologists.[5] For this reason, I prefer to speak of abusive relationships where physical violence may or may not occur. Abuse is always, to some degree, a violation of the other person. Because we have tended to associate violence with the use of physical force resulting in physical harm, actual abuse often goes undetected and unacknowledged.

THE MORAL PARADOX IN ABUSIVE BEHAVIOR

In the previous chapter I attempted to show that negative self-esteem is grounded in a sense of powerlessness caused by resistance to the instinct for self-gratification. The fusion of the need

Need

for self-fulfillment with the instinct for self-gratification when coupled with a sense of being "all-powerful," causes the self to compensate through behaviors that are manipulative, controlling, and finally abusive.

A further dimension to this analysis can now be provided. Persons who are apprehended and brought to account for acts of family abuse and violence often express a sense of moral outrage as the motive for such actions.

On one occasion, a man, whom I will call Ralph, charged with assault against his wife for inflicting physical injuries which necessitated her hospitalization, came to me for pastoral counseling. Ralph considered himself to be a strong Christian and was an active participant in the life of the church. As he recited the events that led up to the physical assault, he told me, "Pastor, I never intended to hurt her. I am truly sorry for what I have done. But she was resisting my authority in the home and putting me down in front of the kids. I only intended to bring her under submission because she was out of control. Isn't that my responsibility as a man and the head of my house. Don't I have a right to expect my wife to obey me?"

I began to realize that he was willing to accept responsibility and to repent for his actions which led to her physical injury, but not for his attempt to "bring her under control." I felt his moral indignation rise when he described what it felt like when she resisted his attempt to "subdue" her and to bring her "under submission" to him. He also cited the Bible as support of his role of exercising authority in the home and marriage.

This experience gave me the first clue that behind some actions of violence in domestic situations there is not only a need to regain power and control, but also a primitive moral reaction to what feels like a "violation" of one's natural rights. Ralph was caught in the double bind of feeling that he had a moral (and scriptural) right to discipline his wife for her insubordination but, at the same time, he was deeply grieved over his actions which led to her physical harm. He sought God's forgiveness for his sin of violence and promised never to do it again. At the time, my instincts told me that he needed more than forgiveness, he needed a deeper healing of God's grace for which I felt quite unprepared to offer.

Ralph was humiliated and contrite; his self-esteem was shattered by the discrepancy between the perceptions he wanted to hold about himself and the violence that he himself actually committed. In looking back on this case, I now think that what he and others might have considered as "high self-esteem" was actually a very negative self-esteem seeking compensation through ideations of spiritual attainment and successful role modeling as a good husband and father.

My first assessment was that he suffered from low self-esteem and thus compensated for this by attempting to "bully" his wife and children. Upon further analysis, I have concluded that he suffered from a crippled self-love complicated by a chronic sense of being robbed of the power that was morally and rightfully his. His self-esteem, that he would have considered to be quite high, was actually very fragile. This made it difficult for him to negotiate the ordinary give-and-take of a relationship. Questions which were intended to provide options and alternatives were taken to be attacks on his authority, prompting hostile reactions. I began to suspect that Ralph actually hated himself and that this self-hatred fueled his anger which led him to hurt others who were close to him.

Attempts to relate low self-esteem with a tendency toward abusive and violent behavior have not been successful. This may be because of a failure to see that self-esteem actually has two standards for measurement. If one uses the high/low measurement, the discrepancy within the self may be concealed. One could conceivably build up a high sense of self-esteem, but deep within the self harbor a sense of failure or unworthiness. Ralph would be considered a person with a relative high degree of self-esteem. This is why his outbreaks of violence were so shattering to him. This is also why recovery of self-esteem was so vital and which was sought through the "quick fix" of repentance and forgiveness, with a promise never to do it again.

If we use the criteria of negative or positive self-esteem, we can access more accurately the underlying perception of the self as to its worth. A perception of high self-esteem may contain within it self-hatred and a deep sense of worthlessness or shame.

My own analysis leads me to believe that negative self-esteem invariably has to do with feelings of powerlessness coupled with a pervading sense of moral outrage.

When negative self-esteem is understood as a diminished sense of power and control, the seeds of violence and abusive behavior become more visible. In more technical terms, this can be called "narcissistic damage" to the self, resulting from a failure to make the developmental transition from self-pleasure to self-fulfillment.

Because the infantile narcissism is a manifestation of the instinct for self-fulfillment grounded in the image of God, there is a powerful sense of moral entitlement which is present along with the narcissism. Resistance to the narcissistic need for self-gratification not only results in a sense of powerlessness, it can lead to a sense of moral outrage. When narcissism is fused with a feeling of omnipotence, Meissner's "primitive moral instinct" arises.

The need to regain power through controlling tactics then rests on a moral basis with the result that abusive behavior can seem to have a moral instinct hidden in its emotional feeling. There is a violence inherent in the moral sense, says Meissner.

> *Moral rules are based on a primitive level of development. They are derived from fear, a response to threats of abandonment, punishment, exposure, or the inner threat of guilt, shame, or isolation. Ethical rules, however, are based on ideals to be striven for. . . . There is a violence inherent in the moral sense. We violate children and arouse them to an inner rage when we keep them from the guidance and support they need to develop fully. Nonviolence means more than the preservation of another's physical inviolancy; it means the protection of his essence as a developing person and personality.* [6]

It is inevitable that each infant will experience frustration of the pleasure instinct to some degree, for the self is incapable in its earliest stages of development to accept delayed gratification of pleasure as a moral value. The fusion of pleasure and a sense of omnipotence takes place before there is a chance for the self to differentiate between the feelings of pleasure and power. Having the pleasure instinct gratified gives one an immediate sense of power. The infant experiences a feeling of omnipotence in receiving gratification from those who have the power to give it.

This sense of being "all-powerful" is an acquired feeling: it is not innate such as is the pleasure instinct. We are not born with a sense of power, but each of us possesses from birth a need for self-fulfillment. At the core of the pleasure instinct is a deep longing for the fulfillment of self through relation to another. This "God-created" longing seeks fulfillment in its source; that is the love of God. Human love and relation is a reflection of that divine image which is experienced as a longing and desire for self-fulfillment. There is, in a sense, a 'moral right" to this fulfillment, so that if it is denied there is a sense of violation and even injury to the self. The earliest experience of this longing for self-fulfillment is the pleasure instinct in the child. The feeling of omnipotence for the child becomes attached to a sense of ownership of space, toys, and even persons.

A schematic diagram which depicts this movement of the pleasure instinct toward violence and self-indulgence when resistance is met would look something like this.

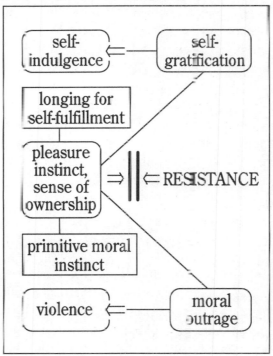

Figure 6.1

Figure 6.1 is read by beginning with the center box in which the fusion of the pleasure instinct and the sense of ownership occurs. When resistance is met, a splitting occurs, with the pleasure instinct moving toward self-gratification and finally toward self-indulgence. The sense of ownership, fueled by a primitive moral instinct, moves toward moral outrage and even violence. In making this response, the self has collapsed in on itself, twisting the moral sense into self-justification, and the longing for self-fulfillment into self-indulgence.

When the self acquires the feeling of being in control and having ownership of what is needed for self-gratification, the moral instinct shifts from pleasure to power of ownership. When the desire for pleasure is frustrated, it is perceived as a threat to the moral right to possess that which is needed for one's gratification. The instinct to recover one's control over the situation can lead to abuse of the rights and person of others. The culmination of this process in acts of violence brings moral condemnation on the abuser.

The moral paradox of abusive behavior lies in the contradiction between the sense of moral outrage felt when denied what is perceived as necessary to self-identity (self-esteem) and the abusive (immoral) behavior that results. When Ralph came to me for counseling, he could not express this moral paradox conceptually, but he was surely caught in the moral self-contradiction of his intentions and actions. What Ralph failed to understand was that abusive behavior does not suddenly spring up out of nowhere. There is a continuum of behavior that begins long before there is an overt expression of it.

THE MORAL CONTINUUM OF ABUSIVE BEHAVIOR

Whenever abusive relationships occur there is a violation of the personal being of one person by another. The risk of abuse is greater when persons are in primary relationships where intimate contact is experienced. This accounts for the high incidence of abuse between family members. Primary relationships tend to be intimate, personal, and sensitive. Secondary relationships tend to be more functional, impersonal, and task-oriented.

The checkout person at the supermarket may be friendly, but basically functions in a secondary type relationship to me. If he is impersonal and quite insensitive to my feelings on that particular day, I do not feel abused, though I may be irritated. We seem to have an instinctive sense of when we are moving out of primary relationships into secondary ones when we leave the company of a good friend to stand in line at the Department of Motor Vehicles! There is a sense of abuse when confronted by the impersonal nature of a bureaucracy, to be sure, but it is quite different from the same treatment by one who professes to love and care for us.

Primary relationships carry an implicit promise of mutual care, respect, and trust. It is only on the basis of such qualities in the relationship that we risk ourselves to the intimacy of sharing our thoughts, personal space, and physical touch. When we form such relationships we expect to feel safe, free to respond, and nurtured in our own need for self-care. The moment that we no longer feel safe or free to respond, a violation has occurred, and abuse has begun.

In pastoral counseling I have discovered that teenage dating patterns reveal tendencies toward abusive behavior under the sanction of accepted cultural roles in the relationship. Because men are often assumed to have the responsibility for initiating a relationship, women can feel disempowered and helpless when confronted with demands for intimacy which feel like a violation of personal integrity. Fearing rejection and possibly the loss of the relationship, the woman may feel pressured to respond. At this moment, the relationship has become oppressive, coercive, and demanding. Men are invariably shocked and defensive when this is pointed out to them. However, women are not always ready to call this abusive behavior. Only after marriage, in many cases, does the more overt abuse become apparent in the form of economic, emotional, and physical forms of oppression and coercion.

Incidents of abuse may appear to be isolated and unconnected, but the deeper pattern is more systemic. The underlying problem of negative self-esteem and a self-perception of powerlessness can pervade all of the relationships an offender has. One case of domestic violence may be closely connected to other acts of violence or abuse in the home. Studies have shown that child abuse incidents are higher in homes where there is spouse abuse.[7]

Without careful empirical studies, it would be impossible to say that negative self-esteem is a contributing factor to such abusive behavior. Anecdotal evidence, however, suggests that there may well be some correlation. The typical pattern in abusive incidents is one in which the need to control is strongly present, coupled with perceptions of self-inadequacy. The victim experiences the offender as oppressive, coercive, demanding, exploitative, destructive, and crippling. These are the negative aspects of an abusive relationship. The positive counterparts are relationships which are safe, responsive, nurturing, productive, and empowering.

If negative self-esteem is rooted in a lack of self-worth and a sense of powerlessness, the need for control, or being controlled, sets the pattern of abuse. The structure of an abusive relationship may include negative self-esteem on the part of both the offender and the victim. In this case, the victim lacks the self-worth and ego strength to set boundaries or, as may well be necessary, to terminate the relationship as the first step in self-recovery from the abusive situation. This may explain the fact that victims of abuse often find it difficult to report abuse or, even when reported, to terminate the relationship.

These can be placed on a continuum of relationships ranging from loving to abusive, correlated with positive and negative self-esteem. Figure 6.2 on page 131 depicts the kinds of behavior which often occurs on the continuum of abuse.

The left side of the continuum represents loving relationships and lists the attributes of healthy relationships noted above. The right side of the continuum represents the abusive side and lists the characteristics of dysfunctional relationships. Note that there is a continuum on which each of the contrasting relationship pairs are placed. When a relationship no longer feels safe, it is already abusive to the degree that it is experienced as oppressive. When one no longer feels free to respond but is coerced into responding, it is abusive.

An abusive relationship is fundamentally based on power dynamics. Where the abuser has a power advantage by virtue of

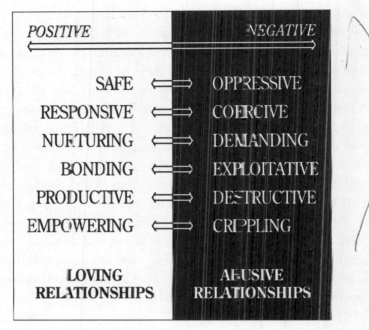

POSITIVE		NEGATIVE
SAFE	⟺	OPPRESSIVE
RESPONSIVE	⟺	COERCIVE
NURTURING	⟺	DEMANDING
BONDING	⟺	EXPLOITATIVE
PRODUCTIVE	⟺	DESTRUCTIVE
EMPOWERING	⟺	CRIPPLING
LOVING RELATIONSHIPS		**ABUSIVE RELATIONSHIPS**

Figure 6.2

gender, role, professional status, or financial assets, controlling type of behavior is extremely effective. When this power differential is coupled with negative self-esteem, the offender may carry a hidden "moral rage" at feeling so inadequate that abusive behavior brings a certain satisfaction to this primitive moral instinct. Gelles and Straus suggest that acts of violence occur when the costs of being violent do not outweigh the rewards.

> *Clearly, the immediate rewards of using violence to work off anger or frustration are quite valuable to some individuals who would rather not wait to see the longer-term benefits of more reasoned and rational discipline and conversation with their children or partners. . . . Power, control, and self-esteem are other rewards of family violence. . . . Being in control, being master (or apparent master) of a situation, increases one's sense of self-worth. For men or parents whose sense of self-esteem may have been damaged or devalued by experiences outside of the home . . . control at home is even more important.[8]*

The recent focus on sexual harassment in the workplace points to the same continuum of abuse. Men are often totally unaware of what constitutes sexual harassment because of the cultural pattern of male sexuality which dissociates intimacy from physical sexuality. When the criteria of what constitutes abusive behavior are applied, as defined above, the issue is not so much the sexual aspect of the relationship but the issues of gender and power. The power dynamics of the workplace tend to place women at a disadvantage with regard to equal opportunity and recognition with men. In the case of sexual harassment, the particular form of the oppression, coercion, and exploitation which serve to preserve the power differential is gender oriented and sexually contrived. When sexual harassment is seen as a form of abusive relationships, it can better be understood and dealt with. A model for the prevention of abuse and domestic violence begins with a process of self-recovery where negative self-esteem is overcome, and positive self-esteem is developed through the empowering of God's grace and love.

The process of recovery which leads to self-empowerment is not an easy one, however, and when it is not completed adequately in the development of the self, some level of abusive behavior can occur in primary relationships.

THE RECOVERY OF SELF-EMPOWERMENT

To make an effective intervention into this moral paradox of abusive behavior, the sense of moral outrage must be transformed into a sense of moral worth. The key to the "re-framing" of negative to positive self-esteem lies in a therapy of empowerment through unconditional love by which the narcissistic damage is healed, and the self-love originally intended by God is restored.[9]

Theologically, self-empowerment is understood as the power of new birth through the Spirit and grace of God. This is not, however, an effort of the self to promote its own well-being and to fulfill its own needs. Such efforts have already been seen to produce failure, powerlessness, and moral outrage. The grace of God does not "dis-empower," but empowers the self, leading to feelings of self-worth and self-fulfillment.

Psychologically, the re-framing process restores a sense of self-integrity and unity. In it, positive ego strength is released as the psychic energy needed to suffer delayed gratification for the sake of more fulfilling relationships and goals. W.W. Meissner suggests that the grace of God can empower the ego to regulate instinctive forces. The pleasure instinct can therefore also be regarded as subject to the ego's management.

> *Grace, therefore, operates to increase the ego's capacity to mobilize its inner resources and to perform effectively the ego-functions that under-lie the regulation of instinctive forces, that reinforce the orientation to reality, that organize and direct the executive functions, and most significantly, carry on the dynamic processes of synthesis and integration within the ego itself, specifically contributing to the consolidation of the self and to its capacity for mature and meaningful relationships.* [10]

The dynamics of self-empowerment must include some form of forgiveness where abuse has occurred or the part of the victim, as well as self-forgiveness on the part of the offender. Beverly Flanigan has made an approach to this important aspect of recovery in her book, *Forgiving the Unforgivable — Overcoming the Bitter Legacy of Intimate Wounds.*

> *People who forgive sever themselves from the past and look to the future. In the emergence of a new self, the person who has gone through major conversions in his beliefs about very central things in his life (like other travelers) ends his journey, unpacks his figurative bags, and gets life back to normal. Whatever he chooses to do, it will be a time when his new beliefs gathered along the journey to forgiveness are consolidated and tested. . . . If nothing can ever be the same, this time around it can be even better.* [11]

From a cognitive behavioral approach, this therapeutic suggestion offers a way to overcome the "cognitive dissonance" caused by the injury to the self. The perception of inadequate self-worth, she believes, can be removed by introjecting a new belief about the self. The emergence of a new self, results from the "gift of forgiveness" by which the old self is forgotten and a new life of the self begins.

The gift of forgiving, then, is the relaxation of vigilance. The new self becomes more relaxed, less defensive and brittle. Forgivers know they can be wounded and have learned to take the idea in as part of their working perceptions of reality. They have experienced the worst of pain. Everything ahead should be much easier. [12]

I have presented this approach to forgiveness by Flanigan as a recent and practical attempt to release the victims of abuse from bondage to grievous injuries to the self. At the same time, such an approach fails to take into consideration the moral issue with regard to abuse. Forgiveness, biblically speaking, is much more than cognitive integration of the fact of injury in the larger scheme of things.

THE MORAL BASIS FOR FORGIVENESS

Any injury to the self produces an instinctive moral judgment, usually in the form of an accusation against the one who caused the injury. Until this moral judgment is resolved it is not possible to talk of forgiveness. Along with the moral judgment, there is the desire to inflict punishment against the offender. A distinction between judgment and punishment is essential in order to understand the role of forgiveness in self-recovery. A judgment is something like a verdict rendered in a court of law. One is pronounced guilty or innocent. Punishment is like the sentence imposed by the court. In determining punishment, extenuating circumstances can be taken into consideration so that not all who are judged as guilty experience the same punishment.

Forgiveness is not absolving an offender from judgment, but is a release of the offender from punishment. For example, a good friend may betray you by sharing some information given in confidence with the result that you suffer shame and humiliation. The act of betrayal is a violation which produces an instinctive moral judgment against the one who committed the offense. If the friend, when confronted with the fact, acknowledges that betrayal indeed took place, then the issue of judgment has been resolved. Forgiveness is now possible because judgment has been rendered and the offense to the moral instinct of the self has been resolved. Releasing the offender from further punishment is what forgiveness does.

Ethel (not her real name) is the wife of a pastor. She had suffered sexual abuse from her brother at an early age and only recently had disclosed this to her husband. Her brother denied the abuse ever took place. Her husband refused to take sides and told her that this was something that only she could resolve through forgiveness and spiritual healing.

Despite more than a year of therapy with a Christian psychologist, she was unable to let go of the anger she felt and was troubled by her inability to forgive. At a pastor's conference where I spoke on the subject of abuse, she approached me and shared her story. When I asked whether or not she had ever had a verdict rendered concerning the offense, she shook her head and said, "No one will take sides against my brother. Even my husband feels that he is in no position to make a judgment as he was not part of the family at the time."

I explained again the difference between a verdict and punishment and told her that I accepted her account as true. "The verdict is guilty as charged," I told her. "Now you can think about the punishment which he deserves. Forgiveness does not nullify a verdict, it only releases the offender from punishment."

Some weeks later, her therapist approached me and said, "Your counsel to Ethel has released her from the anger and sense of personal shame that we have been working on for months. She is now working on forgiveness out of her own sense of empowerment as a beginning of spiritual healing."

In a domestic violence or child abuse case there is a deep-seated moral offense which has been committed against the person abused. The victim will need to be supported and affirmed in making a judgment against the offense, as well as against the offender, that addresses the moral issue in the abuse hidden within the pain. Once this judgment has been rendered as rightfully directed against the offender, the victim no longer is caught in self-blame. The feelings of outrage have now been dealt with. The feelings of anger can be allowed to be processed as emotion. Outrage is grounded in a moral sense, while anger is primarily an emotion which is capable of cognitive re-framing. Bringing forth a judgment against an offender draws the outrage to a conclusion. To continue to express condemnation once the judgment has been rendered is not necessary to satisfy the moral instinct.

Judgment and punishment can sometimes become blurred in the feelings of the victim. Moral outrage and anger are not clearly distinguished at the emotional level. Judgment and punishment are actually part of a two-step process. To judge another who has abused you as morally wrong is to satisfy the moral instinct of the self. To inflict punishment is a step beyond judgment. Punishing an offender for a wrong done may often be beyond the power or competence of the victim.

The Bible does not prohibit us from passing judgment against moral wrong. At the same time, it warns us about exacting vengeance against the offender. "Beloved, never avenge yourselves," writes the Apostle Paul, "but leave room for the wrath of God; for it is written, 'Vengeance is mine, I will repay, says the Lord'" (Rom. 12:19; cf. Deut. 32:35).

Once judgment has been rendered, the moral issue has been resolved and the basis for outrage removed. Anger, of course, continues to be a factor, as do the feelings that the offender should suffer for the wrong done. Forgiveness does not excuse the wrongdoing nor does it bypass judgment. Forgiveness is only possible when the moral judgment has been rendered and supported. Forgiveness is itself a moral and spiritual achievement when it can be exercised. It is an acknowledgment that justice has been rendered through the moral judgment made and moves the self toward recovery through the building of positive self-esteem.

Suppose the offender in the case of abuse denies the offense, as typically happens. When an offender does not acknowledge the wrong done through abuse, it is difficult, if not impossible, for forgiveness to be expressed. This is because forgiveness demands a moral threshold upon which to stand, ordinarily established when a judgment has been rendered.

James Leehan reminds us that it may be inappropriate to expect the moral behavior of "forgiveness" from the victim of abuse. The moral virtue of forgiveness offered to an offender requires a reciprocity of relation as a moral context for forgiveness, which is not always present. In the case of child abuse, for example, victims of such trauma may be expected to express forgiveness as a moral or religious virtue.

> *To expect forgiveness to be their initial response to abusive parents is to deny the reality of what was done to them. They need to deal with that reality in order to heal the scars which mar their lives. To berate them for their behavior may well convince them that they are not able to live up to the moral expectations or religious beliefs of any church or synagogue.*[12]

Those who have been the victims of abusive behavior need an advocate to enter in and empower them to render a moral judgment against the offender, whether the offender acknowledges wrong or not. This intervention serves to authenticate the outrage done to the self and serves to render a moral judgment against the offender and on behalf of the victim. This does make forgiveness possible in the sense of giving over to God the punishment (vengeance) and freeing the self to be healed of the hurt and anger.

Behind all injuries to the self, regardless of the cause, there is a moral need for justice to be done. This can take the form of expressing a moral judgment on behalf of the injured person, even if the offender will not acknowledge responsibility.

When small children argue over the possession of a toy, and one strikes the other when robbed of the toy, the violence against the offender conceals the deeper moral injury done to the one whose toy was taken. In this case, a parent's response should not cause the child who committed the physical violence to feel guilty of a crime! Rather, the child should be assured, "It was wrong of Bobby to take your toy. He should not have done that to you." By saying this, the child's sense of moral outrage is addressed. At the same time, Bobby can be told, "It was wrong of Timothy to bite you. He should not have done that." It will take some time for the feelings of anger to subside so that forgiveness can be offered and received. To force a child prematurely to say, "I am sorry," compounds the feelings of moral outrage. Confession of wrongdoing and the offer of forgiveness both require positive self-esteem and the recovery of the self from the outrage experienced.

The matter of taking punishment into their own hands can be dealt with in good time, in the hope that they will learn how to forgive based on the judgment rendered against the offense. It doesn't actually work that easily, of course, but the example illustrates the point that all injuries to the self produce moral outrage and that this moral instinct demands that a judgment be rendered.

When an offense against us has produced the emotion of anger, the anger is actually a form of moral outrage and becomes a strong defense of the vulnerable self that has been wounded. To berate a person for that anger and attempt to move one quickly to a position of passivity and acceptance is to take away what appears to be their strength and leave them weak and even more vulnerable. "If survivors of abuse seek pastoral counseling and again are told not be angry, they are being told that they are not worth caring about. . . . We must accept and even encourage their anger as an appropriate response to the injustice that has been done to them. We must support their feelings and share our own anger about the way they have been mistreated."[14]

When we have not been empowered to render judgments fairly and accurately, we tend to resort to punishment in order to compensate for the hurt we have suffered. Unfortunately, punishing others or ourselves never really satisfies the moral offense and never produces healing for the injured self. We cannot forgive ourselves or others until judgment has been fairly rendered. But we cannot do this without assistance and affirmation.

THE SPIRITUAL SOURCE OF SELF-EMPOWERMENT

Empowerment of the self must come from a source outside the self. This is not only a theological truth but also a psychological reality, as the "relational" psychologists have told us. The emergence of psychologies based on interpersonal constructs of the self point toward a dynamic of empowerment as a source of self-esteem. When, instead of resistance to the self, which produces negative self-esteem, the self experiences positive reinforcement, we find the pathway to self-recovery opened up.

Figure 6.3 shows the difference that can result when the empowerment of love is directed toward the self through the experience of resistance. In this case, the pleasure instinct, grounded in a God-created longing for self-fulfillment, produces a sense of self-worth leading to self-fulfillment and happiness. At the same time, the sense of ownership, with its primitive moral instinct, leads to moral self-worth, resulting in intentions and actions of love, self-sacrifice, and fulfilling the ethic of love.

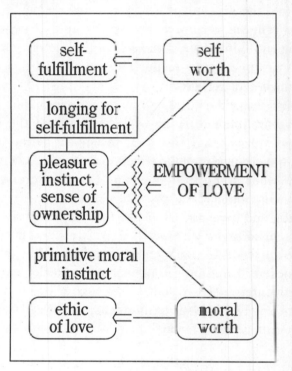

Figure 6.3

Notice the effect of love's empowerment upon the core of self-identity. The self internalizes the love projected by the other so that a sense of self-worth is experienced leading to healthy self-love, or what we have called positive self-esteem. At the same time, the self internalizes the love projected in such a way that moral worth is claimed by the self, leading to the ethic of love as a positive basis for relationship and community.

Sooner or later, all children moving into adulthood will be confronted by experiences which require the surrender of right of ownership for the sake of self-fulfillment. At these times, there needs to be a shift which will feel unfamiliar and unnatural to the self. It is a leap of growth when the self learns to experience the moral worth and the fulfillment received through empowering the life of another.

In making this movement, the self moves away from the primitive moral instinct, which has become fused with ownership, to an ethic of love. We long for love which is not an innate instinct of the self, but which is the highest possibility of the self. Love means acquiring the capacity to experience ultimate meaning and fulfillment of the self in the life of another. There is an innate moral right to this fulfillment, and this is the seed from which love can grow.

If negative self-esteem and inadequate formation of personal identity contribute to family violence, both on the part of the abuser as well as the victim, then one should define strategies of family ministry and therapy which identify the problem as early as possible and provide opportunities for intervention and growth. Developmental aspects of personal identity at the psychological and psychosocial level have been extensively clarified and described by Erik Erikson.[15] W.W. Meissner, however, faults Erikson's attempt to construct a developmental approach to personal identity based on ego psychology as inadequate. Erikson's developmental model includes a process of moral development which is largely a dynamic of internalization of ego conflicts. Says Meissner of Erikson's model:

> *One of the deepest conflicts in life is the hate for the parent who serves as the model for development of the superego — the organ of moral tradition. Inconstancy in parental morality produces a suspiciousness and evasiveness which when linked with the absolute quality of the superego makes "moral" man a potential danger to his own ego and to his fellow men. The formation of the superego requires a submergence of the infantile rage leading sometimes to a self-righteous intolerance or moralism that inhibits rather than encourages initiative in others. In turn, the initiative of "moral" man can break through the boundaries of self-restriction (conscience) and permit him to do to others what he would never permit to be done to himself.[16]*

The individual must pass from the morality learned by the child to the ethics of the adult. Erikson's genius, says Meissner, is that he has been able to embrace the fundamental insights of psychoanalysis and integrate them into a higher and broader view of the human without doing violence to these basic insights. Under Erikson's model, the human person has become a creature open to and involved in the social and ethical structures of life that persist to the end of the life cycle. Nonetheless, Meissner argues that Erikson's model is too restricted to the dynamics of ego development. Value formation as a part of identity formation, says Meissner, must undergo a shift from the aggressive moral and punitive forces in order to become a more effective arbiter of ethical conduct.[17]

Meissner, of course, builds his theory of identity formation more along the lines of object relations theory (cf. Guntrip, Winnicott). Where parents or primary caregivers embody in practice spiritual factors of identity, such as grace, faith, and hope, identity formation of the child, including superego formation, rests on the quality of these "objective" introjects.

It would then seem to be the case that models for family life which reduce the potential for violence should not depend upon a "moralizing" approach to abusive behavior. This approach only drives aggressive and defensive instincts deeper into the ego, with the superego now the guardian of self-preservation and the "rights" which belong to the self at all costs—even violence against others. Rather, as Meissner has carefully shown, the positive value of the self is to be reinforced through healthy, or "good enough" object relations within the family structure. including dealing realistically with one's own propensity to sin and evil.

The empowerment of love is one form of the grace of God directed toward the self through human parents, the ministry of Christ in Word and Spirit, and the effective intervention of Christian therapists. The longing for self-fulfillment is not the root of sin. Rather, sin emerges through the inherited sense of ownership and autonomy with regard to the Word and Law of God. Although a strong sense of omnipotence develops when the pleasure instinct is gratified without setting the boundaries of love, the key to fulfillment is not to annihilate the self but to rediscover the self as an object of God's love. This leads to self-worth and moral worth, with self-fulfillment gained through the intentions and actions of love.

A sense of shame is one factor in negative self-esteem. Shame is a form of emotional self-abuse and can be more devastating than a feeling of guilt. The difference between guilt and shame and how shame can be overcome, as well as guilt, is the subject of the chapter which follows.

SUMMARY

In summarizing this section let me make the following points:

- Domestic violence is a form of abusive behavior which has higher risk with increased levels of intimacy.
- Negative self-esteem is experienced as lack of self-worth and a sense of powerlessness, leading to feelings of having lost some essential aspect of one's personal being.
- A primitive moral instinct is aroused by the feeling that one has been deprived of the worth that belongs to the self. One's basic "rights" seem to have been violated.
- Abusive behavior, leading to violence, takes place on a continuum where safe, nurturing, and empowering relationships tend to be oppressive, demanding, and crippling.
- Recognizing and overcoming negative self-esteem through the act of unconditional love empowers the self toward self-worth and the ethic of love.
- Self-empowerment is the restoration of the image of God in the form of positive self-esteem through the intervention of God's grace and love mediated by significant others.
- In this way, self-empowerment is the beginning of spiritual healing.

PRAXIS

The pastor received an urgent call from the chaplain at the hospital. Linda, a member of his church, had just been admitted with serious injuries due to a physical beating by her husband. The husband was in shock and making a scene in the waiting room. When the pastor arrived, he found that Linda had no broken bones, but would be in the hospital for several days recovering from lacerations and bruises. Al, her husband, was crying and protesting that he did not mean to harm her, but that he had just lost control. The next day, Al came to the pastor's office for an appointment as he had promised. Al confessed, "I admit that I hit her but had no intention of hurting her. As God is my witness, I love her. I have asked God to forgive me and I want to pray with you that I will receive his forgiveness and yours." The pastor did not immediately respond. After a few moments he asked, "What really was your intention then?" Al replied, "She was mouthing off to me in front of the kids. She does not really respect my authority in the home. I had to do something to stop her. Pastor, don't I have a right to have my wife respect me and to expect that she will honor my role as the Bible says?"

- Al claims to love his wife, Linda. How is it possible for love and violence to exist in the same relationship?

- Al admitted that he was wrong to hurt his wife and put her in the hospital. At the same time he claimed that he had a right to discipline her. Using the diagram in this chapter, explain why Al could feel morally justified in using coercion against his wife.

- What response can be given to Al when he argues that the Bible says that the wife should submit to her husband's authority in the home?

- How should the pastor respond with regard to Al's request for forgiveness?

7

Shame:
Letting Go of Emotional Self-Abuse

Most everyone walks through a valley of shame now and then. Some of us, however, take a lifelong lease on shame; it is our permanent home. We are shame-bound. . . . Some of us are so hooked into shame that we are afraid we would be lonely without it. . . . If we lost our shame, we would not recognize ourselves. (Lewis Smedes)

I have received only a few traffic citations over the past twenty-five years and, while I cannot recall the date, I can remember precisely the details of each incident. I know exactly where my car was stopped by the flashing red light. I can visualize clearly the scene, handing over my driver's license, standing behind the car waiting for the officer to write out the ticket while other cars went speeding by. I remember word for word the brief conversation, and have replayed the tape many times in my mind trying to insert new explanations into the script, sometimes being sarcastic, sometimes humorous.

In each case, I paid the fine immediately and, as far as the law was concerned, I was no longer guilty and had nothing to fear from any traffic officer, at least with regard to that offense. The receipt which indicated that the fine had been paid in full was my assurance that whatever guilt I had incurred for the violation had been removed.

Why then was I unable to erase the incident from my mind and let go of the emotions which the incident produced? I have attempted in vain to recall other experiences of joy and pleasure from the past which must have been deeply moving at the time, but which mingle now with positive aspects of the self to produce wholeness of life. My guess is that the feelings of pleasure were integrated into the healthy core of the self. The feelings of humiliation and embarrassment when "caught in the act" have their own secret places in the psychic jungle.

THE FEELING OF SHAME IS A POWERFUL SECRET

As I have reflected on the growing literature on shame and its effect on the self, I think that I understand more clearly what happened to me. I was startled to discover that I carried deep within me such a vivid recollection of the incidents and, in particular, the same sensations and feelings I had at the time. I wondered why incidents like these had such power as to virtually burn into my psyche the details of the incident, as well as the feelings I experienced. I only have to recall each incident to experience once again the feelings of humiliation at being caught, exposed to the merciless gaze of the other motorists and, in some cases, curious bystanders.

I also discovered that my pattern was never to disclose the incident to others and to act as though it had never happened. While it was a matter of public record for strangers to look at, it was also a secret to be kept from those whose affirmation I valued the most. There was nothing to fear from the law, but the possibility of exposure and further humiliation was a fearful threat to my self-esteem.

What I have felt in recalling the traffic violations was the power of shame and its relentless attack upon the vulnerable core of the self. The incidents with the traffic officers penetrated through the normal defenses and found a chink in my psychic armor. A primitive sense of shame, no doubt experienced in childhood, was activated and used this new incident to abuse the self and inflict new wounds, further entrenching itself in the psychic core.

I share my own experience as one that most of us have had, in one form or another. Common to all of us are the feelings of shame when we have felt exposed to the scrutiny of others in a moment of personal failure. What we are concerned about in this chapter is not the general feeling of shame that comes and goes, but the destructive and crippling power of shame that rises up within ourselves, causing us to feel unworthy, disgusting, or rejected. Feelings of self-condemnation often follow instances where shame will not permit us to forgive ourselves, nor to accept the forgiveness of others.

WHY IT IS IMPORTANT TO HAVE A CAPACITY FOR SHAME

Not all feelings of shame are so destructive to the self. Indeed, the capacity to feel shame seems to be part of the self's maintenance of a healthy sense of limitation and even the core of humility. To be called "shameless" is to be judged to be without a sense of discrimination concerning appropriate and inappropriate behavior. "In the past the capacity to experience shame was valued," says Robert Karen.

> *To be capable of shame meant to be modest, as opposed to exhibitionistic or grandiose, to have character, nobility, honor, discretion. It meant to be respectful of social standards, of the boundaries of others, of one's own limitations. And, finally, it meant to be respectful of one's need for privacy.* [1]

John Bradshaw also speaks of a healthy and nourishing shame that keeps us within the boundaries of our own humanity. This capacity for shame is the foundation for humility and a source of spirituality.

> *Shame is a normal human emotion. In fact, it is necessary to have the feeling of shame if one is to be truly human. Shame is the emotion which*

gives us permission to be human. Shame tells us of our limits. Shame keeps us in our human boundaries, letting us know that we can and will make mistakes, and that we need help. Our shame tells us that we are not God. Healthy shame is the psychological foundation of humility. It is the source of spirituality.[2]

I must confess that it is difficult to think of shame as normal and even necessary to healthy human existence. Perhaps this is because we always think of shame as something that we experience as a loss of well-being, as a negative and not a positive feeling.

"There is a nice irony in shame," says Lewis Smedes, "our feelings of inferiority are a sure sign of our superiority, and our feelings of unworthiness testify to our great worth. Only a very noble being can feel shame."[3]

How do we reconcile the fact that to have no sense of shame is a sign of inappropriate understanding of the self and yet the experience of being shamed is so negative and even destructive?

"Our shame tells us that we are not God," says Bradshaw. I do not think that it is shame that tells us that, but the capacity to *sense* shame as a consequence of overreaching our human limits. The psalmist says: "O Lord, my heart is not lifted up, my eyes are not raised too high; I do not occupy myself with things too great and too marvelous for me. But I have calmed and quieted my soul, like a weaned child with its mother; my soul is like the weaned child that is with me" (Ps. 131:1-2).

The capacity for shame has a spiritual basis, says Smedes. To have a sense of shame is akin to feeling God's presence.

Spiritual shame may come as a tremor after a close encounter with God, but unhealthy shame is a godless shame. Undeserved shame may come from religion, but it only gets in God's way. Religion without grace can tie shame around our souls like a choke chain and never offer relief. The pain we feel is not even a distant cousin to spiritual shame.[4]

In order to understand the concept of healthy shame, let's take the concept of a limit, or boundary, as Bradshaw suggests.

If a child attempts to impersonate an adult by doing some action beyond its ability, it will surely fail and experience shame.

If the child has a capacity for shame that could result from such an attempt, she will stop short of the act, and think to herself, "I'm just a child. I am not big enough to do that."

Having a capacity for shame keeps us from doing something that causes us to *be* shamed. It is our capacity for shame that enables us to live comfortably within the boundaries and limits set for us by our capabilities, our relationship with others, and our own sense of dignity and self-worth. A capacity for shame keeps us from violating our dignity by exposing ourselves in such a way as to cause discomfort and offense to others. Having a capacity for shame keeps us from the foolishness of doing something shameful, as Smedes reminds us. "Our shame may be our best defense against our folly. When it comes down to it, most people do the right thing because they would be ashamed of themselves if they did the wrong thing."[5]

WHEN SHAME BECOMES A SECRET

In the Creation story, the first man and woman "were both naked, and were not ashamed" (Gen. 2:25). But could they know that they were not ashamed without some sense of what shame is? I believe that they indeed were created with a capacity for shame and that in the security of the intimacy of their relationship, they could be open and exposed to each other without shame actually being felt. Immediately upon overreaching their limits and attempting to "be like God" (3:5), they "knew that they were naked; and they sewed fig leaves together and made loincloths for themselves" (3:7).

At this point, they actually felt shame in the presence of each other and, we assume, in the eyes of God, for they hid themselves from His presence in the garden. Adam blamed God for giving him the woman, and the woman blamed the serpent for beguiling her.

It is one thing to have a keen sense of shame as a possible consequence of an action. It is quite another thing to actually *feel* shame because we have been shamed. Being shamed is a violation of the self which occurs with human interaction. Wherever there is blame there is shame. One continually feeds on the other.

Because of the need to conceal the shameful act, shame is buried as a secret within the self. Fear of exposure drives the self deeper into hiding in a desperate attempt to preserve some semblance of decency. When we have been shamed, we put on "fig leaves" to maintain a sense of decorum and acceptability.

It appears that our capacity for shame has lost its innocence and insight. We do not understand the shame that "keeps us within our boundaries," so we cower behind the fig leaves of our own creation. Rather than admitting our mistakes and asking for help, we abuse ourselves with stinging rebuke and merciless condemnation. The fig leaves can hardly be removed before the hurtful shame is taken away, and we are finally able to recover a sense of self-worth and value our humanity.

In his perceptive essay on shame in *The Atlantic Monthly*, Robert Karen identifies several kinds of shame.[6] *Existential shame* arises from suddenly seeing yourself as you really are—too wrapped up in your own bitterness to allow yourself or anyone close to you to be happy. *Narcissistic shame* is a sense of personal defect, feeling inferior, burdened with a negative self-portrait. *Class shame* is a function of social power; it has inflicted a sense of unworthiness upon the poor, ethnic minorities, and women since the beginning of civilization. *Situational shame* is a passing shame resulting from incidents of rejection and humiliation. *Universal shame*, says Karen, is typical of the teaching of medieval Christianity; it is the belief that all are unworthy and deficient of the righteousness which God expects. This concept of unworthiness can be used to bind the community, to maintain spiritual focus and, perhaps, to drain off some shame that might otherwise have become individual and narcissistic.[7]

If shame is used as a "binding" concept in the community, it nonetheless contributes to the loss of personal identity. The individual who finds belonging in the community on the basis of the common denominator of universal shame will find it difficult to gain a sense of spiritual identity that is not also shame-based.

When one's spiritual life is based on an excessive concentration on guilt consciousness, a deep sense of unworthiness may be deemed a necessary condition in order to be accepted by God. A pervasive feeling of shame may thus have its roots in a certain kind of piety. Exploitation of this condition in the name of religion may lead to spiritual abuse where individuals are kept from true spiritual health by the very tenets of a theological confession.[8]

Lutheran theologian Dietrich Bonhoeffer had nothing but scorn for a religion which attempted to make people feel shameful before offering the "good news" of salvation.

> *Of course, we now have the secularized offshoots of Christian theology, namely existentialist philosophy and the psychotherapists, who demonstrate to secure, contented, and happy mankind that it is really unhappy and desperate and simply unwilling to admit that it is in a predicament about which it knows nothing, and from which only they can rescue it. Wherever there is health, strength, security, simplicity, they scent luscious fruit to gnaw at or to lay their pernicious eggs in. They set themselves to drive people to inward despair, and then the game is in their hands. That is secularized methodism. . . . The ordinary man, who spends his everyday life at work and with his family, and of course with all kinds of diversions, is not affected. He has neither the time nor the inclination to concern himself with his existential despair, or to regard his perhaps modest share of happiness as a trial, a trouble, or a calamity.[9]*

Bonhoeffer saw clearly the crippling effects of a Christian experience based on a presumption of personal weakness. He called for a Gospel which did not first of all shame people into submission. Forgiveness in Jesus Christ should empower persons rather than weaken them. The appeal of Christ is to those who find in Him a meaning and purpose which satisfies the deepest yearnings for life and self-fulfillment.

THE DIFFERENCE BETWEEN SHAME AND GUILT

The experience of being shamed has no motivating power toward health. Once we feel shamed, the capacity for shame no longer functions in a positive sense. Feeling shamed, we are likely to blame and condemn ourselves as though we were guilty of some terrible offense.

Guilt has to do with an act which is measured against an objective standard, or against another person. Guilt is the consequence of a violation of this standard. Guilt is removed when one has satisfied the penalty imposed, been pardoned from the wrong, and/or forgiven. The objective nature of the offense is removed from one's record.

The removal of guilt may not remove the feeling of shame, which is subjectively rooted in the feeling that the self has no worth. The confusion between guilt and shame can be the source of much self-condemnation. Often when we continue to feel guilt, we are experiencing shame.

When I paid the traffic ticket, the penalty for violating the law was fulfilled and satisfaction made. There was no longer an objective basis for guilt. Guilt is removed by paying the penalty or seeking pardon.

Shame has to do with a loss to one's identity and being. Long after the guilt has been removed objectively, one can still be caught in the dehumanizing grip of shame. The guilt I feel for having broken a traffic law long after the ticket has been paid is really shame. I experience a loss of personal integrity. My self-worth is threatened. Paying the penalty removes the guilt, but does not restore my sense of personal worth.

Shame does not necessarily disappear even though guilt as an objective offense standing between God and human persons is removed. Shame, as the deeper problem of the self, means that one has suffered loss of being, not merely loss of status. The purpose of divine forgiveness is not only to pardon sin as a legal or objective fault, but to overcome shame which has weakened and destroyed the inner fabric of the self.

When we think of atonement for sin as a removal of guilt we must also understand that it has not produced wholeness and health within until the effects of shame on one's personal being have been overcome.

Smedes captures this thought well when he says, "Most of us feel shame not for our too-badness but for our not-good-enoughness. Not measuring up to snuff hurts us more than when we violate a law."[10]

The confusion between guilt and shame is not only a psychological problem, but a theological error. The failure of historic Christian theology to recognize the devastating effects of shame in its solution to the problem of guilt is certainly lamentable, but curable.

AN ATONEMENT FOR SHAME
AS WELL AS GUILT

The doctrine of the atonement in orthodox Protestant theology is based upon a concept of sin as an objective offense against God's honor and His law, for which a penalty must be paid. Based on the thought of the early twelfth-century theologian, Anselm of Canterbury, this tradition, adopted by the Reformers, views the death of Jesus Christ on the cross as a sacrifice to God sufficient to satisfy His judicial sentiment and free Him to grant pardon to all who accept Christ's death as a substitutionary atonement for their own sin. Immediately upon conversion to Christ and the receiving of the new nature, born of the Spirit, sinners are justified—"just as if they had never sinned," we are told. Being made free from the condemnation of sin, Christians no longer are guilty before the Law. All of this is freely given by God's grace to be received by faith.

Because Anselm's view of sin was primarily that of an offense which robbed God of the honor due to Him, the satisfaction to His honor through Christ's sacrifice removes the judgment of guilt for all who receive Jesus as Savior. However, it must be said that the *forensic* model which Anselm developed and which became the orthodox doctrine of atonement for the Reformers, failed to deal with the effects of sin in the form of shame. The payment of a debt to the justice of God was seen to remove the legal guilt which sinners incurred and for which they were under condemnation. But shame remains where guilt has been legally removed.

C. Norman Kraus argues that the Western approaches have dealt almost exclusively with the relation of the cross to guilt, as the moral and legal basis for removal of a penalty. The atonement must also be seen, argues Kraus, as effective in dealing with shame as well as with guilt.

The Christian doctrine of forgiveness and reconciliation, then, must deal
with the social disgrace and exclusion (objective shame) as well as the
subjective feelings of failure and unworthiness Further, it must deal
with the intrinsic consequences of guilt—both its internal and external
consequences, and it must do this in such a way that it does not condone
or augment the objective fault. The intention of forgiveness is to nullify
shame and guilt so that reconciliation and a new beginning become
possible. The shamed person must find new identity and personal worth.
And the guilty person must find expiation. Both objective alienation and
hostility which have been institutionalized in our social and legal systems
and the subjective remorse and blame that so inhibit personal fulfilment
in human relationships must be overcome.[11]

The traditional theological approach has been to interpret
the atoning death and resurrection of Jesus Christ as offering
pardon from sin. Guilt has to do with an act which is measured
against an objective standard or another person. Sin is the violation of this objective standard; guilt is the consequence of this
violation. Guilt is removed when one is pardoned from the wrong
and/or forgiven. Shame has to do with a loss to one's identity and
being. Long after the guilt has been removed objectively, one
can still be caught in the dehumanizing grip of shame.

Kraus suggests that the removal of sin as objective offense
standing between God and human persons does not yet remove
shame as the deeper problem of the self. Shame means that one
has suffered loss of being, not merely loss of status. The purpose
of divine forgiveness is not merely to pardon sin as a legal or
objective fault, but to overcome shame which has weakened and
destroyed the inner being of the self. Thus, atonement must also
deal with the overcoming of shame.

In no way can shame be expiated through substitutionary compensation
or retaliation. . . . Only a forgiveness which covers the past and a
genuine restoration of relationship can banish shame. What is needed is
a restoration of communication. The rage which isolates and insulates
must be overcome. Reconciliation and restoration of mutual intimate
relationship through a loving open exchange is the only way to heal
resentment and restore lost self-esteem.[12]

When Christians are told that they no longer have any basis for feeling guilty because that guilt has been removed through Christ's death, they can still be left with the deep wound to the self which shame causes. The continued feeling of shame, as Robert Karen suggests, is a "victimless crime."

> *If guilt is about behavior that has harmed others, shame is about not being good enough. Shame is often, of course, triggered by something you have done, but in shame, the way that behavior reflects on you is what counts. Shameful behavior is thus often a victimless crime; and shame itself is less clearly about morality than about conformity, acceptability, or character.*[13]

The restoration of personal being and the recovery of a sense of self-worth, as Kraus suggests, is a process of restoration through communication and community. Shame isolates, recovery must restore relation. Shame causes inner rage and fury against the self; recovery must disarm that abusive emotion. Shame eats away at the tender and vulnerable narcissistic core of the self, turning even self-love into ritual abuse. Recovery must stop the self-abuse of shame and release the power of Christ's resurrection life into the innermost cells of the self's secrets. While shame is sensed as humiliation before others, it does its vicious work of self-destruction in secret. Recovery is breaking the code of secrecy through which the abuse of shame takes place.

SHAME AS SELF-ABUSE

Shame is not an emotion. It is self-abuse, with the emotions used as instruments of flagellation. Shame attacks the self in the name of the self, inflicting punishment for the sake of crippling, not to correct. Robert Karen says of shame:

> *It is crippling, because it contains not just the derisive accusation that one is a wimp, a bully, a runt, or a fag but the further implication that one is at core a deformed being, fundamentally unlovable and unworthy of membership in the human community. It is the self regarding the self with the withering and unforgiving eye of contempt. And most people are unable to face it. It is too annihilating.*[14]

This kind of shame has been called pathological, or toxic shame, to distinguish it from a more benign sense of shame which is intrinsic to the self's awareness of limitations. "Pathological shame is an irrational sense of defectiveness," says Karen. "a feeling not of having crossed to the wrong side of the boundary but of having been born there."¹⁵ This kind of shame is what John Bradshaw calls toxic shame.

> *Toxic shame, the shame that binds you, is experienced as the all pervasive sense that I am flawed and defective as a human being. Toxic shame is no longer an emotion that signals our limits, it is a state of being, a core identity. Toxic shame gives you a sense of worthlessness, a sense of failing and falling short as a human being. Toxic shame is a rupture of the self with the self.*¹⁶

A classic case of pathological shame can be seen in the person of Søren Kierkegaard, the nineteenth-century Danish philosopher and theologian. His brilliant and probing analysis of the human condition was the result of a psychological autopsy on his own tortured soul. On the occasion of his twenty-first birthday, he was told by his father that a curse had come upon the Kierkegaard family. When he was just a young boy, the father confessed, he had shook his fist at God because he was left alone out in the field, abandoned by his own father. As a result, his father told Sören there was a divine curse upon the family. In addition, his father confessed that Sören had been conceived before he married his mother. This was a shame which the father had concealed all these years and now confessed to his son!

As a result, the son was thrown headlong into a brief period of sensualism and wanton living. He recovered himself sufficiently to complete a university degree and the requirements for ordination as a minister in the Danish state church. Kierkegaard then began his literary career, applying his pathological brilliance to the task of overturning the reigning philosophy of Hegel, on the one hand, and exposing what he considered to be the hypocritical posturing of the Danish church on the other hand. Falling in love with a young woman, Anna Regina, he finally broke off the engagement as he explained, because he did not wish to inflict upon her the melancholy of his own soul.[17]

The Concept of Dread, one of Kierkegaard's most perceptive works, was his analysis of the phenomenon of dread *(angst),* a space through which the self must move in order to achieve faith and develop spirit. At the end of that book, he concluded by saying that his attempt had not been to describe the condition of a healthy soul, but of a sick one, and in so doing, show the way to true selfhood by the "leap of faith" in which one could gain freedom from the despair which crippled the self in its attempt to "be the self." "If I had had faith," he once said, "I would have married Regina."[18]

A significant factor in the shame which tormented Kierkegaard, and prevented him from living what he considered to be a normal life of faith, was that it was transmitted to him through his father. This is the "toxic shame" of which Bradshaw speaks, passed on from one generation to another.

> *Toxic shame is multigenerational. It is passed from one generation to the next. Shame-based people find other shame-based people and get married. As a couple each carries the shame from his or her own family system. Their marriage will be grounded in their shame-core. The major outcome of this will be a lack of intimacy. It's difficult to let someone get close to you if you feel defective and flawed as a human being. Shame-based couples maintain non-intimacy through poor communication, non-productive circular fighting, games, manipulation, vying for control, withdrawal, blaming and confluence. Confluence is the agreement never to disagree. Confluence creates pseudo-intimacy.*[19]

To be shame-based is not only to live with a deep sense of personal deficit, but to experience oneself as caught in a web of shame that conceals a secret hidden in one's family of origin. In the case of Kierkegaard, he discovered this secret only on his twenty-first birthday. But the shame of the father had become systemic and had its effect long before the secret was disclosed. In many families, the secret dies with a previous generation while the shame continues. Freedom from this kind of shame requires intervention into the systemic nature of shame. The discovery of the secret does not produce freedom from shame, as

Kierkegaard discovered. This means that the cause of shame is of less importance in recovery than the pattern of shame. Only when the pattern of abuse is broken and the self begins the process of recovery is there an end to this kind of shame.

The abuse of shame in a shame-based system is difficult to discover and deal with because the system operates in what appears to be a normal and structured way. Bradshaw reminds us of this when he says, "Shame-based families operate according to the laws of social systems. When a social system is dysfunctional, it is rigid and closed. All the individuals in that family are enmeshed into a kind of trance-like frozenness. They take care of the system's need for balance."[20]

Shame is a form of self-abuse. This is what makes recovery so difficult. Shame cannot be removed by retaliation against others, nor by punishing an offender. Shame does not disappear when one is freed from guilt, nor can it be relieved by reassurances that there is no objective reason for these feelings of self-recrimination. There is no one who is hurt more by shame than the one who feels it. Karen describes it as a "victimless crime," where the self is both the abuser and the victim of the abuse.

The need for professional psychotherapeutic intervention into the abuse of shame is quite clear. Shame is not overcome through "self-help" techniques, although growing out of shame is a process of "self-recovery." The splitting of the self into accuser and victim lies behind the power of shame to abuse the self To stop this abuse, the self must recover its sense of personal worth, unity, and belonging in a non-shame-based relationship.

This is why intrapsychic therapy alone will not ordinarily restore the self when it has become isolated and alienated through toxic shame. The core of the self is grounded in its existence as a social construct, as I explained in chapter 2. The steps to recovery thus entail a "resocializing" of the self through encounter with non-shame-based persons.

LETTING GO OF THE SHAME THAT HURTS

There is no one hurting more from shame than the one feeling it. The self becomes the primary victim of punishing shame, as both abuser and victim. At the same time, shame spreads its poison through the family system and creates shame-based relationships.

Shame is not overcome through "self-help" techniques alone, although growing out of shame is a process of self-recovery. Professional psychotherapeutic intervention into the abuse of shame is often necessary. Along with therapeutic intervention, however, recovery from the self-abuse of shame requires a resocializing of the self with non-shame-based people.

Recovery from the destructive power of shame means letting go of the shame which abuses, while retaining a capacity for shame. The goal is not to become shameless, but to value and esteem the self as not shameful. Three elements of this process can briefly be described. *Uncovering* is first, followed by *recovering*, and finally *discovering*.[21]

1. Uncovering the secret of shame

Shame thrives on secrecy, and secrecy is its most powerful defense. What shame fears most of all is the uncovering of the self in its wretched and disgusting condition. It is instructive that, in the first recorded instance of shame in the Bible, Adam and Eve covered themselves with fig leaves when "they knew that they were naked" (Gen. 3:7). When God found them hiding in the garden and called out to them, "Where are you?" the man explained, "I heard the sound of you in the garden, and I was afraid, because I was naked: and I hid myself." "Who told you that you were naked?" replied God (3:9-11).

The relation of nakedness to shame no doubt has more than a literary origin in this text. Nakedness is a metaphor of a self-perception rather than of physical exposure. To "know that one is naked" is a self-perception which causes fear of exposure to arise. Thus the clothing of oneself is a further metaphor of the self's desperate attempt at concealment. This is the beginning of the ritual abuse of shame. Any threat of exposure causes the self to turn against itself and force into hiding what is deemed too ugly to reveal.[22]

Self-recovery begins when a pattern is broken. This may result from an encounter with another person sufficient to stop ritual abusive behavior. Shame isolates and alienates as the self ritualizes self-condemnation, even though one is bound to some social system. Encounter means a breakthrough by which one is arrested in one's tracks and stopped from continuing an action which is destructive and self-defeating.

Consider this example. "I was yelling at my son for not having the guts to stick to his commitment to the track team," a man once confided to me. "Suddenly, I heard my six-year-old daughter say to me, 'Daddy, you're hurting him!' Thanks to her, I caught myself in time and recovered my perspective. I was supposed to be encouraging him, not punishing him.'

The uncovering of shame came as a realization that he was projecting onto his son his own lack of self-worth. The self-condemnation of shame spilled over into a verbal tirade against his son for what he perceived to be a weakness. Shame often leads to blaming of others as a projection of self-blame.

The father who shared his experience with me had begun the first step of recovery. He realized that it was not enough to stop the shaming of his son as a projection of his own self-abuse of shame. He had a lot of uncovering to do to continue the work of self-recovery. This work was begun in our counseling, but soon it had to be extended into other relationships in his life.

I hesitated to encourage him to do recovery work with his own family. The family was much too bound up in shame-based relationships. Instead, I encouraged him to join a support group with whom he could begin the process of uncovering what his shame had forced into hiding. These were feelings of shame that needed to be opened up and shared, not incidents or actions.

With this group he found reinforcement for positive affirmations about himself that did not depend upon keeping his shame feelings secret. At the same time, he recovered the capacity for shame as a positive indicator of the integrity and honesty he had achieved with them. He now could anticipate the shame that would follow from any action of deception of these men by failing to be honest with his feelings. This healthy sense of shame empowered him to maintain the integrity of those relationships and to build a new base for his self-concept as worthy of being known and trusted.

With the uncovering of his shame as a feeling of unworthiness, this man began the journey toward the recovery of a healthy capacity for shame based on his self-worth rather than self-blame.

2. Recovering the capacity for shame

I was "stopped in my tracks" by the traffic officers, and I still feel to this day the burning shame of being made to feel like a little boy caught doing something wrong by his father. I guess that those incidents made me a more cautious driver due to the threat of being caught again. I have learned to use my rearview mirror more consistently when driving with the pack on the freeway. I admit I relish the feeling when I see another get caught and forced to go through what I did. But this is not recovery!

Recovery has to do with catching myself in the act of shaming myself. When that process begins, I am in recovery if I "catch myself in time" and shift from self-condemnation to self-evaluation. "Why am I doing this to myself?" I ask. "Am I not supposed to like rather than hate myself?"

"Why are you hurting yourself?" is the voice that I need to hear. But this voice must come from someone who has the power to intercept the blind and brutal assault on the self by the self. The man who shared with me his own recovery moment, admitted that if his wife had said the same thing, he probably would have turned his rage on her as well. The six-year-old girl had access to a vulnerable part of him, but also stood outside the pattern of shame in which he was caught.

Recovery cannot begin until the most vulnerable part of our self-image is opened up with the innocence of a child's question. There was no perceived blame in the child's question, nothing to stir the hidden shame into reaction or to cause further shame. Rather, the child, by her intervention, actually empowered the father to recover his own sense of shame at what he was doing.

Recovery is about having a capacity for shame without feeling shamed. This is almost impossible to do when shame has already produced self-imposed alienation and isolation. The capacity for shame has become distorted and twisted into an instrument to be used in the ritual abuse of self-shaming.

Recovery begins with an intervention into this self-abusive dynamic. I believe that it can only happen when someone or something touches the most vulnerable part of us with sufficient innocence to cause us to recover, for a moment at least, a capacity for shame. The painful but accurate insight that one suffers from shame as a form of self-abuse must be linked to the assumption that one has the power to do good because one is actually good. This involves recovering the capacity for shame as a positive and healthy core of the self.

Recovery can only follow from uncovering the shame which binds the self and blinds it to its own essential worth. Once the penetration has been made into the vulnerable core of the self and the self has recovered, "just in time," from its programmed ritual of self-abuse, the process of recovery can continue.

Recovering a capacity for shame based on a positive valuing of the self results from the affirmation of a non-shame-based network of relationships. Uncovering the secret of hidden shame is the first step. Recovering a capacity for healthy shame through the renewal of self-worth is the second. "Only a very noble being can feel shame," Smedes reminds us.

Recovering a sense of nobility is a humbling and yet empowering discovery. The recovery of self-worth, says Smedes, is what the grace of God does when it heals our shame. "A grace that makes us feel worse for having it is an ungracious grace and therefore not really grace at all. If grace heals our shame, it must be a grace that tells us we are worthy to have it. We need, I believe, to recognize that we are accepted not only in spite of our undeserving but because of our worth."[23]

3. Discovering the blessing of freedom from shame

The goal of recovery is discovery. This is the awakening to the reality of self-recovery, similar to the experience of breaking through to the crest of a hill after a steep climb and seeing the expanded horizon of new vistas opened up to one's gaze. New possibilities emerge out of the discovery that the self is anchored in place by a positive unity of perception and affirmation.

On occasion, in the process of pastoral counseling, I have had a person come in for an appointment after many weeks of struggle and exclaim: "I don't know what has happened. But I awakened this morning and the feeling that I had a weight tied around my neck was gone! I feel free from the burden that we have been trying to get rid of and full of hope and expectation such as I have not had for years."

To tell the truth, I was as surprised as the person who experienced it! It was not as though I concluded the session a week prior with the knowledge that next week would produce the breakthrough. It was only in retrospect that I could look back and see the signs of recovery which had led to the discovery of a newfound sense of peace and wholeness. Discovery has to do with the realization that a transformation has taken place deep within the self.[24]

The biblical concept of blessing was surely meant to empower the self with a sense of worth and value. Shame produces what some psychologists have called a "narcissistic injury" to the self. The self-love which is a God-created image in the human self through which we seek fulfillment and pleasure, is wounded and crippled by shame. In our desperate search for happiness we seek rights and benefits when what we really need is blessing.

The feeling of being blessed can only be described, it cannot be defined. It is something that one must experience. It cannot be taught but it can be learned. There is no technique by which it can be achieved, but there is a pathway that leads toward it—it is more of a discovery than a discipline.[25]

When the Apostle Paul contemplated his life through the lens of acceptance in Jesus Christ, he saw that his recovery began when he was intercepted on the Damascus road by the Spirit of Jesus Christ. Having been "stopped in his tracks" by this encounter, he heard the voice of Jesus ask him why he was hurting himself. "Saul, Saul, why are you persecuting me? It hurts you to kick against the goads" (Acts 26:14). Thus began his recovery followed by his "uncovering": "I was formerly a blasphemer, a persecutor, and a man of violence. But I received mercy" (1 Tim. 1:13).

Paul was well aware of the terrible consequences of attempting to fulfill his own need for righteousness. He confessed that he became a "wretched man," captive to h s desperate desires so that the "law of sin" was working within him. Yet, in the midst of this confession he cries out, "I delight in the law of God in my inmost self" (Rom. 7:22). At the very core of his being, Paul does not deny or devalue himself. He feels that God loves him and has called him to be His child. "We boast in our hope of sharing the glory of God," Paul wrote, "and hope does not disappoint us, because God's love has been poured into our hearts through the Holy Spirit that has been given to us" (Rom. 5:2, 5).

When Jacob fled from his brother Esau, after conspiring to rob him of the birthright, he was in a state of turmoil and uncertainty. He had acquired the birthright, but had not gained the blessing of inner peace. What appeared to be flight from the only place that he had known and the only family that he had, dysfunctional as it was, turned out to be a pilgrimage to promise. Falling asleep in the wilderness, with a stone for a pillow, he dreamed of angels ascending and descending on a ladder that reached into heaven. Awakening, he cried out: "Surely the Lord is in this place—and I did not know it." (Gen. 28:16) The hard stone of shame became a ladder of blessing through a vision of God's grace in his life.

Jacob set up the stone as an altar to God, naming the place Bethel—house of God. While this marked the spot as a religious shrine, the greater significance was the discovery deep within himself that he was really blessed by God. Up to that time he no doubt felt shame at the means used to secure the birthright at the expense of his brother Esau. Whatever the wrong done to that relationship and the guilt incurred—and later he would make recompense for that—it was nothing compared to the shame which he carried away in his soul.

Jacob's discovery was the internalizing of the blessing which now came directly from God's own word. He arrived at the place under the burden of shame and left with the blessing in his heart. Now he has the blessing, and the shame is gone, with its power of self-condemnation.

It is not enough to overcome feelings of shame. We need restoration of the positive value of the self, which can only occur through personal empowerment and spiritual healing. One way of experiencing this healing is through the gift of blessing by another. We cannot bestow a blessing upon ourselves. At the same time, we need to receive this blessing and thus, "bless ourselves." Shame keeps us from blessing ourselves and thus from receiving the blessing of others. Spiritual healing transforms shame into self blessing and results in personal empowerment.

There is a blessing for us, when the hard stone of crushing shame and self-condemnation can be turned into a ladder with angels carrying manna from heaven to feed our starved souls! It is wise for us as well to have an outward point of reference for the inner experience of blessing. Bethel marks the place of discovery and the beginning of recovery. There is freedom to continue the journey knowing that the blessing is abiding in our hearts and the stone remains to mark the place.[26]

When Jacob received the blessing he was empowered to continue the journey. But the journey away from his family and brother Esau would eventually lead back. Esau felt that he had been tricked out of his birthright by Jacob and betrayed by his brother. Betrayal takes the consequence of shame to a deeper level of offense. In the next chapter we will see why betrayal is only possible where there has been a covenant of love and friendship. Recovery from betrayal is a journey in itself, for both the betrayer and the one betrayed.

SUMMARY

● A capacity for shame is necessary and healthy in order to prevent violation of relationships with others and one's own inner integrity.

● Shame differs from guilt in that shame is a feeling of unworthiness while guilt is the result of violating a law or commandment. Shame is a loss of one's own sense of self-worth. Removal of guilt through pardon does not always bring healing from shame.

● Shame is not an emotion, it is a form of self-abuse in which emotions are used as instruments of self-condemnation.

• Shame may become part of a social structure, so that, for example, a family may be shame-based, passing this shame on from one generation to another; this is called toxic shame.

• Recovery from shame involves restoration of one's sense of self-worth. This can only come through relationships which are not shame-based. The grace of God through the atonement of Jesus Christ not only brought pardon from sin, but healing from shame through the blessing of restored personal communion and fellowship with God and others.

PRAXIS

When Linda returned from the hospital after having been severely beaten by her husband, Al, the pastor met with both of them over the next several weeks for counseling. At the same time, Al had agreed to enter group therapy and was faithfully attending his sessions. Linda assured her husband that she had forgiven him and expressed hope that Al's contrition was genuine and that the incident would not happen again. Al, it appeared, had accepted her forgiveness but admitted that he felt deeply ashamed over what he had done. "It was not only that I did wrong to her," Al said, "but now the whole church knows about it. I don't think I can ever face these people again. Nothing that I can do will ever restore my reputation as a good husband and father."

• If Al has experienced genuine forgiveness for the wrong that he did, both from God and from his wife, why does he still feel shame?

• In what way is shame different from guilt and why can one be pardoned from guilt and still experience shame?

• What really is the cause of the shame that Al feels?

• What clue can you find in what Al has said that his shame is not due primarily to the wrong that he has done to his wife?

• What strategy should the pastor now take to help Al overcome his sense of shame and find restoration and acceptance with the other members of the church?

8

Betrayal:
An Irreparable Tear in the Fabric of Friendship

It is not enemies who taunt me — I could bear that; it is not adversaries who deal insolently with me — I could hide from them. But it is you, my equal, my companion, my familiar friend, with whom I kept pleasant company; we walked in the house of God with the throng. . . . Even my bosom friend in whom I trusted, who ate of my bread, has lifted the heel against me (Pss. 55:12-14; 41:9).

When Jerry and Paula (not their real names) asked me to work with them in preparing for their marriage, they made it clear that this was a second marriage for both of them. Each had gone through the painful process of a failed first marriage and worked through the grief process. They were survivors, they told me, and were now ready to make a commitment to each other in hopes that this time they could be more realistic.

As we read over the marriage vows, we came to the phrase, "so long as we both shall live." Jerry protested and said, "I cannot say that. I failed in my first vow and do not feel that in all honesty I can make such an unconditional promise again. It is not fair to Paula." As we discussed the implication of what was being said, he suggested an alternative reading: "As long as we both shall love." In his mind, this conditional vow of love had more integrity than an unconditional one. He was attempting to be realistic, acknowledging the fact that love can die. Paula was disturbed by the conditional character of his suggestion and was quite willing to have the original form of the vow used.

I suggested that the very nature of love is unconditional and that trust in each other was grounded in a commitment which reached beyond the failures of the past. In the end, he allowed me to proceed in accordance with the original vows, though he personally held to his reservations. As it turned out, after no more than three years, the marriage came to an end. Paula left the relationship over problems in the marriage which Jerry acknowledged to be largely his fault. He continues to insist that he loved her, while she says that love has died.

What Jerry never really grasped, apparently, was that "as long as we both shall love" really was a condition which left *him* an escape clause in the marriage, but not for her! The shock of the failed marriage is a blow to him. His pain and grief are deep and devastating. The fact that she no longer loves him does not diminish for a moment the sense of loss and betrayal he feels.

Jerry considered himself to be a survivor through the failure of his first marriage. He sought to protect himself from further pain by qualifying his commitment and making his promise conditional on love. His assumption was that if love dies then there would be no loss, or at least, the loss would be less devastating and destructive. But it doesn't work that way! The death of love is always an unqualified loss. The breaking of a promise is a tear in the fabric of friendship. The failure of another to fulfill expectations or to keep a promise is experienced as a betrayal.

Paula felt betrayed by Jerry's lifestyle and irresponsible behavior which left her feeling abused and threatened. Her response was to protect herself by initiating a separation and then a divorce. Jerry felt betrayed by Paula's unwillingness to forgive him and begin anew. Both felt betrayed and, in some strange way, each felt like a betrayer.

The act of "betrayal" is a dirty deed—with connotations of treachery and falsehood—no less easy to accept if another has betrayed us than if we have betrayed someone else. Judas comes to mind immediately when we think of a betrayer. He was a trusted disciple of Jesus, one of the inner circle of the Twelve. Yet in the end, he betrayed Jesus with a kiss for the price of thirty pieces of silver. When he realized what he had done, he threw the money back, confessed that he had betrayed an innocent man, and went out and hung himself.

THE JUDAS SYNDROME: WHY BETRAYAL IS OFTEN FATAL

I saw it in a men's rest room in a restaurant in San Francisco. It was printed in block letters with a blue felt pen across the top of the mirror: JUDAS COME HOME, ALL IS FORGIVEN. The name of Judas, who betrayed Jesus with a kiss, has become a synonym for an act so treacherous and so fatal to the self that recovery seems impossible. Having betrayed the one who chose him and loved him, Judas could not find the grace to recover from the injury which he had inflicted upon himself.[1]

When I first read this, I pondered the possibility of recovery for even one like Judas. What remained with me was the thought that there may be a bit of Judas in each of us. As much as we want to find a Judas to become the scapegoat and to blame for the intrusion of evil into the good, we cannot pretend our own innocence. In fact, is it possible that those whom we trust the most could also end up as *our* betrayers?

With the capacity to love comes the possibility of betrayal. This is an incredible statement. Only those who dare to love have the power to destroy that love through betrayal. Betrayal is a secret which every promise pretends not to see. How could we make promises and trust another person implicitly with our deepest secrets, not to mention our dearest love, if we permitted the thought of betrayal to enter our minds?

We do not expect to be reminded of betrayal at the exchange of wedding vows. The illusion of "perfect love" is like a wedding garment cast over the naked reality of imperfect lovers. These are injured selves making promises not to hurt. These are selves capable of deadly violence making vows to promote safety and serenity. These are persons who do not fully trust themselves entrusting their happiness to another.

We inoculate children against the most deadly childhood diseases, while entrusting them to parents whose best intentions carry the virus of violence and abuse. We bless the children with sacramental grace as a sign of divine favor and, in some cases, with the hope of the implantation of a spiritual nature. Yet, experience teaches us that they are born with selves which carry the seeds of hatred as well as of love, as well as a capacity for self-inflicted injury that is not washed away in the baptismal font nor with the most selfless devotion of human love.

While we suffer much from the actions and failures of others, we inflict the most grievous injury upon ourselves. Why is it that we can begin life with such idealism and optimism and end by losing or destroying the very things we cherish the most?

With the death of a loved one there may be anger, self-pity, regret, and even feelings of blame and self-accusation. "If only. . . ." "Why didn't I . . . ?" The death of love, however, has its own kind of grief.

With the breaking of a promise, there is a sense of failure and betrayal that cuts both ways. We can never be absolutely certain that we are not the ones to have failed. There was only one betrayer of Jesus, but each of the disciples shuddered with the possibility that he was the one! "They began to be distressed and to say to him one after another, 'Surely, not I?'" (Mark 14:19) When love has died and promises are broken. each one is an accomplice of the betrayal of a vow.

Betrayal is like a fault in an otherwise perfect diamond It is not a scratch on the surface that can be rubbed out. Hurts can heal, sometimes with only the faintest scar. But when a fault occurs, like betrayal, what was once a jewel can look like junk. This is what makes recovery so difficult. In our despair, we are tempted to trash our treasures.

THE ANATOMY OF BETRAYAL

The suggestion that love contains the seeds of betrayal cries out for an explanation. We want to think that the act of betrayal is caused by some alien spirit that enters the sacred sphere of love and destroys it. Even the Apostle John, after Judas betrayed his Lord, in retrospect explained it by saying, "Satan entered into him" (John 13:27).

In Peter Shaffer's play, *Equus,* Alan Strang is a young boy who was sent by the court to a psychiatrist for examination after he had blinded the eyes of several horses with an iron spike. As the psychiatrist unravels the troubled youth's past and, in particular, his relationship with his religious mother and his atheistic father, it becomes clear that the boy's problem has something to do with his own religious obsession with the head of a horse as representing the god Equus (the Latin name for horse). In blinding the eyes of the horses he sought to blind the eyes of his god who had witnessed his sexual dalliance with a young woman in the stable.

During a visit to the hospital where the boy is being treated, Dora, his mother, creates an angry scene with her son and then reacts defensively to the psychiatrist's probing.

> *Look, Doctor: you don't have to live with this. Alan is one patient to you: one out of many. He's my son, I lie awake every night thinking about it. . . . We're not criminals. We've done nothing wrong. We loved Alan. We gave him the best love we could. . . . Whatever's happened has happened because of Alan. Alan is himself. Every soul is itself. If you added up everything we ever did to him, from his first day on earth to this, you wouldn't find why he did this terrible thing—because that's him: not just all of our things added up. . . . You've got your words, and I've got mine. You call it a complex, I suppose. But if you knew God, Doctor, you would know about the Devil. You'd know that the Devil isn't made by what mummy says and daddy says. The Devil's there. It's an old-fashioned word, but a true thing. . . . I'll go. What I did in there was inexcusable. I only know he was my little Alan, and then the Devil came.*[2]

That is one explanation, to be sure. I do not doubt the existence of an alien spirit, called the devil, whose intention is to distort and destroy what God created to be good. In the very beginning, in the Garden of Eden, the innocence of the first man and woman was invaded by the guile of the serpent and they were seduced into claiming the forbidden fruit.

But betrayal soon came to have its own power as that first attachment of human love came to grief over the consequences of their fall. When questioned by God as to his actions, Adam responded, "The woman whom you gave to me to be with me, she gave me fruit from the tree, and I ate" (Gen. 3:12). This was more than blame, it was betrayal. And the devil had no need to prompt Adam to surrender her to judgment to save his own skin. Betrayal is now an instinct of survival when one's personal life and value is threatened.

Let us see how the seeds of betrayal are already sown in the promises we make and the vows we take.

THE SEEDS OF BETRAYAL ARE SOWN IN THE SOIL OF LOVE

The reality of love grows where the intentions of the heart are focused and shared. Attachments are also forms of commitments, and we are bound to one another through shared promises and expressed love. But in that love is also found the source of betrayal and the seeds of treachery. We can do injury to a stranger, but this is not betrayal. A manufacturer may fail to honor a warranty on a product. I am angry at the injustice, but this is not yet betrayal. A robber may break into my house, steal my property, and violate my space. I am outraged but I do not feel betrayed. It is easier to forget a crime than to forgive a friend.

Jerry, for whatever reason, was unable to keep the vow he made in his first marriage. He took that failure to heart and determined that he could never again trust himself to love another unconditionally. In a sense he was saying, "I cannot promise more than I can deliver. As long as I love, I can be faithful to my vow. But when love dies, the promise comes to an end." Jerry assumed that love was insurance against betrayal when, in fact, the seeds of betrayal are already sown in the bonds of love.

The very concept of betrayal requires that there be something to betray. And in betrayal it is love that is both the source and the object. We betray when we feel that our own love is betrayed by the failure of others. We become treacherous when we test the vision of love and find it different than our own. When we feel betrayed, we turn the passion of love into raging violence and ruthless vengeance when that which we love seems to fail our expectations and resist our demands.

How else do we explain the fact that domestic violence and child abuse is treachery against the people that we have promised to love? What could account for the fact that "normal" people abuse and seek to destroy those with whom they live other than the fact that before there was betrayal, there was love? Only when trust is first formed through shared life can it be broken. And only the sense of outrage, fueled by a primitive moral instinct, and carried out with the passion of love's despair, can wreak the havoc and destruction in a family and among friends that betrayal causes.

At the core of the psyche of the betrayer is failed love, not an evil spirit. Betrayers need more than forgiveness which issues from the love of another. Both the betrayer and the betrayed need the recovery of a love within themselves that has gone awry. This is why it is so difficult for those who have betrayed others to be received back into fellowship through repentance and forgiveness. For betrayal has torn the flesh of fellowship and friendship away, leaving only the skeleton of love's despair visible. This is too terrible to look upon and too revealing, of the fear that hides in our own love, for us to tolerate.

When we make promises and seal them with a vow of love and friendship, we acknowledge an attachment to others that has the power to break our hearts and destroy our trust in the goodness of life. Some of these attachments are involuntary, created through the daily life of family, beginning with the earliest experiences of caregiving and receiving. Other attachments result from our conscious choices and intentional acts of shared life. Regardless of how they are formed, attachments to others become part of our personal identity. We invest more of ourselves in them than in any other contractual obligation or social relationship.

The loss of an attachment which has enabled one to form a self-identity in relation to another threatens the very core of the self. It is one thing to feel an existential sense of aloneness and separation. It is quite another to mourn the death of a loved one, the loss of a relation, or the betrayal of trust. A broken promise cuts deeper into the self than unfulfilled desire. I can weep for something which may never come to pass, but my heart is broken when the love which came to pass is taken from me. We may survive such losses, but find it difficult to recover the capacity to love and trust again.

HOW DID IT ALL BEGIN?

The cycle of life is one of separation, attachment, loss, and survival. Torn from the fetal cocoon and separated at birth from the nourishing cord of common life by the snip of a scissors, the human infant is set adrift both physically and emotionally on the ocean of humanity. However tranquil the waters may be in the snug harbor of the caregiver's calm, the sensitive self of the newborn feels the stirring of distant storms and trembles in anticipation. Seismic tremors of future shock are silently recorded on the psychic Richter scale of the anxious self. It will be a journey not without some loss.

Before the psychologists, who only arrived after the damage was done, there were the theologians. Before the theologians, who tend to misread psychic distress as religious yearning, there were the astrologers. Before the astrologers, who explained human tragedy as cosmic fate, there were the storytellers. When we listen to them, we hear the heartbeat of our natal companion and feel the pulse in the finger of God.

The biblical story of human origins replicates the life cycle of the self from its natal alienation and subsequent bonding through a near fatal loss and consequent survival. The account of the origin of human life is cast in the form of a drama in Genesis 2.

First, there is the solitary form of the human brought on stage, with no companion. There is a stern warning given concerning the fruit of a certain tree, of the knowledge of good and evil. "In the day that you eat of it you shall die," came the whisper from offstage (2:17). A word of wisdom if one is prone to be cautious, a shiver of excitement if one is inclined to be curious. But what is this talk about death? In the innocence of spiritual puberty, what could be known about death that it should be a possibility if not an inevitability? For the moment, these questions hang in the air. A more immediate concern arises.

In the divine soliloquy, we hear the words, "It is not good that the man should be alone; I will make him a helper as his partner" (Gen. 2:18). As the animals are brought forth out of the dust of the ground and taken to the man to see what he would call them, there is rising expectation, only to be brought crashing down to the dust again by these words: "But for the man there was not found a helper as his partner" (2:20). The man is put to sleep, ending the loneliness created by the absence of something he had never known. With the deft hand of the divine surgeon, a woman is fashioned as the counterpart to the man and then the silence is shattered!

"This at last is bone of my bones and flesh of my flesh," cried the man, awakening out of his primordial trance and solitary silence, "and they became one flesh" (Gen. 2:23-24). The figure of the divine is in the background, slightly offstage, writing the script as the drama unfolds. The author and the actors are part of a piece; in their respective roles, each alike embracing the whole.

Thus occurs the first human attachment, arising out of a primordial womb of isolation and separation. The "good" of human encounter and relationship is preceded by the "not good" of aloneness and alienation of the self from the uncreated other. In the bond of human companionship and partnership, there is hidden the knowledge of a fatal slip back into that "not good." Our fate is always in the hands of the other. How do we know this?

Ah, the storyteller reminds us, we always know more than we can tell.[3] There is a knowledge at the core of the self for which we will never have words. It rises up within us without our bidding and cannot be forgotten or erased by the most strenuous act of the will, nor by the most delirious ecstasy of emotion.

In the bond of love and attachment experienced by the first man and woman, each has a knowledge of the absence of the other. In the narcissistic pleasure of life's most gratifying moments, there is a knowledge of the passing away of that life, and that is death. In the most self-assured managing of one's possessions in life, there is the knowledge of their impending loss.

When the forbidden fruit was eaten (Gen. 3), the consequence was no surprise, though the pain of the loss was incomprehensible. "Cursed is the ground because of you; in toil you shall eat of it all the days of your life.... By the sweat of your face you shall eat bread until you return to the ground, for out of it you were taken; you are dust, and to dust you shall return.... therefore the Lord God sent him forth from the garden of Eden ... " (Gen. 3:17, 19, 23). However, as we see in the next chapter, life goes on: "Now the man knew his wife, Eve, and she conceived and bore Cain, saying, 'I have produced a man with the help of the Lord' " (4:1).

Yes, they survived even this tragic loss. And so the cycle is complete. Human life does not begin in a vacuum; the self does not emerge without shadows of the darkness to which it is prone. Bonding to another satisfies the deepest longing of the self for connection, but creates its own pain of separation and loss. Love intensifies the suffering when love is lost. "Yet no one loves another without becoming vulnerable to the other, without being affected by the other, and, if need be, suffering with the other; hence one who loves, especially with a steadfast love, will necessarily be changed in the loving relationship."[4]

We can no more split the joy of love apart from the pain of loss than we can cut the story of our origins out of the narrative of our lives. There was no age of innocence without a knowledge of death and no joining of the self with another without the "not good" of being alone and disconnected.

As the biblical story goes, they did not "live happily ever after." The seeds of betrayal were already sown in the joyful affirmation of love and companionship. The consequences of their mutual act of disobedience, and defiance of the terms that God had set for their good, were devastating and divisive. Feeling self-conscious in the presence of each other, they covered themselves with fig leaves to cover their nakedness and hid themselves from God. Confronted by God, the man stood back from his companion and partner and said, in effect, "She is the

guilty one; if someone has to die, let it be her." The consequences of betrayal are often fatal to a relationship and the
wound to the one betrayed as well as to the betrayer is seldom,
if ever, healed.

Can recovery take place when the losses of life are so pervasive, so permanent, and so painful? The answer is yes, but the
key is finding the place to begin and the resources to help.

RECOVERING FROM BETRAYAL

In every act of betrayal there are two victims, the one(s) betrayed and the betrayer. Let us consider each in turn.

1. Those of us who have been betrayed

When we have been betrayed, we experience an injury which no
punishment of the offender can heal. The violation of trust by
another can cause irreparable damage to the core of the self. No
amount of punishment of the offender can repair this damage.
Healing must come from another source.

Betrayal, as I have indicated above, is quite different from all
other offenses in that it constitutes a tear in the fabric that
binds the inner self to the outer world. When one cannot bridge
the gap between the self and the external world, the self retreats
into itself and becomes inaccessible. In its most serious form,
this can result in an autistic disorder, one of the most difficult
mental problems to treat.

What we call trust is not a volitional act as much as it is the
freedom of the self to allow external stimuli to enter through
sensory experience resulting in a sense of well-being, security,
and pleasure. This "trust-full" openness of the self is a fragile
but firm basis for feelings and actions of love, commitment, and
shared life. In a normal or "good enough" caregiving environment, infants grow in their capacity to trust and, through bonding and attachment experiences, are capable of making binding
commitments to others as they mature.[5]

This is what I have called the "fabric" that binds the inner
self to the outer world. When this fabric is torn, the self is cast
into a dilemma. The openness to others which brought pleasure

and expanded dimensions to the self, has now become an instrument of pain and violation. The betrayer cannot be isolated as merely an untrustworthy person, as one would pick a rotten apple out of a sack and throw it away. Betrayal ruptures the sack itself so that all of the apples spill out. The self perceives that it is not just the one apple, but the sack itself that is dangerous. For in allowing oneself to be "gathered up" in the lives of others, one has become vulnerable to all.

To choose another metaphor, trust is something like having a telephone installed by which one can call out and make contact with others, but also a way in which others can call in to invade the privacy of one's own space. One "trusts" that when the telephone rings the person calling will at least respect one's personal life, if not also be a friend with whom one can share a pleasant and fulfilling moment. If, however, one receives a threatening or obscene phone call, which violates one's personal being and security, the phone now becomes untrustworthy! The dilemma is, when the phone rings, how does one know whether to answer it or not? To protect oneself from further abuse, one can simply choose not to answer the phone, or to have it removed. But that also means the loss of contact with all others.

I am afraid that the metaphors that I have chosen each have their limitations. But each is intended to make this single point. An act of betrayal attacks the core of the self at the trust level and thus creates an injury which can only be healed by the recovery of trust, not by punishing the betrayer. Because the injury caused by betrayal is to the trust level of the self, it can only be healed by the rebuilding of this trust.

Once again, trust is not a volitional act, so that we cannot simply decide to start trusting others. Trust is a capacity of the self to allow access and for the self to venture (risk) engagement with others at a deep personal level. This capacity can be regained when it has been lost, but it can only take place through relationships where trust is experienced as openness to others in ways that protect and affirm the integrity of the self.

We now see why the self is cast into a deep dilemma when betrayal occurs and why the process of recovery from betrayal is difficult to initiate. How does one trust those who are necessary for the recovery of trust when it has been destroyed? Let me make some suggestions.

First, shared pain is possible when shared trust is not. The pain of betrayal is not unlike the pain which other victims experience, whether it be from abuse, loss of a loved one, or rejection by others. While betrayal itself is unique in that it attacks the core of the self's trust capacity, the pain it causes is not. There are a variety of support programs, twelve-step programs, and other resources where persons come together with the common experience of personal pain and loss.

We only begin to trust one who can share our pain — the guilty do not trust the innocent! And the dying do not trust the living! The sympathy of those who recognize our hurt and wish to help is not sufficient. Those who are vulnerable at the level of their own pain create access to our pain, and thus to the very core of our being, without requiring a commitment or a promise. Without the experience of shared pain, those who have had trust shattered cannot find a point of beginning.

Second, the reality of shared pain creates an implicit bond which requires explicit recognition and affirmation. Once we have experienced bonding through shared pain, there is a further step now possible. The implicit bond of companionship and shared life has now taken the place of the distrust which served as a protective mechanism against risking further hurt. While there is not yet a capacity to make promises that require trust, there is "ground under one's feet," so to speak. The ones who provided unconditional acceptance through their own shared pain now stand with us and for us. There is less risk involved in saying "yes" to the reality of a bond already established than the attempt to create a new one "out of nothing."

Third, the reality of shared life in a common bond creates a new basis for trust. The "yes" to the reality of shared life creates implicit trust. The undeniable reality of this trust provides a basis for belief. Belief is the content of hope based on experienced trust and reaches out through faith to expand the horizon of life beyond shared pain to shared promise.

Fourth, entry into community with others is a shared promise as an expression of love. One has recovered the capacity to trust and love when one can risk betrayal again! As Craig Dykstra has said:

> *It is not the failure to keep promises, in and of itself, that destroys family. Such failure happens in every family and can be expected. Family can remain family in the midst of unfulfilled promises. What destroys family is the collapse of promise-making. It is when the very making of promises is no longer believed and believed in that families die.*[5]

Recovery from betrayal finally occurs when we are able to make promises again and enter into a promise-making community. This may not lead to reconciliation with the one who is the betrayer, for the one who betrays another must also go through a process of recovery. Reconciliation is an ultimate goal; recovery is a penultimate gain which may or may not lead to reconciliation. Let us consider now the recovery process for the betrayer.

2. Those who have betrayed others

For the betrayer, an act of betrayal is a crime for which self-abuse is the only atonement. The case of Judas, who betrayed Jesus, makes this point with devastating consequences. Immediately following his treacherous act of betrayal, Judas went to those who had paid him to point out Jesus so that He could be arrested and confessed that he had done wrong to betray "innocent blood." He threw down the thirty pieces of silver and went out and committed suicide by hanging himself (Matt. 27:3-5).

When I wrote the book, *The Gospel According to Judas*, I put these words in the mouth of Judas:

> *I perished from this earth by my own hand, as you have been told. It need not have happened. But that can only be true in retrospect At the time, the relentless accusations of my heart against myself because of my sin of betrayal became unbearable. . . . I cannot blame others for my own desperate act, however. In destroying another's life through betrayal, I felt that I had committed an act for which only my death could atone. It would not save him, of course, but it would put a merciful end to the spiral of accusation, remorse and guilt. I assumed that only I could pay the penalty for my own act.*[7]

The inner logic of betrayal, as I have explained above, is grounded in the trust which is created through intentional commitment. In the case of Judas, it was the call of Jesus to be a disciple and the response of Judas that created the possibility of the betrayal. As I have also pointed out, however, betrayal is not a violation of an external law so much as it is a violation and destruction of the very foundation for the self's relation to others and the world.

This is what makes it so difficult for both those betrayed and the betrayer to recover. In the case of the betrayer, self-accusation can become a relentless form of self-abuse. All attempts at reconciliation and healing fail under the onslaught of this inner torment. Whereas for the ones betrayed there is mainly the pain and the loss of trust, for the betrayer there is a crime committed against the very nature of love and trust. Forgiveness, even self-forgiveness, is not possible until a verdict has been rendered, for forgiveness has to do with setting aside punishment.

The verdict demanded by the self-accusing conscience of the betrayer is to subject the self to relentless remorse. Death, as in the case of Judas, becomes one way to stop this torment. And, because the verdict and torment is self-imposed, suicide is felt to be the appropriate means to render satisfaction and make atonement.

Not everyone who betrays another goes to such desperate lengths, of course. But the inner logic is the same. Recovery in this case must restore self-love or a sense of self-worth as the only basis for the recovery of self-empowerment and spiritual healing.

In the end, as the dialogue I created between the resurrected Jesus and Judas came to its climax, I traced the inner movement of recovery for Judas as follows.

I thought I could see, but I was blind. Through your eyes I see that my life is no longer flat and one-dimensional. The door I closed has become transparent. I — I see a different Judas on the other side.

It's not enough to use my eyes, Judas, I have touched yours so that you may see yourself, and for yourself, that you are my friend.

I saw my guilt, but not the shame that blinded me and angered me.
I confessed my sin of betrayal and threw the money back at their feet.
But something in me cowered like a child caught stealing coins from the
box for the poor.

You have discovered what many have yet to see, Judas,
that each failure is not merely an offense against God, but a
loss of dignity and esteem for the self. Long before you met
me, you wove a veil of shame to shield your eyes from the
sight of that emaciated child.

Even in my betrayal of you, I sought to protect myself from
exposure through a too-quick confession, as though I could merely undo
a wrong. But I could not keep the shame from burning through and
tormenting me to death. In the end, I crept within it and killed the child
that could not be healed.

You are that child, Judas, and of such is the Kingdom of
God![8]

The spiritual healing necessary when we have betrayed another only becomes possible when we can find release from the
terrible torment or self-abuse. This is why the figure of Judas is
so pathetic and, at the same time, so powerful an example of the
need for divine grace and spiritual healing. Every act against the
core of the self, and betrayal is ultimately such an act, is also a
tear in the fabric of the image of God in which each of us was
created.

The restoration of that divine image is a process of spiritual
healing. Our own human spirit must be touched and renewed by
the Spirit of God. To whom can we go for this healing? To those
who themselves have experienced the healing power of divine
grace and love. Only the forgiven can mediate forgiveness.

For those who are victims of abuse and caught in the addic-
tive power of substance abuse, the first step in a twelve-step
program is to come to the end of one's own resources and reach
out to others. For those who have been betrayed, there is a point
of healing and recovery in making this step.

For the betrayer, however, even that first step is difficult.
For an intervention must be made into the relentless logic of
self-abuse and self-condemnation before one can begin the pro-

cess of self-recovery and self-empowerment.

Here is where the reality of spiritual healing can actually begin. That intervention has been made through Jesus Christ into the vicious cycle of self-condemnation. Jesus, by the power of the Holy Spirit, can make the intervention with surgical skill and sensitive heart.

"Do not say in your heart, 'Who will ascend into heaven?' (that is, to bring Christ down) or 'Who will descend into the abyss?' (that is, to bring Christ up from the dead). But what does it say? 'The word is near you, on your lips and in your heart.' The Scripture says, 'No one who believes in him will be put to shame' " (Rom. 10:6-8, 11).

The "step before the first step" has been taken by Christ toward us. Together, Jesus Christ goes with us to the place where healing begins. This is the end of betrayal and the beginning of life.

For some, the experience of tragic loss and suffering feels like the ultimate betrayal of trust in the providence of God. In the midst of a personal crisis or unrelieved suffering, the question is often asked, "Why does God permit suffering and evil when he has the power to intervene?" The question of God's goodness and the problem of evil arises as a crisis of faith for many people. In the chapter that follows we will trace out the promise and presence of God in the midst of the tragic in life.

SUMMARY

• Betrayal is a violation of the trust which binds people together in covenants of promise and love. These covenants can be implicit as with children and parents and explicit as in the case of marriage and vows of friendship. Only where there has already existed commitment and trust can betrayal occur.

• The seeds of betrayal are sown in the soil of love. Betrayal has such a devastating effect because it attacks the very foundation of human social relations. One act of betrayal shatters the bond by which all are bound by common life and promise.

• Recovery from betrayal begins with the reexperiencing of trust by sharing the pain of betrayal with those who have their own pain. Shared pain is the building block of shared trust.

● For those who have betrayed others, self-atonement through desperate acts of self-condemnation is futile, as Judas discovered. Reentry into a community which provides empowering grace and demands unconditional love is God's provision through the body of Christ.

PRAXIS

Bill, Mary, and Lisa are brother and sisters. Their older brother, Walter, is an attorney and offered his services as executor of the estate when their wealthy parents died. Several years later, it was revealed that Walter had violated this trust and had diverted the majority of the funds in the estate into his own account and had squandered the fortune through gambling losses. The family were members of the church, and the two sisters and their brother Bill came to the pastor for counsel. "We are not financially destitute," Lisa said. "We each have enough money for our own use and our families. So it is not just that our brother Walter stole the money that belonged to us, but that he betrayed the trust that we placed in him." Bill added, "Walter has admitted what he did was wrong and wants us to forgive him and accept him back into our family saying that he lost his own marriage over this and that he has no one else to call family. Our problem is that we now realize that he was always a loner in our family and that he was unscrupulous in many other ways. He betrayed us and we can't find it possible to trust him again, even as a brother."

● Why is betrayal perceived as a greater wrong than embezzlement by those who have suffered the financial loss?

● If a stranger had embezzled the money, there would be the same financial loss but not the devastating consequence of betrayal. Why is this so?

● How can persons who enter into commitments with one another based on friendship or kinship protect themselves against the possibility of betrayal?

● In what way does Walter represent the "Judas syndrome," as discussed in this chapter?

● What should be the pastor's strategy in dealing with this issue and how should it involve Walter as well as his three siblings?

9

Tragedy:
An Invisible Tear in the Eye of God

My anguish, my anguish! I writhe in pain! Oh, the walls of my heart! My heart is beating wildly; I cannot keep silent; for I hear the sound of the trumpet, the alarm of war (Jer. 4:19).

Sooner or later, each one of us will utter in our own way, the cry of Jesus from the cross: "My God, my God, why have you forsaken me?" (Matt. 27:46) "Why, God?" "Why me, God?" "How could You let this happen, God?" These are some of the questions I have heard over and over again in pastoral ministry to persons caught in personal tragedy.

WHEN SUFFERING PRODUCES A CRISIS OF FAITH

Some years ago, I was asked to make a pastoral call to counsel a woman who was dying of cancer. She was a young mother in her middle thirties, with three small children. Her husband was in denial of her illness; he would not discuss it with her and even avoided coming into her bedroom where she lay, too weak to get up. As we talked she raged in anger over the fact that God was allowing this to happen to her. "How can God let me die with these small children to care for?" she demanded. "I have prayed, but my prayers go unanswered."

I attempted to enter into her feelings of anger and agreed that what happened to her was a terrible injustice and a great tragedy. I asked if she was afraid to die, and she replied, "Yes, because I don't know who will take care of my kids, and I have lost my faith in God." Then, looking directly at me, she demanded again, "Tell me, pastor, how do you explain God's absence and His failure to heal me and prevent this terrible thing from happening?"

My formal theological training melted away like a sand castle washed with a cresting wave. To give a defense of God at that moment was beyond my competence. The enormity of the reality of her situation exposed my carefully prepared "textbook" responses as superficial and inane. Venturing into unexplored territory, led only by the flickering light of her own desperate honesty, I replied, "I don't think that God can do anything about it. I think that He feels as helpless and perhaps as angry as you do."

"You can't say that," she protested. "Don't we believe that God is in control and has the power to do anything He wants?" She had learned her theology well, as it turned out. She knew what one was expected to say about God, but had little idea of what God had to say about her.

"The only God that I know was present when His own child was suffering and dying on the cross," I replied. "He was powerless to intervene and remove Him from the cross, for His love is His power, and it took a powerful love to enter into sickness and death in order to provide a way through it for us."

I went on to talk about the reality of God as present in the pain and suffering of His Son, Jesus Christ. I suggested that our concept of power as absolute control over everything from outside was really a very superficial and empty concept of power. She was quiet for a long time. Then she said, quietly and with deep feeling, "I can believe that. I just had to have some point of contact. I couldn't reach Him when I thought of Him being powerful and distant. But I can trust Him if He is willing to die with me."

After a prayer with shared tears, I asked her, "Are you afraid?" And she replied, "Not so much now. I guess that God is with me. I don't feel so alone."

WHEN GOD'S POWER SEEMS TO FAIL

As I later reflected upon what had happened in that room, permeated with pain and shadowed by suffering, I realized that a concept of a God who is viewed as omnipotent and all-powerful places Him outside our perceptions of reality and beyond the reach of our powerless faith. Instead of destroying her faith in God by suggesting that God was not the all-powerful figure she had in her mind, God was made more real to her and, in a paradoxical kind of way, more powerful in relationship to her own suffering than she had ever experienced before.

What she came to realize is that the power of God is not an abstract kind of power as control over everything, but a power of personal presence even in a time of suffering and dying.

To experience tragedy is to have one's faith in God severely tested. Not everyone survives the crisis of faith. The shocking intrusion of an unexpected and catastrophic loss can appear so irrational and evil that the self's connection with God is broken off at the core.

My concern in this chapter is not primarily with the psychological effects of a crisis produced by tragic and catastrophic loss to the self. Rather, in addition to the psychological trauma to the self, there is a theological trauma which the self experiences, usually in the form of questions raised with regard to the failure of divine intervention.

For many people, one role of God in the face of uncertainty and unpredictability is that of assuring that there is some ultimate order and meaning to life. The self cannot really cope with the feeling that life is subject to sheer randomness of disease, destruction, and death. If God is no longer in control, then some evil power must lie behind such brutality and horror. If the devil did not exist, he would have to be invented to provide some explanation for the evil which strikes at the good with such deadly aim. But if we use the devil to account for evil, what will account for the freedom of this evil one to run rampant over God's good earth and wreak havoc amid God's children?

The biblical writer does not attempt to provide an analytical model of the self. Rather, the life of the self is depicted in dramatic form, with a plot and characters. The focus is not upon some idyllic Garden of Eden inhabited by perfect humans like Greek sculptures, glazed with impermeable but transparent lacquer designed to deflect contrary moods and invading spirits.

The Greeks idealized the human form while projecting into their gods tragic imperfections who spun a web of intrigue into which humans were ineluctably drawn. The Hebrews, on the other hand, preserved a concept of a God who was good, if not ideally perfect, and allowed humanity to bear the burden of passion and the risk of failure. This is why the Old Testament views human suffering as a crisis of faith in the justice and goodness of God, not as a philosophical problem to be analyzed.

The simplistic formulas by which humans attempt to divide life into moral categories of good and evil, prosperity and suffering, fail under the undeniable reality of personal pain. Why do the righteous suffer? (Ps. 73:1-3) Is suffering so relentless and pervasive that there is nothing to hope for? (Job 19:1-12)

CAN WE BELIEVE IN A GOD WHO PERMITS EVIL?

Does God permit evil? Dostoyevsky's Ivan Karamazov does not think so. Ivan challenges the theology of his brother Alyosha, a novice in residence to become a monk. Ivan recounts incidents of the torture of children and one case of where a general set his dogs on a boy and they caught him and chewed him to bits before the eyes of his mother. When Alyosha protests and suggests that this horrible crime can only be explained by submitting to the inscrutable will and purpose of God, Ivan responds.

Listen! If all must suffer to pay for the eternal harmony, what have children to do with it, tell me, please? It's beyond all comprehension why they should suffer, and why they should pay for the harmony. Why should they, too, furnish material to enrich the soil for the harmony of the future? I understand solidarity in sin among men. I understand solidarity in retribution, too; but there can be no such solidarity with children. And if it is really true that they must share responsibility for all their father's crimes, such a truth is not of this world and is beyond my comprehension. . . . Oh, Alyosha, I am not blaspheming! I understand, of course, what an upheaval of the universe it will be, when everything in heaven and earth blends in one hymn of praise and everything that lives and has lived cries aloud: "Thou art just, O Lord, for Thy ways are revealed." When the mother embraces the fiend who threw her child to the dogs, and all three cry aloud with tears, "Thou art just, O Lord!" then, of course, the crown of knowledge will be reached and all will be made clear. But what pulls me up here is that I can't accept that harmony.[1]

Ivan cannot accept the theological answer to the problem of evil that God will finally reconcile all things to Himself and reveal a pattern of perfect justice that will vindicate Him and produce a final harmony. Not even retribution against the offender will satisfy the injustice that this horrible evil was permitted. No forgiveness and no atonement can wipe away the *fact* that a grievous wrong was done.

You see, Alyosha, perhaps it really may happen that if I live to that moment, or rise again to see it, I, too, perhaps, may cry aloud with the rest, looking at the mother embracing the child's torturer, "Thou art just, O Lord!" but I don't want to cry aloud then. While there is still time, I hasten to protect myself and so I renounce the higher harmony altogether. . . . What do I care for a hell for oppressors? What good can hell do, since those children have already been tortured? And what becomes of harmony, if there is hell? . . . I don't want the mother to embrace the oppressor who threw her son to the dogs! She dare not forgive him! . . . Is there a being in the whole world who would have the right to forgive and could forgive? I don't want harmony. From love for humanity I don't want it. I would rather be left with the unavenged suffering. I would rather remain with my unavenged suffering and unsatisfied indignation, even if I were wrong. Besides, too high a price is asked for harmony; it's beyond our means to pay so much to enter on it. And so I hasten to give back my entrance ticket, and if I am an honest man I am bound to give it back as soon as possible. And that I am doing. It's not God that I don't accept, Alyosha, only I must respectfully return Him the ticket.[2]

Like Ivan, many have "given back their ticket" and turned away from a God who has the power but not the compassion or will to eliminate suffering and intervene when innocent people suffer. Attempts to defend God in the face of such monstrous evil, for many, makes atheism a more attractive alternative.

The standard theological textbooks miss the only starting point for coming to grips with the reality of suffering and the reality of God. Instead of beginning with the "crucified God," as the theologian Jürgen Moltmann suggested, the traditional attempt to justify the existence and power of God in the face of evil led more in the direction of atheism than to the God of Abraham, Isaac, and Jacob and finally, to the Son of God, Jesus Christ, who died on the cross![3]

The older theologians tended to discuss the problem of evil and suffering under the category of theodicy—the defense of God's goodness in the manifestation of evil. The problem was formulated in this fashion:

If God is all powerful, but has not the will to prevent evil, then He is a cruel and malicious God;
If God is loving and good, but lacks the power to prevent evil, then He is a weak and impotent God;
If God has both the will and the power to prevent evil, then whence evil?

The answer from the mainstream of Christian theology has been to uphold the sovereignty of God and to suggest that evil arose in a perfect world due to human sin. God allows the suffering and evil to continue for reasons which we cannot question but which will be revealed in the age to come. John Hick, in his seminal work on *Evil and the God of Love,* looked at human suffering from the divine side: "Whatever tends to promote the attain-

ment of [the divine purpose] will be good and whatever tends to
thwart it will be bad."[4] The evangelist Billy Graham speaks out
of this tradition when he says:

> *We may not fully understand why God — who is all powerful and*
> *loving — permits evil in this world. But whatever else we may say, it*
> *must be stressed that man, not God, is guilty for the evil of the world. It*
> *is man that bears the responsibility, because man was given the ability to*
> *make free moral choices, and he chose deliberately to disobey God. The*
> *world as it now exists is not the way God intended it to be.*[5]

This, of course, is precisely what Dostoyevsky calls into
question through the impassioned repudiation of such an "ultimate harmony" by Ivan. The concept of God's absolute power in
the face of human suffering continues to cause a crisis of faith.
But in the modern view of God, contrary to the Old Testament
view, the crisis is resolved through a concept of a finite and
limited God who lacks the power to prevent evil but who is
strong in compassion for those who suffer. In this view, God sits
helplessly on the sidelines, wanting to help, but unable to
intervene.

WHAT KIND OF GOD LETS CHILDREN DIE?

Rabbi Harold Kushner struck a responsive chord in the hearts of
many people with his best-selling book, *When Bad Things Happen*
to Good People. His son died at the age of fourteen, following
extended illness due to progeria, the "rapid aging disease." Attempting to answer why God would permit such a tragedy if He
had the power to prevent it, he arrived at the following conclusion.

> *I believe in God. But I do not believe the same things about Him that I*
> *did years ago, when I was growing up or when I was a theological*
> *student. I recognize His limitations. He is limited in what He can do by*
> *laws of nature and by the evolution of human nature and moral free-*
> *dom. I no longer hold God responsible for illnesses, accidents, and*
> *natural disasters, because I realize that I gain little and I lose so much*

when I blame God for those things. I can worship a God who hates
suffering but cannot eliminate it, more easily than I can worship a God
who chooses to make children suffer and die, for whatever exalted
reason.[6]

When I ask my students to read this book and respond to
Kushner, a great deal of anxiety is produced. Most feel sympa-
thetic toward the Rabbi, but rush to defend God's sovereignty.
Some suggest that because Kushner is not a Christian and does
not understand that God destroyed the power of sickness and
death through Jesus Christ, he is unable to retain a concept of
God's sovereignty. Invariably, they end by some kind of appeal
to God's permissive will during the interim time, where suffering
continues due to sin, but for which there will be compensation
in the end. I often urge them never to offer this bit of wisdom to
someone who is actually suffering!

Whatever our concept of suffering and the reality of evil, we
do well to remember that for the one who suffers, it will always
be perceived as evil and not as good. Paul Schilling reminds us:
"It is not easy to distinguish between real and apparent goods
and evils, though we dare never forget that events perceived as
evil by the one experiencing them must be treated seriously
because they are evil for him."[7]

In response to a discussion of Kushner's book in *The Los
Angeles Times*, John B. Cobb, Jr. and David Ray Griffen from the
School of Theology at Claremont, California presented a view
quite similar to that of Kushner. At the time, Cobb was director
and Griffen executive director of the Center for Process Studies
at Claremont. Process theology views God as participating in the
struggle against evil with assurance that He will eventually triumph over it, but will Himself be changed in the process.[8]

The problem of God's relation to evil is usually couched in terms of the
first image of power. People want to know, therefore, why God does not
snatch a child out of the way of a backing car, stop a bullet that is
about to kill an innocent person (or stop the finger that was about to
pull the trigger), or prevent the operation of the Nazi death camps.
Superman is pictured as doing things like that. If God is even more

powerful than Superman, why does God stand idly by? We would despise Superman if he did so. . . . We should not think of God as a super-Superman, out-coercing the coercive forces of the world. Rather, God has the evocative, inspiring, transforming power needed by the all-pervasive, loving, creator of the universe. This is the power to evoke order out of chaos, life out of inanimate matter, consciousness out of mere life, love and concern for justice out of hate and indifference, global consciousness out of tribalism, and a resurrected life beyond death.[9]

Process theology has rejected the notion of a transcendent God who resides in untouchable serenity and absolute power outside the world of His creation. God is bound up in the historical process of change in such a way that whatever is meant by the term "god" awaits the final outcome of the struggle between good and evil. One *hopes* that there will be a God in the end and that goodness will survive in the contest with evil, but in the meantime one should not expect intervention by this God. Faith in the ultimate survival of God as the power of goodness over evil is seen as the power to evoke hope and trust in the human subject and thus provide a coping mechanism to endure pain and suffering.

In my estimation, process theology has accepted too quickly the formulation of traditional theism constructed more along Greek concepts of deity rather than the Hebrew understanding of God as a covenant partner. As a result, the resolution of the problem is dictated by the terms in which the problem is set up. Once the power of God has been set up in an abstract way, with absolute power to control every event, the conflict between goodness and power is inevitable.

CAN WE ACCEPT SUFFERING AS HAVING REDEEMING VALUE?

For the Christian who suffers, and who is shocked and grieved over the tragedy and pain of others, there may well come a crisis of faith. I have developed some of the theological issues in this crisis of faith without attempting to provide conclusive theological answers. At the same time, I have suggested that suffering has what we might call a hermeneutical function. Hermeneutics is an attempt to interpret and provide meaning.

The young woman dying of cancer discovered that her earlier concepts of God were inadequate to provide her with a foundation of faith and trust in the context of her pain and anguish. Her only point of contact with God was her anger and accusation against Him. Yet, out of this existential crisis of faith emerged the profile of a suffering God with whom she could identify in her own anguish.

God's power is made manifest in weakness, wrote the Apostle Paul, following his own experience of unanswered prayer with regard to his "thorn in the flesh." This is the power of Christ who has Himself entered into the domain of suffering and evil and has overcome that power with a greater power of divine love and restoration to life (2 Cor. 12:8-9).[10]

This is not to suggest, as some have, that suffering produces character or that good can come out of evil. The older concept of suffering as a "vale of soul-making," was often offered as counsel to those who were afflicted. In a paper on suffering prepared for the Church of Scotland (1981), this "song was sung to a heavy heart" (cf. Prov. 25:20).

> *Without the experience of suffering, a man's nature remains shallow. Pain that has been lived through gives to character a depth that seldom comes from the experience of happiness. No one dare speak glibly of the spiritual consolation of such experience, yet the strong have often to confess to seeing in the less fortunate, a fortitude and a beauty that they cannot understand.*[11]

Graham Monteith, minister in the Church of Scotland, and himself physically disabled, questioned the logic which makes the one who suffers a source of inspiration to others. In response to this paper he wrote:

> *The earth seen as a "vale of soul-making" seems to be good in intention, but cruel in actual fact. It is difficult to argue that any good comes out of disability. It may, in fact, be true, but the disabled, myself included,*

do not wish to hear it. . . . Thus far I have said that I have not been
sustained by a mission, or by any mitigating circumstances, or by the
challenge of suffering for Christ, nor indeed that I merit a particular
place in the Church because of my disability. So what has sustained
me? . . . Christ suffered vicariously. What He did for us was not of
His own asking. . . . Therefore, in His sufferings Christ suffered for
and with man because the parameters of suffering were set by
man. . . . At no point did He abandon God's mission to save us by the
sacrifice of His own son. I believe that this is the message which has
sustained me and is the beginning of any understanding of the theology
of the disabled.[12]

To tell a woman that the death of her young child was God's
plan to develop in her a deeper spiritual life and a stronger
character will likely provoke the response, "I would rather have
my child and remain weaker in character, given the choice."
Some who have gone through the cycle of self-development,
experiencing grief and loss and who finally survive, may well
testify to a faith and hope that is stronger by virtue of having
stood the test. But only they have the right to make such a
statement. As one such person said, "Yes, I am a survivor, but
someday God is going to have a lot to answer for!"

In the Old Testament, the Prophet Habakkuk was prepared
to call God to account for the injustice he saw all around.

Your eyes are too pure to behold evil, and you cannot look on wrongdo-
ing; why do you look on the treacherous, and are silent when the wicked
swallow those more righteous than they? (Hab. 1:13)

I will stand at my watchpost, and station myself on the rampart; I
will keep watch to see what he will say to me, and what he will answer
concerning my complaint. Then the Lord answered me: . . . Look at the
proud! Their spirit is not right in them, but the righteous live by their
faith (2:1-2, 4).

This was probably not the kind of answer Habakkuk expected! He was challenged to remember what the Hebrew people
had known from the beginning. Their God demanded righteousness of those who belonged to Him by covenant, but He was not

the God of the righteous only. He sends the rain upon the righteous and the unrighteous (Matt. 5:45).

God does not duck and dodge the reality of evil, attributing it to human sin and blaming it on the devil. God is the author of the drama, in which pain and pleasure, suffering and joy, and good and evil are part of the plot. Faith means that we as human participants know that there is an author and that the drama is being constructed even as we live it out. The righteous do not live by their righteousness, God reminded the Prophet Habakkuk, but by faith. God takes full responsibility. This, at least, is a start.

The theological question with regard to suffering is: What does it mean to say that God takes responsibility for evil and that we can have faith in Him to do this? The biblical tradition has no view of evil as a problem outside of the concept of God's providence. God's overarching providence is expressed through His partnership with human persons in suffering, which is the divine power to be present as our advocate for redeeming those who suffer. The providence of God is bound to His promise. This promise is a miracle and mystery of divine love. Suffering and injustice can produce a crisis of faith, leading us directly to God as the one who must ultimately take responsibility. In His taking responsibility through participation in the dilemma of evil, God provides redemption from it, not a solution to it as a problem.

This is why, for example, the dramatic story of Job is told in such a way that the devil is permitted to inflict Job with catastrophic losses, and yet is limited by God as to the destruction of Job himself. God is the author of the drama of life, and He can allow the characters He has placed in the story to run the course of their role and live out the part assigned to each. At the same time, God has the "story under control," so to speak. And this, in the end, is the message of the Book of Job.

We are troubled by the fact that the devil and God seem to conspire against Job and that God would allow such evil to exist. We want a different story, where we can sort out the good and the bad from the beginning and ensure that we are always on the good side! But we are not the author. For the Hebrew people, it was sufficient to know that God was not only one who could enter into the story at will, but who also had the story under control. They knew that salvation was not in a perfect world, but in God who kept the story under control and who could be trusted to preserve their lives in the end.

THE SUFFERING OF GOD AND
THE RECOVERY OF FAITH

For the Christian, Jesus Christ is not only a human person caught up in the same suffering that befalls all people. He is the actual presence and reality of God taking upon Himself the evil, pain, and suffering that alienates and isolates humans from each other and from the life of God.

Jesus Christ enters the human drama as the one who experiences for Himself the power and destruction of evil and, at the same time, becomes the mediator of grace and hope. God's providence is expressed through the event of redemption in which He takes evil upon Himself so as to deliver, once and for all, human persons from the power of evil to separate persons from His covenanted purpose and goal.

There is a pastoral question with regard to evil: How can we mediate this presence and divine power in the face of evil and with those who suffer? This cannot be done by defending the power of God as an abstract concept of divine sovereignty. Nor can it be done by limiting God to the constraints of the finite world and so render Him powerless, albeit, full of sympathy and compassion.

We cannot mediate God's presence and power in the face of evil by resorting to a concept of divine providence that ordains suffering for some and blessing for others. God's providence is seen through the life of Jesus and ultimately in His death on the cross. What appears to be a triumph of evil over good is an event of unspeakable horror wrapped in the arms of God. The crisis of faith drives us toward the God who Himself cries out with the anguish of the "godforsaken." It was from the cross that Jesus took upon His lips the lament of the ancient Hebrew: "My God, my God, why have you forsaken me?" (Matt. 27:46; Ps. 22:1) In so doing, Jesus took the depths of human despair into the very heart of God.

"Only the suffering God can help," wrote Dietrich Bonhoeffer, when he experienced the collapse of the good and the evil of Hitler's program of destruction.

> *The God who is with us is the God who forsakes us (Mark 15:34). The God who lets us live in the world without the working hypothesis of God is the God before whom we stand continually. Before God and with God we live without God. God lets himself be pushed out of the world on to the cross. . . . Here is the decisive difference between Christianity and all religions. Man's religiosity makes him look in his distress to the power of God in the world: God is the deus ex machina. The Bible directs man to God's powerlessness and suffering; only the suffering God can help.* [13]

We must "watch with Christ in Gethsemane," Bonhoeffer wrote to his friend, Eberhard Bethge, and reminded him of the poem which captured the same theme, which he had recently sent to him, titled: "Christians and Pagans."

> *Men go to God when they are sore bestead,*
> *Pray to him for succour, for his peace, for bread,*
> *For mercy for them sick, sinning, or dead;*
> *All men do so, Christian and unbelieving.*
>
> *Men go to God when he is sore bestead,*
> *Find him poor and scorned, without shelter or bread,*
> *Whelmed under weight of the wicked, the weak, the dead;*
> *Christians stand by God in his hour of grieving.*
>
> *God goes to every man when sore bestead,*
> *Feeds body and spirit with his bread;*
> *For Christians, pagans alike he hangs dead,*
> *And both alike forgiving.* [14]

Faith reaches for the hand of God and finds it torn by the nails which bound Christ to the cross. Faith cries out to the heart of God and finds it bruised and broken by the anguish of betrayal. Faith looks up to the face of God and sees the tears of sorrow for unbearable pain. When Jesus wept at the tomb of Lazarus, these were tears in the eye of God (John 11:35).

This can no longer be a godforsaken place. Here is a divine pathos so powerful that pain, by comparison, is weaker and grief, in contrast, is shallower. Even the demons draw back from the holiness of this divine outpouring of suffering love, and the devil turns aside as though to gaze upon such beauty would blind the eyes of evil.

Human sorrow and pain is not itself evil. Our grief is, after all, human grief and seeks the comfort and healing of a divine sorrow. Grief can be so devastating, however, that it can isolate us from the most well-intentioned human consolation and separate us hopelessly from the divine presence. Left to itself, human pain and unrelieved grief conceives unbelief and gives birth to atheism.

Evil, by whatever name and in whatever form, seeks out pain and makes its home in grief. That is its business. The devil is a parasite that attaches voracious tentacles upon the vulnerable underside of faith, sucking up the bitter broth of human anguish as the sweetest nectar this side of hell. Unhealed grief can become the host for this bloodless parasite whose power is increased as the threshold of pain is raised to the shrieking point. Human pain devoid of divine presence becomes a sickness of the soul and a fertile womb for the demons of doubt and despair.

Against this sickness, the perfections of divine complacency and the motionless wings of angels have no power.

One thing, and one thing only, will cause the tormenting corruption of evil to flee, and that is divine pathos poured out into the cup of human sorrow. Where the suffering God walks, there are no demons and no darkness. The holiness of this divine grief whispers with the muffled thunder of divine wrath against all that destroys, all that corrupts. The devil is evil, but cannot suffer and has no compassion. God is good, and His power is in His suffering and compassion. Where God is present, there may be suffering, but no evil. Where God is present there may be pain, but no despair.

SELF-EMPOWERMENT IN THE
FACE OF TRAGEDY

The exorcism of demonic spirits as practiced by Jesus was only one form of God's redemptive and healing presence in the midst of human tragedy, brokenness, and suffering. There is no reason to suppose that the same demonic phenomena do not occur today, alongside of other forms of evil, such as poverty, homelessness, and hunger. The focus of God's power, however, is not upon evil nor upon the demonic as much as it is upon empowering humans to recover the sanity, serenity, and security that God intends for His children. Where the demons go when they are forced to vacate the premises of the human self is of little concern to Jesus. Questions as to the origin of the devil and why he should be allowed to afflict human life are not generally addressed in the Bible.

I believe that our focus should be upon the empowerment of the self and restoration to health, wholeness, and hope. Removal of the effects of evil is the exorcism of evil wherever it occurs. We should not follow the demons back to their lair. They feed upon our attention and are strengthened by our resistance. When we cannot eliminate suffering, with faith in God's presence as our advocate, we see evil banished.

In the healing of the demoniac possessed with a "legion" of demons, Jesus "allowed" them to enter the swine who subsequently perished in the sea. Our curiosity is aroused by this graphic incident, but the focus of the Gospel story is upon the tormented man, who now is pictured as sitting at the feet of Jesus, "clothed and in his right mind" (Mark 5:15). Driving out the demons did not by itself restore the man's selfhood. He is now "clothed" and in his "right mind." Formerly, he had been driven out of the community and was wandering among the tombs, naked and mutilating himself. Now he has been clothed and restored to the community. Clearly the focus of the story is meant to demonstrate the power of God in restoring this man to his life in community. Physically, socially, and spiritually (mentally) this man experienced self-recovery.

In other instances, Jesus empowered persons through a kind

of "transfer of spiritual power." The transfer of spiritual power is not a literal movement of energy from one person to another; rather, it is a process of empowerment which results in moral and spiritual health. When a woman who had suffered years of physical affliction touched the hem of His garment, she was healed instantly. Jesus "felt power go forth from him," and sought her out (Mark 5:30). When she acknowledged that she had indeed touched Him, despite the "uncleanness" of her medical condition according to the Law of Moses, he said, "Daughter, your faith has made you well; go in peace, and be healed of your disease" (Mark 5:34).

Jesus could have said: "See, I do have power to heal, and you were right in touching Me." Instead, He attributed her healing to her own faith! He thus empowered her to live out of the wholeness of her own self and to live out of the peace that she was indeed a "daughter" of God.

FORGIVING GOD AND
TRANSFORMING FAITH

The human self has a capacity for loss and the pain of grief, and also for recovery, for it is endowed with the image of God. Susie is a former student and my friend. Afflicted with cerebral palsy since birth, she cannot dress or feed herself. She talks with difficulty and in words which emerge as twisted and tortured as the spastic motions required to force them out. With a passion for life that exceeds most others less restrained by birth boundaries of their own, she completed college and a master's degree in theology, including several courses sitting in my classes. When she received her degree, I asked her what she intended to do, perceiving her within the boundaries which I had set for her. "Perhaps you will have a significant ministry to others who suffer handicaps in life," I suggested. "No," she said, "most of them haven't forgiven God for who they are, and I have."

Forgiving God for who I am! Indeed! Who should she hold responsible for the constricting birth boundaries which imprisoned her free and joyous spirit within a body she could not control? She expanded the horizon of her complaint, like Job of old, and laid the offense at the throne of God. When the Lord who created her did not dodge or duck, she concluded that the only freeing thing left was to forgive. Having lodged the charge against God with all of the emotional power at her disposal, she discovered that she also had the power to forgive Him.

Susie had no sense that God had caused her birth deformity nor did she feel that He had willed this condition for some inscrutable purpose of His own. Her dealings with God were not theological, but deeply existential. She sought to touch with her feelings the face of God and trace out there the profile of one who would take responsibility for her life without looking away. What she found encouraged her, that in holding God responsible she found an ally in her predicament. Releasing God from blame became possible when God assumed responsibility. Her life now had two sides to it. The one side of her life was restricting and confining. The other side was open and freeing. This is what she meant by forgiving God for who she was. She let God become the other side to her life. She made the outward journey and discovered a new horizon for her inner self.

Personal-empowerment and spiritual healing is not an inward journey alone, but also an outward journey. The journey begins when we discover the growing edge midst the grieving process.

"You have kept count of my tossings; put my tears in your bottle. Are they not in your record?" (Ps. 56:8)

Who would think of saving tears! They are such unlovely mementos of moments we hasten to forget. Ah, but the value of tears is not to the one who weeps, but to the one who cares.

What would be only a vial of self-pity if kept on the shelf with our other secret treasures, becomes a precious token of shared loneliness—a pledge that the weeping was not desolate nor the pain a barren thorn.

It is not pain that we fear—but barrenness.

The life of the spirit pours out of the open wound that is our heart. The uncontrollable expression of love too long measured out carefully— according to necessity—is a sighing of the body, a spending to be spent.

The pain of this extravagance is not the giving but the undesignated gift. Who is able to receive such an offering?

What green thing grew these tears? [15]

Every loss must be grieved, and each loss has its own special shade of grief. Grief has a healing power when it is comforted by grace. When we get stuck in grief, we use pain as an attempt to recover what has been lost rather than grieve through to the healing power of grace. In the chapter that follows, we will discover how this takes place.

SUMMARY

● If we play God's goodness off against God's power in the face of evil in this world, we can only preserve a notion of a good God by viewing Him as powerless.

● The crisis for faith is directly related to our concept of God. If God's power is understood to mean control over every event, as though He sat at a computer console, the apparent inaction of God will cause anger and even unbelief.

● If we view suffering as having some intrinsic redemptive value, then we are in danger of attributing to evil a power to produce good. It is God who works good in the experience of pain and suffering, not the pain itself.

● It is in the suffering of God through Jesus Christ, the cross and the resurrection, that we find both the power of God and the presence of God as a redemptive force in our suffering.

● When faith stumbles and God appears to disappear behind the inscrutable shadow of the tragic, the recovery of faith and the reality of God is found in the power of the God who suffered, died and was raised. At times, as Dietrich Bonhoeffer discovered, "only a suffering God can help."

PRAXIS

Cynthia sat in the adult Sunday School class clenching her fists in anger. The leader of the class was teaching from Romans 8 and was expounding on verse 28: "We know that all things work together for good for those who love God, who are called according to his purpose." "Nothing happens but that God has determined it in order to produce some good in our lives," he explained. "Even what we consider to be a tragedy God uses to strengthen our faith and make us better people." Only six months ago,

Jimmy, the two-year-old son of Cynthia, had contracted a fatal disease and died. Cynthia and her husband had prayed for healing and finally had given up hope. Now, as she reflected upon what she heard from the class leader, she could stand it no longer. Standing up, she said to the class: "If God needed to kill our child in order to produce some good, I would rather have my child than whatever good could come of it." With that she turned and left the room. The leader was stunned. What had seemed such a reassuring biblical teaching had now blown up in his face.

- What concept of God was presented in the interpretation of the biblical text as given by the class leader?
- What will be the likely consequence to Cynthia's spiritual life and faith if she rejects this concept of God?
- Many people testify to the redemptive value in suffering through a tragic loss. How might this be of help to Cynthia?
- In this chapter the concept of the suffering of God was presented as a point of contact for us when tragedy strikes. How might this be of help to Cynthia?
- The leader feels that he must approach Cynthia in order to offer an interpretation of Romans 8:28 which takes into account her statement. How should this be done?

10

Grief:
From Mourning's Night to Morning's Light

My joy is gone, grief is upon me, my heart is sick (Jer. 8:18). For the Lord will not reject forever. Although he causes grief, he will have compassion according to the abundance of his steadfast love; for he does not willingly afflict or grieve anyone. (Lam. 3:31-33)

In Christopher Fry's play, *The Boy with a Cart*, Cuthman has been sent by his father out to guard the sheep while they graze. In his simple faith, he talks with God and even has God assist him in guarding the sheep, by drawing a circle around them with his crook. "It is so! Not today only, but other days God took the crook and watched them in the wind." Informed by a neighbor that his father has suddenly died, Cuthman is at first disbelieving, and then defiant. "Let me alone. No; if I come you'll take me to a place where truth will laugh and scatter like a magpie. Up here, my father waits for me at home and God sits with the sheep." After the neighbor leaves, Cuthman expresses his grief.

> *What have I done? Did I steal God away
> From my father to guard my sheep? How can I keep*

Pace with a pain that comes in my head so fast?
How did I make the day brittle to break?
What sin brought in the strain, the ominous knock,
The gaping seam? What have I done to him?
Father, if you are standing by to help me —
Help me to cry.

(The People of South England, a voice chorus in the play,
chant in unison to Cuthman.)

How is your faith now, Cuthman?
Your faith that the warm world hatched,
That spread its unaccustomed colour
Up on the rock, game and detached?
You see how sorrow rises, Cuthman,
How sorrow rises like the heat
Even up to the plumed hills
And the quickest feet.
Pain is low against the ground
And grows like a weed.
Is God still in the air
And in the seed?
Is God still in the air
Now that the sun is down?
They are afraid in the city,
Sleepless in the town,
Cold on the roads,
Desperate by the river.
Can faith for long elude
Prevailing fever?[1]

When confronted with the sudden and tragic loss of a loved
one, the shock to the self is catastrophic. The psychological effects
are well-known and produce typical responses of stress and crisis
trauma. A crisis has been defined as: "A state in which people have
failed to resolve a problem, are in disequilibrium, and exhibit the
first four of the five characteristics of a crisis — symptoms of stress,
attitude of panic or defeat, focus upon relief and decreased effi-
ciency."[2] The fifth characteristic of crisis, "limited duration," is not
determined for a particular crisis until the crisis is over.

The built-in coping mechanisms of the self kick in and the first level of response is often some form of denial, as exhibited in the response of Cuthman to news of his father's death. The self then attempts to process the information and seeks to restore some equilibrium and composure. Usual coping mechanisms at the external level enable persons and groups to maintain equilibrium by adjusting to problems and making compensations. Secondary coping mechanisms involve the use of strategies and resources not ordinarily used in normal and ongoing adjustment to problems. Equilibrium does not mean absence of crisis situations or experiences, nor absence of stress; rather, equilibrium is maintained through adequate balancing factors in the face of stress or problems as against inadequate attempts to balance or compensate.

In Fry's play, Cuthman returns home, builds a cart, places his mother in the cart pulled by two oxen, and sets off on a pilgrimage of faith to build a church in the place where the "withies" (ropes) which pull the cart break; there he will build the church and work out his grief in thanks to God. He finds compensation and equilibrium in the midst of his carefully constructed world which is crashing down. His story is the crisis of faith and its recovery in the finding of a task which pulls him forward into life.

THE GOODNESS OF AN IMPERFECT WORLD

The pronouncement of goodness upon this creation by the Creator was not for the purpose of creating a dialectic between good and evil. The script includes all of the possibilities with the characters clearly defined, including a devil. The contrast is not between good and evil, but between the story and the author. But the Creator/author is also an actor who is able to move in and out of the story line with a freedom that opens the plot to creative innovations. It is a *good* story, not because the characters are perfect, but because the plot has its source in the goodness of God. Here there is realism without pessimism; life is bound to God in such a way that a vision of hope can be renewed and sustained. There is determinism without fatalism; temporal life has the appearance of finality as events pass into history, but God is the Lord of history as well. There is freedom without chaos; despite the randomness and capriciousness of nature, the presence of God is creative, not chaotic.

The story of Job makes clear the fact that he was not surprised at the loss of all that once lay within his power of possession. "Naked I came from my mother's womb, and naked shall I return there; the Lord gave and the Lord has taken away; blessed be the name of the Lord. . . . Shall we receive the good at the hand of God, and not receive the bad?" (Job 1:21; 2:10) In pouring out his sorrow and lamenting the fact of his own birth, Job confessed, "Truly the thing that I fear comes upon me, and what I dread befalls me" (3:25). The truth was, Job's prosperity and apparent complacency were shadowed from the beginning by an apprehension deep within himself, that it all could be lost. He did not use God to stave off the bad and as a guarantee of the good. Rather, God was an accomplice in all that happened, something that Job was not about to let God forget!

The Pulitzer-Prize-winning author, Ernest Becker, began his treatise on the nature of human existence by creating two alternatives. One view is that of the healthy-minded self, in which human existence is taken to be without pain and anxiety at the core. In this view, suffering and loss enter in as alien to the self, a threat to be resisted and even denied. The other view, which Becker confessed to be his own, was that of the anxiety-driven self, where human existence is at its very core grounded in a knowledge of its finiteness and mortality. In Becker's view, the self is in denial of its own existential reality unless it becomes aware of and comes to terms with its inevitable collapse into the void of nonbeing along with all of nature. Only when the self thrusts itself outward toward some transcendent source of life in an act of faith, can it live with this knowledge.[3]

Becker's concept of the self is grounded in the existential paradox of Kierkegaard, with its incline toward the individual. I have dealt with Kierkegaard earlier in this book, and have developed my own concept of the self as essentially social in nature rather than follow the existential and individualistic paradigm of Becker and Kierkegaard. Nonetheless, there is something in

Becker's analysis of the self that is compelling. A sense of the tragic is not absent from the very core of love.

In the biblical drama, the human characters are more than pale reflections of an ideal. They emerge deeply wounded by their encounter with evil in the guise of self-fulfillment. The devil does not make his appearance so as to terrify and repel. Nor are the sources of evil to be found in some ugly and alien part of the self. The devil is not an author, he is part of the plot. And whatever goes by the name of evil cannot be traced to some cosmic counterpart to God. "This is my story," says God, "and I am responsible for all of the characters and their actions." "I form light and create darkness, I make weal and create woe; I the Lord do all these things" (Isa. 45:7).

The origins of the self are caught up in the process of discovering the "fatal attractions" which insinuate the pleasure of self-fulfillment while creating the pain of impending loss. In the cycle of the self, bonding is the perfect resolution to the primeval loneliness, but this is a perfection which raises the stakes of separation and loss to new levels of pain. When Adam and Eve clasp each other in the ecstasy of self-fulfillment, the inevitable separation and loss lurks beneath the cresting of the wave.

Ann Morrow Lindbergh saw too that perfection carries within itself the seeds of fragmentation and loss when she wrote:

> *Within the hollow wave there lies a world,*
> *Gleaming glass-perfect, rising to be hurled*
> *Into a thousand fragments on the sand,*
> *Driven by tide's inexorable hand.*
> *Now in the instant while disaster towers,*
> *I glimpse a land more beautiful than ours;*
> *Another sky, more lapis-lazuli,*
> *Lit by unsetting suns; another sea*
> *By no horizon bound; another shore,*
> *Glistening with shells I never saw before.*
> *Smooth mirror of the present, poised between*
> *The crest's "becoming" and the foam's "has been"—*
> *How luminous the landscape seen across*
> *The crystal lens of an impending loss![4]*

My point is this. A Christian view of the self must not begin with an abstract concept which diagrams perfection and imperfection in such a way that their boundaries are precise and unambiguous. When we begin with a view of the self as intended by God to be free of pain and impervious to loss, we end up with a caricature of both God and human beings God is viewed as so abstractly good and powerful, that He no longer has a place in a world that is neither. The human self becomes idealized and no longer has any relevance for persons attempting to find their identity in the multiplicity of self-images. Only the devil has tangible and concrete reality, for evil is omnipresent, sickness and death reach into every relation, and pain follows the nerve endings to the cortex of every brain.

In the face of the pervasive reality of suffering and grieving life's losses, we face two temptations. First, we can give way to the inevitability and apparent certainty of suffering by giving up whatever concept of God sustained us in the past. "Theism tends to atheism when what God accomplishes can also be accomplished without him. If he takes no decisive action in the fact of evil, he is not necessary to the process, and someone less pious will soon come along to eliminate God as superfluous."[5]

An alternative response is to mask the reality by inventing a coping mechanism of denial, or avoidance, which is really a false hope. Pretending not to see or to feel the evil or pain is a form of self-deception. Temporary relief from the anguish caused by a tragic loss or broken promise by turning to the platitudes and promises of a future hope breaks us off from the real world. Christian Beker, professor of biblical theology at Princeton Seminary, warns against such superficial hope when he says:

When such perceptions of reality become too threatening or are deemed too pessimistic, we create forms of hope which are simply false hope, a result of our unwillingness to see the real world as it is. Thus they are based on the foundation of an illusion. Hope which is nourished by repression, illusion, blindness, or self-deception becomes false hope. Indeed, expectations and hopes which separate themselves from the realities of suffering in our world become demonic hopes; they cast a spell over us and mesmerize us. They are as destructive as the illusory hopes

*engendered by a drug trip. It is indeed characteristic of the apocalyptic
climate of our time that just as the question of suffering numbs us, so the
question of hope is divorced from any meaningful relation to suffering.*[6]

I have attempted to counter this tendency toward denial in
the Christian theological tradition by a return to a biblical understanding of the self. The Hebrew view of reality does not split
good and evil, happiness and suffering, into separate metaphysical entities. Personal loss and painful grief are part of a larger and
longer cycle of the self. Recovery in the form of self-care is more
than reduction of pain and the healing of grief. Personal-empowerment is the first step by which the self finds its place in the
drama, once again. Suffering isolates and pain alienates the self
from the human community. It is in one's participation in the
community in which the cycle of the self is being enacted and in
which recovery can take place.

BEYOND SURVIVAL TO RECOVERY

The cycle of self-development, I have suggested, is one of separation, attachment, loss, and survival. Whatever we may think
about the emerging self of an infant cradled in our arms and held
secure with the bonds of love, the sense of attachment experienced by the self has already passed through the anxiety of
separation. Many of the relational psychologists who view the
caregiver as an object by which the self of an infant develops its
own internal "self-identify," point to the crisis of separation as a
critical stage in identify formation.[7]

When the attachments which offer the self an orientation in
the world give way and break apart, the self experiences more
than the natal separation anxiety. The loss of the attachments
which have enabled the self to form an identity in relation to
others threatens its very core. It is one thing to feel an existential sense of aloneness and separation. It is quite another to
mourn the death of a loved one, the loss of a relation, or the
betrayal of trust. A broken promise cuts deeper into the self than
unfulfilled desire. I can weep for something which may never
come to pass, but my heart is broken when the love which came

to pass is taken from me. We may survive such losses but never fully recover the capacity to love and trust again.

I see now that the cycle of self-development is not intended to end with survival. Most of us finally do survive the losses we experience in life. In the case of a death of a loved one, for example, the "window of excruciating pain" is rather short, according to most psychologists. Within a few hours, or at the most two or three days, the self normally attempts to make an adjustment by repressing the sharpest feelings of loss and picking up some of the necessary functions of life. The journey of survival has begun. As is often the case, the opportunity to deal directly with the raw feelings of pain has passed, and the process of grieving has begun. The grieving of a loss, however, may never lead to recovery of the creative joy experienced in our first love.

In a lament over the destruction of Jerusalem following the Captivity, the Hebrew psalmist wrote:

> *By the rivers of Babylon — there we sat down and there we wept when we remembered Zion. On the willows there we hung up our harps. For there our captors asked us for songs, and our tormentors asked for mirth, saying, "Sing us one of the songs of Zion!" How could we sing the Lord's song in a foreign land? If I forget you, O Jerusalem, let my right hand wither! Let my tongue cling to the roof of my mouth, if I do not remember you, if I do not set Jerusalem above my highest joy (Ps. 137:1-6).*

The process of grieving a loss is paradoxical in its intention. Through grief one seeks to heal the pain of loss, let go of what can no longer be kept, and face the reality of living with only a memory of what once was. At the same time, there is a sense of responsibility not to forget what was lost. 'If I forget you, O Jerusalem," the psalmist cries out, "let my tongue cling to the roof of my mouth . . . if I do not set Jerusalem above my highest joy." Can we give ourselves permission to experience the "highest joy" without abandoning a former one?

The paradox in grieving the loss of a loved one is that recovery from the loss can be seen as betrayal of the one who was loved. C.S. Lewis, following the death of his wife, wrote in *A*

Grief Observed of his intense need to remain in grief for his wife as a way of remaining in contact with her. At first, after her death, to let go of his intense grief was to feel that he was abandoning her.

> *We don't really want grief, in its first agonies, to be prolonged; nobody could. But we want something else of which grief is a frequent symptom. . . . we want to live our marriage well and faithfully through that phase too. If it hurts (and it certainly will) we accept the pains as a necessary part of this phase. We don't want to escape them at the price of desertion or divorce. Killing the dead a second time.*[8]

Through his own painful process, however, Lewis discovered, passionate grief does not link us with the dead but cuts us off from them.

In the cycle of self-development, attachment carries implicit commitment and the promise always to be there when needed. In this bond is the premonition of a future loss. In many cases this loss does not occur through the death of a loved one, but through a succession of broken promises and finally the death of love.

GRIEVING THROUGH TO GRACE

It is the self which has been wounded in every loss, whether through death of a loved one, the death of love, or the searing pain of betrayal. All losses need to be grieved, no matter how trivial they may seem to others. Each person's loss is greater than that of others. For losses are personally weighted, not progressively graded. It is the experience of divine grace, often mediated through the care and love of others, that finally enables us to recover from loss. Grief is the process of reaching that grace.

Grief has to do with feelings, and feelings are the self, as I suggested in chapter 3. Self-care begins with finding those feelings which lead directly to the core of the self. The self is formed through a cycle of separation, attachment, loss, and survival. This means that the core of the self must always be prepared to integrate separation into attachment and loss into survival. Most people survive out of necessity as much as out of grace.

The self is capable of its own survival under normal circumstances in an amazing way. In the same way, the physical body is capable of healing itself—a miraculous thing when we think about it! The goal is to get back on your feet and run the race, even if you can no longer finish first. Physicians, physical therapists, and psychotherapists count on this phenomenon more than on their technical skills!

When recovery has survival as its main goal, however, it is like getting back on a horse immediately after having been thrown off. The thing to overcome is the fear of horses, even if we have not increased our skill in riding.

I suspect that the reason a higher percentage of marriages fail the second time around is related to the same phenomenon. A second marriage can be an attempt to prove to oneself that one is not afraid of marriage, even though one has not recovered the skills necessary to form a lasting relationship. Surviving loss is not the same as recovering the creative life of the self.

When the self is hurting, the felt need is reduction of pain. Therapists tell me that the single most inhibiting factor in self-recovery is the need to feel better rather than to follow the pain back to the core of the self. Clients want their therapists to reduce pain, not to probe the hurt and clean the wound.

When we are caught in the throes of grieving a loss, it is sometimes hard to grow out of the grief. The intense feeling of grief can sometimes be the only way to remain connected to what has been lost. When this happens we get stuck in the loss cycle of recovery, unable to move on to survival. Grief becomes a ritual of attachment to what no longer exists, hindering our growth toward the grace of recovery.

Just the opposite can happen as well. The feeling of grief can be so great that it becomes repressed, and a "will to survive" takes over. "I'm a survivor," these persons like to say, as if to assure themselves that, while they have suffered loss, the game of life is not over.

There is a kind of self-therapy that works the same way. The coping mechanisms that enable the self to survive the onslaught of anxiety, pain, and grief provide the skeletal structure for survival. Around this structure, denial and suppression of feelings build layers of psychic muscle which reinforces the will to survive. What forces one to get back on the horse having been thrown off, despite the paralyzing fear, is the need to overpower the shame and regain recognition among one's peers. This is survival, not recovery. The psychic energy it takes to maintain the defenses against anxiety and emotional pain for the sake of survival depletes the self of its resources for recovery.

Grieving through to grace goes beyond survival to the recovery of the self's capacity to love without fear and to be loved without shame. Grace is growth, and growth moves through phases, each adding strength to hope and faith. Grace empowers the self, enabling it to retain the memory of what was lost while letting go of the object that was lost.

Grace comes from outside the self as empowering love and resides within the self as the "courage to be."[9] The will to survive may express defiance in the face of a loss. "Courage to be" expresses acceptance of the loss through an expansion of the horizons of the self. Survival narrows life to the single task of defeating the enemy. Grace expands life by stitching a loss into the mosaic of the patterned quilt which we are creating to bequeath to those who follow us.

Because grace is creative it has its source in a Creator God. Because grace is restorative it has its power in a Redeemer God. Because grace is inspiring it communicates its life through the Spirit of God. Through grief we apprehend the grace of God, and by the grace of God we recover the courage to be.

Walk with me through the passageway from grief to grace, and discover the contours of recovery.

THE PHASES OF RECOVERY

Recovery moves in phases, not in progressive steps. Recovery is not like climbing a ladder or drawing by the numbers. I have high regard for the numerous variations of the twelve-step programs for recovery. But my own view is that recovery is more like moving through phases of growth than progressing through stages of behavior modification.

What makes the twelve-step concept work, in my judgement, is not the steps alone, but (1) the unqualified abandonment of self-therapy, including an intolerance for self-deception, (2) the unconditional acceptance by others, including a structure of accountability, and (3) an expanding self-horizon, including the courage to be. There is often a spiritual component in these programs, not as a clearly defined doctrine of God, but as an assurance that there is a capacity for renewal and hope within the self that can directly tap the resource of a divine, higher power.

A physical therapist will require that a patient exercise the muscles in order to facilitate the phases of recovery through the body's own resources for wholeness. Manipulation of body parts does not heal, it only forces the body to function in a way that promotes health. Recovery, in this sense, is a process of going through the phases of growth which lead to the restoration of life at its optimum possibility, given whatever limits and restrictions still apply.

C.S. Lewis, during the process of his recovery from the death of his wife, reports:

> Something quite unexpected has happened. It came this morning early. For various reasons, not in themselves at all mysterious, my heart was lighter than it had been for many weeks. For one thing, I suppose I am recovering physically from a good deal of mere exhaustion. And I'd had a very tiring but very healthy twelve hours the day before, and a sounder night's sleep: and after ten days of low-hung grey skies and motionless warm dampness, the sun was shining and there was a light breeze. And suddenly at the very moment when, so far, I mourned H least, I remembered her best. Indeed it was something (almost) better than memory; an instantaneous, unanswerable impression. To say it was like a meeting would be going too far. Yet there was that in it which tempts one to use those words. It was as if the lifting of the sorrow removed a barrier. [10]

Lest we conclude from this that Lewis had finally "gotten

over" his sorrow, he is quick to remind us that recovery is a process of moving through phases that recur. One never takes steps that leave behind what once was essential to the self and now has been lost. "Tonight all the hells of young grief have opened again; the mad words, the bitter resentment, the fluttering in the stomach, the nightmare unreality, the wallowed-in tears, for in grief nothing 'stays put.' One keeps on emerging from a phase, but it always recurs. . . . They say 'The coward dies many times'; so does the beloved. Didn't the eagle find a fresh liver to tear in Prometheus every time it dined?"[11]

1. The abandonment of self-therapy

The dark shadows of a critical loss of love and trust cause us to move toward the light in hopes of ridding our lives of pain and healing the sickness of grief. Self-therapy includes all of our attempts to overcome pain, conceal the hurt, and clothe the self with new images of purposeful and productive life. The critical point in recovery occurs when all such attempts are abandoned, and one's life is exposed to a greater healing power, whatever that may be.

The power of self-deception is what makes self-therapy appear to work. When self-deception is exposed and no longer tolerated, the self is stripped of its most effective defense against the truth and prepared to see what had been hidden by the false light of self-therapy.

In the biblical story of the healing of a man blind from birth, a subplot emerges in the controversy which ensued between Jesus and the religious authorities (John 9). They denied at first that the man was really blind and that a healing had occurred. The man himself was not deceived. "One thing I do know, that though I was blind, now I see" (v. 25). In refusing to believe the man's story, they themselves, as it were, had become blind. "If you were blind, you would not have sin. But now that you say, 'We see,' your sin remains" (v. 41). Their "sin" was the blindness of self-deception and failure to recognize the grace of God which brought healing and hope to the blind man.

There are phases of recovery in which darkness enters again so that the cycle of the self may be fully integrated in its growth toward wholeness and health.

The moon is not always luminous and full, nor does it become permanently stuck in a phase with only a sliver of its self showing. Perhaps this is why primitive people were more attuned to the phases of the moon than the rising and setting of the sun. The sun has no phases. It is either burning so bright that one cannot bear to look directly at it, obscured from view by clouds, or gone completely in the "dead of night." The moon, as we all know, not only passes through its phases corresponding to the cycle of the self, but it is our companion in the night.

In his play, *After the Fall*, Arthur Miller provided a brilliant analysis of the journey to self-recovery in the form of the lead character, Quentin. After failed marriages and the betrayal of his commitment to love Maggie, Quentin speaks:

> *You ever felt you once saw yourself—absolutely true? I may have dreamed it, but I swear that somewhere along the line—with Maggie, I think—for one split second I saw my life; what I had done, what had been done to me, and even what I ought to do. And that vision sometimes hangs behind my head, blind now, bleached out like the moon in the morning; and if I could only let in some necessary darkness it would shine again. I think it had to do with power.* [12]

My father used to plant potatoes every spring. First we would cut them into pieces, making sure that each piece had an "eye" in it, as he called it. From this "eye" a sprout would form and then the pieces were ready to be placed in the ground. One thing remained, however, before we could plant. To ensure a good harvest of potatoes, my father said, we must plant them when the moon is full. So we would wait until the propitious time, and then place them in the ground.

We always had sufficient potatoes, come fall, as I recall. In those days, I did not venture to submit this folk wisdom to a scientific test by deliberately planting some during another phase of the moon. I doubt that he did either. It was probably the only superstition that I recall my father ever including in his otherwise commonsense approach to the tilling of the soil and the husbandry of our livestock.

Even as I write this, why do I feel a sense of uneasiness in making such a clear distinction between superstition and common sense? He would not have been happy with such a charge. For him, the working of the soil was a participation in a cycle of sowing and reaping, suffering crop failures, and rejoicing at bountiful harvests. He never disclosed his inner feelings, neither of grief at his losses nor joy at his successes. I gather now that he lived a self-life in communion with the seasons of nature, with the rhythm of birth, life and death and, yes, by the phases of the moon! This may be the most common of all senses.

2. Unconditional acceptance by others

A second phase of recovery from the grief of loss moves us into relationships which offer unconditional acceptance. Actually, this phase overlaps with the first for, without this offer of unconditional acceptance, the abandonment of self-therapy cannot move forward to grace. Grace, as I have suggested, comes from outside the self as empowering love. Only love which is experienced as unconditional acceptance empowers the self.

Self-acceptance is always conditional because it is qualified by feelings of unworthiness and knowledge of our own failures. If self-acceptance becomes unconditional then it is based on self-deception. It is only the experience of being loved and accepted by someone else without qualification and with no strings attached, that frees us from self-deception and, at the same time, empowers us to love and accept ourselves.

Unconditional love does not reward our strengths and punish our weaknesses. Unconditional acceptance does not say, "You are important to me and I care for you, but you must get over this loss and get on with life." No, unconditional acceptance says, "Because I am committed to you, I will share your grief and feel with you the pain of your loss."

We cannot grieve through to grace without the experience of unconditional love and acceptance, for grace *is* unconditional in giving the gift of love.

It has often been said, "We must love the sinner but hate the sin." I wonder if people who say that have any idea of how destructive and downright ungracious that concept is! Whatever my sins and failures may be, that is who I am! You cannot love me without accepting the whole of me, painful and threatening as that may be.

Love is not a virtue that must be protected by abstractions from the concrete reality of the unlovely. Grief is not a beautiful thing to behold in another and the anger and despair it creates is not conducive to growth in grace by itself. It takes unconditional grace expressed through the presence of others for us to find and feel the acceptance we need. Blessed are those whose moon passes into this phase!

When others make unconditional commitments to accept us as we are, no strings attached, a structure of accountability is also created through which we can measure our growth. The counter side to "I will be there for you" is, "you will always have me to certify your growth." Accountability is corrective and creative. Accountability is what keeps us from slipping back into self-deception. It is the means of our recovery and the measure of our growth.

Through unconditional acceptance by others, we are drawn out of the narrowness of grief confinement into the spaciousness of grace completeness. The third phase of recovery begins when we begin to think about seeds to sow in the freshly dug soil of self-acceptance.

3. An expanding self-horizon

Grief recovery includes an expansion of the self, allowing time for the fragments of the self to "grow their own eyes" and then find a place in the nourishing soil of the human family. Recovery begins with the discovery that what appeared to be a gaping hole in the seamless robe of our fragile happiness is the edge of darkness caused by the setting of the sun. There is no grief that does not have its home in the capacity of the self to suffer loss and still be the self. Grief does not have to kill in order to be grief.

Awakening in the midst of the "dead of night," where the soul lies still and the heart is silent, there is the rising of the moon, now in the luminous phase of fullness. At last comes the time for sowing, even a second or third time, as Anne Morrow

Lindbergh poetically puts it, after losing her own son in a tragic kidnapping.

> *For Whom*
> *The milk ungiven in the breast*
> *When the child is gone?*
>
> *For whom*
> *The love locked up in the heart*
> *That is left alone?*
> *That golden yield*
> *Split sod once, overflowed an August field,*
> *Threshed out in pain upon September's floor,*
> *Now hoarded high in barns, a sterile store.*
>
> *Break down the door;*
> *Rip open, spread and pour*
> *The grain upon the barren ground*
> *Wherever crack in clod is found.*
>
> *There is no harvest for the heart alone;*
> *The seed of love must be*
> *Eternally Resown.* [13]

Grieving through to grace opens up the vault where grief stores its treasures and ritually mourns its losses. When the golden grain we have harvested, sometimes prematurely, from the first sowing of love becomes new seed for sowing, we are in recovery.

We sow seeds by making promises, making friends, making commitments, and giving the gift of ourselves as a living plant to grow in another's garden.

The seeds which we now sow are those which we have reaped from the sorrow and tragedy of earlier losses. This is what the cycle of life teaches us. Watch for your moon, move with its phases, and trust the mystery of life as holding the promise of God.

From the beginning of this book to its conclusion, I have

urged the reader to consider the intrinsic power and possibilities of the self as empowered by the Spirit and power of God – love and grace. Recovery is more than wiping away our tears, overcoming a problem, and attempting a new beginning. It is that too, but it also means the discovery of a new and growing edge to life. The chapter that follows may be the most important one in this book. It points toward the spiritual healing which opens up life to the greatest gift of all—a future which begins on this earth and comes to completion in the creative life of the eternal God.

SUMMARY

• The goodness of God's created world included both loss and gain. Grief is God's way of dealing with loss and creating new life. Human life goes through a continual cycle of separation, attachment, loss, and survival.

• The grace of God enters into each phase of this cycle. Grief is one way of having access to this grace and moving ahead in recovering the original promise.

• The self is endowed with amazing powers of healing and recovery of hope. The grace of God empowers the self by unleashing the spiritual potential of faith in the midst of the "dark phase of the moon."

• Recovery from tragic loss begins with the abandonment of self-therapy and moving with the rhythm of life with its promise of a harvest with every sowing of new seed.

PRAXIS

It had been one year since the accidental death of Jeff, the eighteen-year-old son of Clark and Angela. As was his custom, the pastor called on the parents at the one-year anniversary of the tragic loss. Clark and Angela were cordial and to all appearances seemed to have made a normal adjustment to the death of their son. When Clark received a phone call and went to his study to talk, Angela asked the pastor to follow her upstairs to the room which her son had occupied. Entering the room, she pointed out that nothing had been disturbed from the time that they received the tragic news one year ago. "Pastor," she said, "I am worried about Clark. He comes up here every evening and sits for an hour or more, just touching some of Jeff's things and staring. I even overheard him talking out loud to Jeff on one occasion. I don't think that he has ever really accepted the fact that he is gone and that we will never see him again. I understand that he is still grieving, but when will it ever end? I have given over Jeff to the Lord, why can't Clark do that?"

● Why does Angela have concern about the way in which her husband is coping with the death of their son? Does not each person handle grief in a different way?

● Angela seems to have accepted the loss of their son and moved on to fill her life with other things. Why is her way of handling the loss more appropriate than her husband's?

● What are the clues from this case which lead one to suspect that the grief process for Clark has become abnormal while Angela's is more normal?

● What approach should the pastor take in counseling both Angela and Clark? What spiritual direction and counsel can he give Clark? What is the role of the church in this process?

11

From Overcoming to Becoming:
Living on the Growing Edge

I keep the Lord always before me; because he is at my right hand, I shall not be moved. Therefore my heart is glad, and my soul rejoices; my body also rests secure. . . . You show me the path of life. In your presence there is fullness of joy; in your right hand are pleasures forevermore (Ps. 16:8-9; 11).

Wait a minute, I'm not finished yet," was the impatient response from my five-year-old daughter when I once tried to get her to leave her coloring book and come to dinner. She is now a grown woman with two children of her own. I hope she still feels that way.

The struggle for recovery is not to overcome the hindrances and problems that beset us yesterday and today, but to become the person that we will be tomorrow. "Wait a minute, I'm not finished yet!"

The goal of recovery is not to emerge from an abusive relationship or traumatic experience as a battle scarred survivor but as a passionate lover of life. "Wait a minute, I'm not finished yet!"

The gift of recovery is not to be plucked out of a whirlpool of emotional distress and planted in a quiet lagoon where the water is so shallow that no wave breaks the surface. Recovery is not to be cast as a survivor upon some deserted beach with the hope that the small island of safety will provide all that is necessary to be self-sufficient. Rather, the gift of recovery is to have the sails repaired, the rudder restored, and one's hand on the tiller with a spanking breeze and a spacious horizon. "Wait a minute, I'm not finished yet!"

THE JOURNEY OF SPIRITUAL HEALING

"Spirituality for survivors is a topic that needs much work in the future," writes James Leehan. "Survivors do not need an emphasis on evil and sin; they have gotten more than enough of that. As victims they were constantly told how wicked and bad they were, and as survivors they are struggling to overcome that image."[1]

The effect of suffering, pain, and experience of loss upon the self is a narrowing one. Anxiety causes the self to tighten up. The flow of blood is restricted. Muscular movements become stiff and constricted. The self retreats into isolation and sets up defenses against the intrusion of further pain. The Latin word for anxiety is *angustia*, a word which means narrowness. The first step toward recovery is to overcome the effects of this constriction of the self and to emerge into the larger space of self-expression and relation with others.

> By overcoming the anxiety (narrowness) imposed upon them, survivors will confront the questions life has presented (an important part of the first movement of the spiritual life), let go of their anger (the forgiveness involved in the second movement), and be freed to receive new life from the God of all life. They will have achieved the holiness that enables them to embrace the whole of life—the abundant life to which they had been called but of which they had been deprived by family violence.[2]

Overcoming in order to be a survivor is not enough. To think of oneself as a survivor may empower the self emotionally and lead to recovery, but it fails to satisfy the deeper yearnings and possibility of the self. Survivors may have conquered an addiction, learned to let go of a tragic loss, escaped from dysfunctional relationships, and be healed of traumatic abuse, but this is still not enough. Beyond overcoming is becoming, the abundant spiritual life of fellowship with God and relation with others. More than emotional repair is needed. Restoration is a spiritual dimension of recovery.

What feels like deep emotion during an intense experience of pain and suffering may actually be only a narrowing of the emotional life by denying the full range of feelings which contribute to the health and creative life of the self. The spiritual core of the self gives direction to the emotions. I have cited the comment of Abraham Heschel earlier in this book, but it bears repeating in this context.

> *Emotion is inseparable from being filled with the spirit, which is above all a state of being moved. Often the spirit releases passion, an excessive discharge of nervous energy, enhanced vitality, increased inner strength, increased motor activity, a drive. While spirit includes passion or emotion, it must not be reduced to either. Spirit implies the sense of sharing a supreme superindividual power, will or wisdom. In emotion, we are conscious of its being our emotion; in the state of being filled with spirit we are conscious of joining, sharing or receiving "spirit from above" (Isa. 32:15). Passion is a movement; spirit is a goal.[3]*

"Wait a minute, I'm not finished yet!" This is the irrepressible spirit of creativity, imagination, and vision that moves the self away from the security of a fixed center toward the growing edge; where faith, hope, and love enable the self to transcend its narrowness, move beyond its own history, and create its own story.

Jacob is a familiar character in the Old Testament. With the help of his mother, Rebecca, he tricked his twin brother Esau out of the birthright and then had to flee from his family in fear of his life. Moving out from the security of the only family and only home that he had known, he fell asleep in the wilderness, using a stone for a place to rest his head. That night, he had a dream, where the angels of God ascended and descended on a ladder that reached up to heaven. The voice of God came to him, affirming the covenant promise and the divine presence wherever he would go. Awakening, Jacob said: "Surely the Lord is in this place — and I did not know it. . . . How awesome is this place! This is none other than the house of God, and this is the gate of heaven" (Gen. 28:16-17).

Jacob is well-known for his cleverness and manipulation of others. He himself was often outwitted and deceived, and he never could forget that his brother Esau had become his mortal enemy. Nonetheless, Jacob's story is not one of what he overcame, but what he became. The promise of God was not vague and ambiguous, but described who he was to become. Jacob was inspired by this promise and never forgot the goal which was set before him in the spiritual vision. When, more than twenty years later, Jacob once again met his brother Esau, a spirit of reconciliation rose from the depth of his emotions, transforming his fear into joyous reunion. Jacob was able to greet his brother Esau with a benediction: "truly to see your face is like seeing the face of God — since you have received me with such favor" (Gen. 33:10).

Some might say that Jacob overcame the tragic experience with his brother and became a survivor. There is more to the story, however, than surviving failure and overcoming a loss. Jacob moved from overcoming to becoming through a spiritual experience in which the ragged broken edge of his life became the growing edge. Here is where recovery gives way to restoration.

FROM BROKENNESS TO WHOLENESS

We are fast becoming a society where brokenness can be seen at every hand. Politicians break their promises, public servants break their trust. Broken marriages, broken families, broken homes, and broken lives provide rhetorical thunder for the preachers of traditional values. To rail against brokenness is to rouse the faithful to moral indignation and to make out failure to be moral tragedy. To be a broken person midst the scarcity of wholeness is to be told: "Yes, you are finished, whether you know it or not!"

The metaphor of brokenness carries a variety of meanings. Those who become casualties of abuse, failed marriages, chemical dependency, moral failure, or excessive grief, are assumed by many to be "broken pieces" floating around the center of the "mainland" of a functionally stable community. Or, to change the metaphor to that of an ocean liner, broken people are like those who "fall overboard" and are either left to drown or pulled back on ship as survivors. Even though they have been "recovered," they bear the stigma of being unstable and can never be fully trusted again.

We often refer to people who have gone through a crisis as "broken people." From the outside, it appears that a divorce leaves one a broken person, or that one becomes "broken down" with grief. In a Christian organization with which I am acquainted, the divorce of a staff member caused the chief administrator to say: "You will have to leave because we already have too many broken people around here." Leave she finally did, hurting as much from this rejection as from the failed marriage. As it turned out, she experienced a deeper brokenness which became the basis for renewal and growth. Today she is living on the "growing edge" of life. Meanwhile, the institution which thought that it could not tolerate "broken people" remains as dysfunctional and self-defensive as always. Its will to survive remains intact. The "broken people" are pushed overboard if they will not jump.

Those who work in the recovery movement know that growth toward wholeness cannot begin until self-deception and self-justification are broken and the self experiences a vulnerability that creates an opening through which real contact with others can occur. The most difficult movement for the self to make in the recovery process is to experience a real breakdown in the defenses which enabled one to survive as a victim. Survival is a powerful instinct of self, but it can often hinder growth. The breaking of the self's survival skills in the face of pervasive abuse and punishing loss is a broken edge which is most painful of all. This is the kind of a broken edge, however, where the spirit of renewal and recovery leads to growth.

Look with me at King David for a moment. Caught in a moment of sensual vulnerability and royal prerogative, he seduced Bathsheba, the wife of one of his army officers. Her subsequent pregnancy caused him to panic and arrange the murder of her husband as though he were a battle casualty. He thus concealed the incident, took the woman as his wife, and a child was born (2 Sam. 11).

Directed by the Lord, Nathan the prophet confronted David with the terrible thing that he had done. "I have sinned against the Lord" (2 Sam. 12:13; cf. Ps. 51:4) replied David, when the full extent of his sin and the consequences became clear to him. Nathan reassured him that he would not die, even though the dreadful consequence of the death of the child would ensue.

So much for the incident. Without further expression of the process by which David recovered from this terrible failure and found restoration, we would read the story as yet another lesson to be learned; when you sin against God you have to suffer the consequences.

"Yes, you are forgiven, David, but for all practical purposes, you are finished."

I have looked into the eyes of those who have lived with the shame of being caught in a moral failure and who have received the assurance of divine forgiveness. What I do not often see is hope. Forgiveness which does not lead to hope and the recovery of the joy of life is not good enough. The human spirit seeks the recovery of hope even though one is spared the consequences of sin and failure. James Leehan suggests that the recognition and articulation of imperfection in one's life can lead to hope rather than despair.

> *In a special way, survivors are people of hope. . . . Hope is the virtue of those who see the imperfection of the present, who recognize the fear, insecurities, and inequalities that exist, and who work for a new order of things. This recognition of imperfection and its articulation are critical aspects of hope. . . .*[4]

Old Testament theologian Walter Brueggemann reminds us

that "hope emerges among those who publicly articulate and process their grief over their suffering."[5]

This is exactly what David did. In two Psalms, 32 and 51, David makes public his confession and expresses his confidence in restoration. "While I kept silence," David writes, "my body wasted away through my groaning all day long. . . . Then I acknowledged my sin to you, and I did not hide my iniquity; I said, 'I will confess my transgressions to the Lord,' and you forgave the guilt of my sin" (Ps. 32:3, 5).

In the second psalm, David again acknowledges his sin but goes on to say: "Create in me a clean heart, O God, and put a new and right spirit within me. . . . Restore to me the joy of your salvation, and sustain in me a willing spirit. . . . O Lord. open my lips, and my mouth will declare your praise. For you have no delight in sacrifice. . . . The sacrifice acceptable to God is a broken spirit; a broken and contrite heart, O God, you will not despise" (Ps. 51:10, 12, 15-17).

"Wait a minute," says David, "I'm not finished yet!" He discovered the growing edge at the broken edge. David's spirit did not break until his self-deception was shattered and he was confronted by the painful reality that his life was exposed before God, even if he thought that it was concealed from others. The painful edge of this broken spirit became the creative and growing edge of his renewal and restoration.

With his confession David also prays for restoration. "Restore to me the joy of your salvation," is his prayer (Ps. 51:12). There is no power in the emotional life to utter such a prayer and to reach for such a goal. This is the power of the spiritual life of the self under the prompting and empowering of the Spirit of God.

David is an example of a person who found restoration and renewal through his moral and spiritual failure. But what of those who suffer through no fault of their own? What if there is no sin to confess and yet one experiences abuse, loss, and suffering?

We have such a person in the case of the Prophet Jeremiah. He is assumed by many scholars to be the author of the book aptly titled Lamentations. Viewing the fallen city of Jerusalem after the people have been taken into exile, like Jesus centuries later (Luke 19:41), Jeremiah begins his lament by saying:

How lonely sits the city that once was full of people! How like a widow she has become, she that was great among the nations! She that was a princess among the provinces has become a vassal. She weeps bitterly in the night, with tears on her cheeks; among all her lovers she has no one to comfort her; all her friends have dealt treacherously with her, they have become her enemies (Lam. 1:1-2).

As he continues his lament over the destruction of Jerusalem, Jeremiah becomes more personal and complains bitterly to the Lord of his own situation.

I am one who has seen affliction under the rod of God's wrath; he has driven and brought me into darkness without any light; against me alone he turns his hand, again and again, all day long. He has made my flesh and my skin waste away, and broken my bones; he has besieged and enveloped me with bitterness and tribulation; he has made me sit in darkness like the dead of long ago.

He has walled me about so that I cannot escape; he has put heavy chains on me; though I call and cry for help, he shuts out my prayer; he has blocked my ways with hewn stones, he has made my paths crooked (Lam. 3:1-9).

Not a few suffering souls have found the lament of Jeremiah to ring true to their own experience, though most do not attribute their pain so directly to God in such eloquent fashion. Like Job of old, Jeremiah knows where to lodge his complaint and whom to blame for his condition. But then, as suddenly as it began, it comes to an end.

The thought of my affliction and my homelessness is wormwood and gall! My soul continually thinks of it and is bowed down within me. But this I call to mind, and therefore I have hope: The steadfast love of the Lord never ceases, his mercies never come to an end; they are new every morning; great is your faithfulness. "The Lord is my portion," says my soul, "therefore I will hope in him" (Lam. 3:19-24).

A multitude of Christians cheerfully sing the hymn, "Great Is Thy Faithfulness," without a thought as to the source of this affirmation of trust and confidence in God!

In a way that is very similar to that of King David, the process of recovery and restoration for Jeremiah begins with brokenness of spirit, confession of pain, an address to God (prayer), followed by the gift of a new spirit and restored hope in God. Like David, this process is part of a communal experience and expression, with an articulation that breaks out of the private world of the self into shared life with others.

The circumstances which cause one to suffer pain and distress of soul may be quite different. For some it comes as a result of their own actions, for others as a victim of abuse or the blind and senseless ravages of natural life. In a very remarkable way, however, the process of recovery and restoration is quite similar.

The brokenness of the human spirit is a deeper and more creative edge than guilt and remorse for sin. A sense of guilt is not creative and produces no positive motivation toward spiritual wholeness. We tend to forget that the cross of Christ only has significance as a place where sin is judged for those who have experienced the power of resurrection and the gift of the Spirit of God. It is true, consciousness of sin can lead to brokenness of spirit and thus to healing and wholeness. But so does abuse, pain, and suffering!

There is no need to make people whose spirit is broken come to Christ by leading them through the condemnation of sin. In fact, this may well bruise the broken spirit and turn what could be a hopeful spiritual experience of recovery of the joy of salvation into a hopeless one. The spiritual goal for the broken spirit is renewal and restoration through the power of God. This is the gift of God through Jesus Christ which comes freely to those who receive the Spirit. "For all who are led by the Spirit of God are children of God. . . . When we cry 'Abba! Father!' it is that very Spirit bearing witness with our spirit that we are children of God . . ." (Rom. 8:14-16).

In the parable of the Prodigal Son, the spirit of the son was not broken by the desperate conditions in the far country, when he was reduced to living with the swine. He returned home with a confession upon his lips but with no joy in his heart. He thought that his life as a son was finished for good, and he was prepared to live in his father's house as a servant. Instead, the father rushed out and kissed him, and proclaimed, "This son of mine was dead and is alive again; he was lost and is found!" (Luke 15:24)

The broken edge was not due to disobedience and sin on the part of the son, but the damaged relationship which only the father could restore. The broken edge became a creative opportunity for the son to become what he had not yet achieved — a life of sonship with an openness to the future. It was there, at the broken edge, that the growing edge of recovery and restoration began.

LIVING ON THE GROWING EDGE

The spiritual dimension in recovery begins where the broken edge becomes the growing edge. All brokenness brings emotional pain for which there is no rational relief. The healing of emotional pain is the spiritual work of the self. Growth does not come through emotional change alone, but through the life of the spirit. It is the spirit which expands and directs the self toward growth. The feelings of the self are the core of subjectivity and individuality. The spirit of the self constitutes the openness of the self to the spirit of others and, essentially and ultimately, to the Spirit of God.

The self *overcomes* obstacles and hindrances through the power of will driven by sufficient emotional resources. But the self *becomes* through spirit and experiences growth as recovery toward the reality that faith and hope envision.

1. Growth is openness to change
A healthy and growing self is one that is in balance and under control. This balance and equilibrium is called homeostasis.[6] In a growing self, the homeostasis is dynamic and flexible, able to absorb shock, to make adjustments under stress, and to shift the center of gravity of the self in order to maintain balance. The sickness of the soul which results from traumatic shock and grievous loss can produce a rigid homeostasis — the self's desper-

ate attempt to maintain balance and control under trauma and stress.

When the self is in retreat it takes a negative direction; it pulls back from shock and refuses to deal with the change which comes about through unexpected events and sudden losses. This is caused by rigid homeostasis, an attempt by the self to restore order and to locate a center that is secure and safe. This coping mechanism of withdrawal is sometimes the only defense left to a person in an abusive relationship. When the abuse is inevitable, but unpredictable, the self creates an inner refuge from the violence, much as a person living amidst urban terrorism places iron bars on the windows and cowers inside. We often think of emotional trauma and pain as a state of disorder in the self. Actually, emotional pain and a dysfunctional relationship constitute the most stable of all systems, and least susceptible to change. To introduce change into a rigid homeostasis structure of the self only stiffens the resistance.

Persons who experience the devastating loss of a marriage or the death of a loved one often find it difficult to deal with the shock of losing something which had become so much a part of self-identity. Like an earthquake fault that splits one's house in two, a sudden and traumatic loss is a seismic shudder which can cause the self to step back from the fault line of pain in order to stop the tremors.

To pull back from pain is to retreat from the broken edge in search of a space which is under control and not subject to change. The paradox is that change is a break in the established pattern and produces momentary disequilibrium to the homeostasis of the self. Before change and growth can occur, the structure of the self must shift from a rigid to a dynamic and flexible homeostasis. This requires a strongly supportive environment so that sufficient balance and stability is provided for the self while experiencing the stress and shifting of the ground under one's feet.

Openness to the spirit of others and to supportive relationships is crucial to a process of growth and change. Self-care means the recovery of the self in relationship, sustained by a spiritual openness to love, faith, and hope. This is the recovery of the original form of the self as created in the image and likeness of God. At the beginning, God said, "It is not good that the man should be alone; I will make him a helper as his partner" (Gen. 2:18). This deficiency was not caused by sin, but rather pointed to the "broken edge" of the solitary life which became the growing edge for self-fulfillment: "This at last is bone of my bones and flesh of my flesh" (Gen. 2:23).

Openness to change is a characteristic of the self which is on the growing edge of life. When brokenness occurs, as it does to all of us, it presents a crisis to the self. Healthy recovery goes through the shock and trauma of pain and loss, but discovers the resources to adjust and adapt to the change. This is the spiritual aspect of self-care, for the self experiences a revitalization of spirit which produces the gift of faith and hope. The reach of the human spirit to the Spirit of God underlies the self's capacity for faith, hope, and ultimately trust and acceptance.

The Apostle Paul had a remarkable openness to change and, therefore, to growth in his life, primarily due to the fact that he experienced a shattering loss of all that he had attempted to build up as a self-righteous member of the religious sect of the Pharisees. Through his encounter with the resurrected Jesus Christ on the road to Damascus (Acts 9), Paul received the gift of a new spirit of faith and life. While others of his contemporaries found it difficult to let go of the rituals and rules by which they had formerly lived, Paul, led by the Spirit of Christ, lived on the growing edge.

Years later, when he experienced a physical illness, which he called a "thorn in the flesh," he sought healing and relief through prayer. After appealing to the Lord three times, he received his answer: "My grace is sufficient for you, for power is made perfect in weakness" (2 Cor. 12:8-9).

The growing edge of life is where openness to change becomes a form of spiritual empowerment. In Christ, Paul reminds us, "everything has become new," though not everything is possible (2 Cor. 5:17).

I think that there is a special gift of the Spirit where life becomes broken. The power made manifest in weakness is the filling of the self with the Spirit of God. When our feelings are numb to that possibility, and our emotions rage against the spirit, we can dare to say, "Wait a minute, I'm not finished yet!"

2. Growth is an interchange of life in community

The growth of the self is not an individual thing. The self is intrinsically a social reality from which individuality is derived as we experience differentiation in relation to others. Even as an infant experiences selfhood and self-identity through encounter with others, the growth and life of the self continues through such interchange.

The Apostle Paul was fond of the metaphor of the human body to express the relationships which Christians have as bound together in Christ. "For just as the body is one and has many members, and all the members of the body, though many, are one body, so it is with Christ" (1 Cor. 12:12). As each part of the body has its life through the interconnection and interchange with the other parts, so it is with the individual as a member of the community of Christ.

In his letter to the Ephesian church, Paul is even more graphic in using this metaphor to explain the interchange of life necessary to healthy growth and life. "But speaking the truth in love, we must grow up in every way into him who is the head, into Christ, from whom the whole body, joined and knit together by every ligament with which it is equipped, as each part is working properly, promotes the body's growth in building itself up in love" (Eph. 4:15-16).

The experience of brokenness and the creative power of spirit takes place within the life of the body and the care which members have for one another. "If one member suffers, all suffer with it; if one member is honored, all rejoice together with it" (1 Cor. 12:26).

With brokenness there is bleeding. Every hurt and each loss is a hemorrhage through which the self bleeds its pain. Left to ourselves, we attempt to staunch the flow as best we can. After a time, the wound seems to be healed, and the pain subsides. Then suddenly, like an aftershock of an earthquake long forgotten, a tremor arises within us and the hurt spills over again, an embarrassment to us and a discomfort for others.

Life in relation to others is no protection against abuse, pain, and tragic loss. In fact, shared promises and commitments raise the stakes of our losses and griefs. There is something in us that wants to avoid this by withholding commitment and reserving our independence. But solitariness (not solitude!) is a form of abuse for the human spirit. And walking alone provides no certainty of never falling. "Two are better than one," wrote the ancient Preacher, "because they have a good reward for their toil. For if they fall, one will lift up the other; but woe to one who is alone and falls and does not have another to help" (Ecc. 4:9-10).

When we experience brokenness within a community of support and care, there is an interchange, a transfusion, if you please, so that what life flows out of us flows back into us, filtered through the fabric of intentional care. Within the life of the self in relation to others, there flows the pain of others as well as the joy of others.

"Wait a minute," my daughter said, "I'm not finished yet." We did wait, I am sure. And what do we have to show for it? Not a finished page in a coloring book—that was long discarded. We have a family where no one is quite finished but where everyone is looking forward to completeness. I think we are experiencing personal empowerment and spiritual healing.

SUMMARY

Personal empowerment and spiritual healing are the work of God's Spirit in the life of the self. The purpose of this book has been to integrate the psychological process of healing and recovery into the spiritual core of the self as created in the image of God and destined to share in the abundant life of God beginning here on earth and with Him in eternity.

• The spiritual core of the self is the source of emotional healing: recovery is a journey toward spiritual fitness and health.

• Recovery is a spiritual journey from overcoming the losses, hindrances, and problems that we suffer, to becoming the person we were created to be: spiritual healing begins with the recovery of hope.

• Hope emerges when the broken edge of life becomes the growing edge of faith: growth begins with openness to the Spirit as the source of change.

• Empowerment for change and growth comes from the liberating Spirit of Christ experienced in a community of faith: community is where each one cares for the other.

• Self-care is a gift of grace experienced as an interchange of faith and love among the members of the body of Christ: we never give up for God's grace is never finished!

PRAXIS

It has been one year since Norm was arrested for indecent exposure. He joined a twelve-step program for sexual addiction and he and his wife, Ella, participated in a group therapy program with a Christian psychologist. "My life has certainly turned around," Norm told his pastor. "I have not only overcome my addiction but have experienced genuine healing and restoration of my inner life. My wife and I have a level of intimacy and communication that I never knew was possible. I have only one question," Norm continued, "why is it that through all of the years in church and my strong belief in God I have finally experienced personal and spiritual healing through programs and resources that are outside the church? Explain to me again how spiritual healing can come through developing a more integrated and effective psychological and social dimension to my life?"

• Drawing upon concepts introduced in the first few chapters of this book, what response would you give to Norm concerning the role of the self in spiritual formation and personal healing?

• The thesis of this book has been that we can move beyond merely overcoming a problem to becoming the person that God created us to be. In what ways has Norm begun that journey?

• If you were the pastor or leader in a church, what does Norm's case suggest about ways in which the church can be more effective in its ministry of recovering authentic selfhood and spiritual healing?

• What difference has reading this book made in your own life?

AFTERWORD

Our journey of self-care begins with taking responsibility for our emotions and allowing the feelings behind them to come to the surface. This is always a difficult process, because emotions are often used to conceal painful feelings. Emotional habits are hard to break. We cannot do it by our own efforts.

Self-care is not a project to be undertaken by the self alone. The core of the self is grounded in relation with another, or others. The picture of the solitary Adam in Genesis 2 is one of self-alienation rather than self-fulfillment. Only when God created Eve could Adam say, "This at last is bone of my bones and flesh of my flesh" (Gen. 2:23). The divine image is not a religious quality of the individual person, but a spiritual reality expressed through the interchange of persons in relation. The sharing of our feelings with those whom we trust to listen and respond is the beginning of self-care.

Where do we find such people and how do we begin if we wish to undertake the journey?

The Apostle Paul would tell us, turn to the brother and sister in the body of Christ. His view of the church was that of a community of fellow travelers on the journey of mutual sharing and encouragement. In his letter to the Christians at Thessalonica he spoke with great feeling of his relationship to them. "We were gentle among you, like a nurse tenderly caring for her own children. So deeply do we care for you that we are determined to share with you not only the gospel of God but also our own selves, because you have become very dear to us" (1 Thes. 2:7-8).

To the Corinthians he wrote: "So I made up my mind not to make you another painful visit. For if I cause you pain, who is there to make me glad but the one whom I have pained? And I wrote as I did, so that when I came, I might not suffer pain from those who should have made me rejoice; for I am confident about all of you, that my joy would be the joy of all of you. For I wrote you out of much distress and anguish of heart and with many tears, not to cause you pain, but to let you know the abundant love that I have for you" (2 Cor. 2:1-4). To Timothy he wrote: "Recalling your tears, I long to see you so that I may be filled with joy" (2 Tim. 1:4).

Tears express feelings, not mere emotion. Paul found in Christian brothers and sisters what he did not find in the law nor among his earlier self-righteous religious companions, the community of self-care. He himself created such communities and expressed his own need for them openly and unashamedly.

Unfortunately, the church in our culture is not often the place where we experience such open and trustful community; at least, not in the official programs and meetings. At the same time, the church is made up of people who silently bear hurts, anxieties, and live with feelings of shame and loss of self-worth. Where there are small groups meeting, this may be the place to begin. There will be risks. Not every small group is open to personal sharing and willing to make the commitment to honesty and growth of the personal life of its members.

Be prepared for failure and don't give up. Many have found the best place to begin is with a twelve-step-support group in the community. The encouragement and commitment to growth found there can be experienced for one's own benefit and transferred into other relationships.

One clue I have found in years of pastoral work is this. Shared pain is often a greater bond than shared joy. It matters little what the source of the pain. Pain is a feeling and not just an emotion. The self *is* what it feels. The pain of grief over tragic loss is not unlike the pain of abuse or betrayal. The pain of unfulfilled desire and dreams is a wound to the self which feels very much like all other hurts.

Ministry to those who were in pain often was my own greatest source of self-care. As my feelings came into contact with the pain of others, I felt myself in communion with the self of others. It was not the pain that created the bond, but the shared feelings which brought our separate selves into communion.

The purpose of this book has been to write a practical theology of personal empowerment and spiritual healing. The practical part of it is the journey which we each experience as pilgrims in a strange land, but as those who have the companion of the Holy Spirit on our homeward journey!

NOTES

Introduction

1. Larry Crabb, *Inside Out* (Colorado Springs NavPress, 1988), 49.

Chapter 1: The Growth of the Self

1. Annie Dillard, *An American Childhood* (New York: HarperCollins, 1988), 11.

2. Peter Shaffer, *Equus* (New York: Avon, 1974).

3. For this overview of the concept of the self, I have drawn upon my article, "Self," published in *New Dictionary of Christian Ethics and Pastoral Theology* (Leicester, Great Britain: Inter-Varsity, 1992).

4. H. Guntrip, *Psychoanalytic Theory, Therapy, and the Self* (New York: Basic Books, 1971); Carl Rogers, *On Becoming a Person* (Boston: Houghton Mifflin, 1961); B.F. Skinner, *Science and Human Behavior* (New York: Macmillan, 1953). For other sources on the concept of the self, see: Gordon W. Allport, *Becoming* (New Haven, Conn.: Yale Univ. Press, 1955); Ray S. Anderson, *On Being Human* (Grand Rapids: Eerdmans, 1982); A. Castell, *The Self in Philosophy* (New York: Macmillan, 1957); David K. Clark, "Interpreting the Biblical Words for the Self," *Journal of Psychology and Theology* 18 (Winter 1990), 309–17; C. Stephen Evans, "Self," in *Baker Encyclopedia of Psychology*, ed. David G. Benner (Grand Rapids: Baker, 1985); M. Gorman, "The Self," in

New Catholic Encyclopedia, vol. 13 (San Francisco: Catholic Univ. of America, 1967), 56–60; William James, *Principles of Psychology,* vol. 1 (New York: Holt, 1890). Benjamin Lee, ed., *Psychological Theories of the Self* (New York and London: Plenum, 1982); and Jerry M. Suls, ed., *Psychological Perspectives on the Self,* vol. 1 (Hillsdale, N.J.: Lawrence Erlbaum, 1982).

5. John Macmurray, *The Self as Agent* (London: Faber and Faber, 1957).

6. *Los Angeles Times,* 17 April 1992, sec. 1.

7. Alistair I. McFadyen, *The Call to Personhood: A Christian Theory of the Individual in Social Relationships* (New York: Cambridge Univ. Press, 1990).

8. For a discussion of the concept of the image of God, see Ray S. Anderson, *On Being Human—Essays in Theological Anthropology* (1982; reprint, Pasadena: Fuller Seminary Press, 1990), chap. 6, app. B.

9. For a survey of recent literature on the concept of shame, see Robert Karen, "Shame," *The Atlantic Monthly,* February 1992, 40–70.

10. For a discussion of the relation of body, soul, and spirit, see Anderson, *On Being Human,* app. A.

11. Karl Barth, vol. 3/2 of *Church Dogmatics,* trans. G.E. Bromiley (Edinburgh, Scotland: T & T Clark, 1960), 378.

12. Cf. Walther Eichrodt, *Theology of the Old Testament,* vol. 2 (Philadelphia: Westminster, 1961), 131–32.

13. Evans stresses the fact of "agent causality" as the core of a Christian view of the human self when he says, "human beings are responsible for their spiritual condition, since they are created by God as responsible agents" (C. Stephen Evans, *Wisdom and Humanness in Psychology—Prospects for a Christian Approach* [Grand Rapids: Baker, 1989], 131).

14. The concept of the self as an agent is the main thrust of John Macmurray's view of personhood in his book, *The Self as Agent* (London: Faber and Faber, 1957). The intentions (and motives) of a person, says Macmurray, are primarily located in one's actions. As a result, the actions of a person are primary to the self while self-reflection is secondary (pp. 197ff, 220).

15. John Macmurray, *Persons in Relation* (London: Faber and Faber, 1961), 150.

16. Ibid., 159.

17. Erik Erickson, *The Life Cycle Completed: A Review* (New York: W.W. Norton, 1982) and *Identity, Youth and Crisis* (New York: W.W. Norton, 1968); James Fowler, *Stages of Faith* (San Francisco: Harper and Row, 1981); Jean Piaget, *Six Psychological Studies* (New York: Random House/Vintage, 1967); Carol Gilligan, *In a Different Voice: Psychological Theory and Women's Development* (Cambridge, Mass.: Harvard Univ. Press, 1982).

18. Romney Moseley, *Becoming a Self—Critical Transformations before God* (Nashville: Abingdon, 1991), 60.

19. Charles V. Gerkin, *The Living Human Document—Revisioning Pastoral Counseling in a Hermeneutical Mode* (Nashville: Abingdon, 1984), 98.

Chapter 2: The Social Self

1. See Søren Kierkegaard, *The Concept of Dread* (Princeton: Princeton Univ. Press, 1944) and *Sickness unto Death* (London: Oxford Univ. Press, 1941).

2. Ernest Becker. *The Denial of Death* (New York: Macmillan/Free Press, 1973). Faith, suggests Becker, is a religious category for the psychological condition of mental health (pp. 158, 199, 202, 204). The self is hopelessly caught in a split between two realms, says Becker, "symbols (freedom) and body (fate)." The neurotic lacks "faith" as a means of transcending this split and coming to terms with both freedom and fate (pp. 44–45).

3. Macmurray, *Persons in Relation*, 150.

4. Martin Buber, *I and Thou*, trans. Walter Kaufman (Edinburgh, Scotland: T & T Clark, 1979), 62.

5. Hans Urs von Balthasar, *A Theological Anthropology* (New York: Sheed and Ward, 1967), 87.

6. For a discussion of the critical difference between a social as contrasted with an existential view of the self, see Peter M. Young, *The Ontological Self in the Thinking of C. Stephen Evans and Ray S Anderson: Towards an Integration of the Individual and Social Aspects of Personhood* (Ph.D. diss., Fuller Theological Seminary, School of Psychology, 1991).

7. William Meissner, *Life and Faith: Psychological Perspectives on Religious Experience* (Washington, D.C.: Georgetown Univ. Press, 1987), 5.

8. Mary Vander Goot, *Healthy Emotions: Helping Children Grow* (Grand Rapids: Baker, 1987), 43.

9. Emil Brunner, *Man in Revolt* (1939; reprint, Philadelphia: Westminster, 1979), 235.

10. Abraham J. Heschel, *The Prophets*, vol. 2 (New York: Harper and Row, 1962), 96–97.

11. Brunner, *Man in Revolt*, 251.

Chapter 3: The Subjective Self

1. Thomas Oden, *The Living God: Systematic Theology, Vol. 1* (San Francisco: Harper and Row, 1987), 330. "The empirical inquiry into religious feelings and the emotive life that proceeds from religious

experience is a quite different subject area called psychology of religion (an important study, but it is not theology), the study of affective experience that emerges when persons are psychologically and interpersonally impacted by God or by religious symbols and communities (William James, *Varieties of Religious Experience*)."

2. See, for example, Jürgen Moltmann, *The Crucified God: The Cross of Christ as the Foundation and Criticism of Christian Theology*, trans. R.A. Wilson and John Bowden (New York: Harper and Row, 1974).

3. See my book, *Christians Who Counsel: The Vocation of Wholistic Therapy* (Grand Rapids: Zondervan, 1990).

4. Wolfhart Pannenberg, *Anthropology in Theological Perspective* (Philadelphia: Westminster, 1985), 259.

5. Abraham J. Heschel, *The Prophets*, vol. 2 (New York: Harper and Row, 1962), 6, 37, 45. "The very word 'pathos' like its Latin equivalent *passio*, from *pati* (to suffer), means a state or condition in which something happens to man [sic], something of which it is a passive victim. The term was applied to emotions such as pain or pleasure as well as to passions, since they were understood to be states of the soul aroused by something outside the self, during which time the mind is passively swayed by the emotion or passion" (pp. 27–28).

6. Heschel, *The Prophets*, 4. The frequent references to the wrath or anger of God, for example, must be understood within the aspect of the pathos of God. "The anger of God must not be treated in isolation, but as an aspect of the divine pathos, as one of the modes of God's responsiveness to man. It shares the features that are characteristic of the pathos as a whole: it is conditioned by God's will; it is aroused by man's sins. It is an instrument rather than a force, transitive rather than spontaneous. It is a secondary emotion, never the ruling passion, disclosing only a part of God's way with man. . . . For all the terror that the wrath of God may bring upon man, the prophet is not crushed or shaken in his understanding and trust. What is divine is never weird. This is the greatness of the prophet: he is able to convert terror into a song. For when the Lord smites the Egyptians, he is both 'smiting and healing' (Isa. 19:22)" (p. 63). "The divine pathos, whether mercy or anger, was never thought of as an impulsive act, arising automatically within the divine Being as the reaction to man's behavior and as something due to peculiarity of temperament or propensity. It is neither irrational nor irresistible. Pathos results from a decision, from an act of will. It comes about in the light of moral judgment rather than in the darkness of passion" (p. 78).

7. Heschel, *The Prophets*, 38.

8. Brunner, *Man in Revolt*, 227.

9. Ibid., 233–34.

10. Archibald D. Hart, *Me, Myself and I — How Far Should We Go in*

Our Search for Self-Fulfillment? (Ann Arbor, Mich.: Servant, 1992) See also, his *Unlocking the Mystery of Your Emotions* (Dallas: Word, 1989).

11. See Macmurray, *Persons in Relation*, previously cited.

12. Warren Shibles, *Emotion: The Method of Philosophical Therapy* (Whitewater, Wis.: Language Press, 1974), 14.

13. Ibid., 142–43.

14. Pannenberg, *Anthropology in Theological Perspective*, 252.

15. Shibles, *Emotion*, 17–19.

16. Ibid., 69–70.

17. William James, *The Varieties of Religious Experience*, cited in Betty Edwards, *Drawing on the Right Side of the Brain* (Los Angeles: J.P. Tarcher, 1979), 46.

18. John Pedersen, *Israel: Its Life and Culture*, vol. 1 (London: Oxford Univ. Press, 1973), 107.

19. Macmurray, *Reason and Emotion*, 26.

20. Vander Goot, *Healthy Emotions*, 23. "Both our feelings *and* our actions need to be brought into balance with our intention to love our neighbors and to be healthy, productive persons ourselves" (p. 24).

21. See my book, *On Being Human* (Grand Rapids: Eerdmans, 1982).

22. Pannenberg, *Anthropology in Theological Perspective*, 259. John Macmurray adds a significant comment when he says: "The promise of the full maturity of religion in human life is put perfectly in Paul's words: 'Then shall I know even as also I am known'; and it is the core of his paean in praise of love. It expresses the perfect and complete mutuality of communion, of mutual emotional awareness" (Macmurray, *Reason and Emotion*, 63).

23. Balthasar, *A Theological Anthropology*, 87.

24. Pannenberg, *Anthropology in Theological Perspective*, 265.

25. Vander Goot, *Healthy Emotions*, 23.

26. Shibles, *Emotion*, 217–18. "It is thought that an emotion names something that must be in us as a feeling is. This we saw can result in naming-fallacy or hypostatizing of entities, and can be unfounded. We may think that such words as love, hate, revenge, and anguish describe or name internal states or discrete entities. They may rather be operational or refer to processes and contain within themselves reference to feelings, objects and situations. One does not just feel jealous of no one. It is not just a feeling that comes over one in any situation. Jealousy has reference to an object and situation as well as to ourselves and our reaction. If jealousy were merely an internal feeling it might be driven away by having a pleasant dessert. Can one fall in love with no one? One does not reply to 'With whom are you in love?' 'No one, I'm just in love' " (Shibles, *Emotion*, 24).

27. Vander Goot, *Healthy Emotions*, 36–37.

28. "Emotion is inseparable from being filled with the spirit, which

is above all a state of being moved. Often the spirit releases passion, an excessive discharge of nervous energy, enhanced vitality, increased inner strength, increased motor activity, a drive. While spirit includes passion or emotion, it must not be reduced to either. Spirit implies the sense of sharing a supreme superindividual power, will or wisdom. In emotion, we are conscious of its being our emotion; in the state of being filled with spirit, we are conscious of joining, sharing or receiving 'spirit from above' (Isa. 32:15). Passion is a movement; spirit is a goal" (Heschel, *The Prophets*, 96–97).

29. Brunner, *Man in Revolt*, 251.

30. Vander Goot, *Healthy Emotions*, 43. Emil Brunner speaks of the fragmentation which cries out for a center as the essential "sanity" of the self as grounded in God. "[In] the unity of personality in man's fallen state. . . . insofar as the disintegration has not taken the extreme form, in the pathological sense of the divided personality and the loss of the sense of unity in self-consciousness of insanity, man is still a unity in the formal sense of self-consciousness and of self determination. But this shell of formal unity has no uniform content; on the contrary, it is extremely contradictory. . . . It is still possible to recognize at least a comparative unity of personality in the 'heart.' But it is the heart which is torn, divided, contradictory. It is the heart which feels the disharmony of existence in its 'sorrow-of-heart.' . . . Unity—yes; but the unity of that which at bottom is in despair. This inward unity which still exists we call spiritual or psychological 'health' or 'normality,' to distinguish it from madness, or insanity. Yet all this health is in itself mad and insane. To place the central point of existence outside God, who is the true Centre, in the 'I' and the world, is madness; for it cannot be a real centre; the world cannot provide any resting-place for the Self; it only makes it oscillate hither and thither" (Brunner, *Man in Revolt*, 235).

Chapter 4: The Responsible Self

1. H.W. Wolff, *Anthropology in the Old Testament*, trans. Margaret Kohl (1974 reprint, Philadelphia: Fortress, 1981), 44.

2. Ibid.

3. Pedersen, *Israel: Its Life and Culture*, 108–9. Pedersen later observes, "When modern logicians have characterized the correct manner of thinking as an interplay of simple, i.e. essentially empty but sharply defined space images, then we see at once the contrast between this and the Israelite way of thinking. The Israelite does not occupy himself with empty nor with sharply defined space images. His logic is not the logic of abstraction, but of immediate perception. . . . The most impor-

tant word for thinking contains the plan, the direction of the mind towards action" (pp. 124–25).

4. Macmurray, *Persons in Relation*, 110ff.

5. Pedersen, *Israel: Its Life and Culture*, 127.

6. "The disparagement of emotion was made possible by ascribing to the rational faculty a power of sovereignty over the objects of its comprehension, thought being the active, moving principle, and the objects of knowledge the passive, inert material of comprehension. However, the act of thinking of an object is in itself an act of being moved by the object. In thinking we do not create an object; we are challenged by it. Thus, thought is part of emotion. We think because we are moved, a fact of which we are not always conscious. Emotion may be defined as the consciousness of being moved" (Heschel, *The Prophets*, 96).

7. Dietrich Bonhoeffer, *Letters and Papers from Prison* (New York: Macmillan, 1971), 8.

8. Macmurray, *Reason and Emotion*, 75.

9. Brunner, *Man in Revolt*, 227.

10. Macmurray, *Reason and Emotion*, 49–50. Shibles says: "There is no black and white distinction between emotion, thought, and feeling. In one respect, reason and emotion are too abstract to yield a clear-cut distinction between them. Their paradigms do differ. The difference between reason and emotion has to do with context and so is a rational sort of thing" (Shibles, *Emotion*, 56).

11. Heschel, *The Prophets*, 5.

12. Heschel, *The Prophets*, 4. The frequent references to the wrath or anger of God, for example, must be understood within the aspect of the pathos of God. Heschel observes, "The anger of God must not be treated in isolation, but as an aspect of the divine pathos, as one of the modes of God's responsiveness to man. It shares the features that are characteristic of the pathos as a whole: it is conditioned by God's will; it is aroused by man's sins. It is an instrument rather than a force, transitive rather than spontaneous. It is a secondary emotion, never the ruling passion, disclosing only a part of God's way with man" (p. 78).

13. "Conscience is . . . the thorn in 'the flesh of my feeling.' Conscience sees to it that faith never becomes mere feeling, in the sense of an enjoyment of God or of an optimistically inclined eudaemonism of salvation. To put it rather better and more theologically, conscience is the thorn which sees to it that faith does not become a self-contained, psychically founded *habitus*, but that instead it remains fixed upon its object, and hence in constant motion towards this object. Faith as a flight to the life of God is thus linked with constant dying to self. The open and mortal wound which constantly gives rise to this dying is conscience . . . conscience, even in the justified man, is always the

place where the peace and comfort of God must be realized and implemented. The comforted conscience is not a 'state' which exists; it is the object and result of a 'promise' which is declared". (Helmut Thielicke, *Theological Ethics*, vol. 1 (Grand Rapids: Eerdmans, 1984), 318–19.

14. Macmurray, *Persons in Relation*, 110ff.

Chapter 5: The Worth of the Self

1. "Death of a Salesman," in *Arthur Miller's Collected Plays*, vol. 1 (New York: Viking, 1987), 221–22.

2. One reason why a causal relation between low self-esteem and deviant behavior may be difficult to establish is the suggestion that positive self-esteem may actually be the result of deviant acts. "If an individual has engaged in deviant acts . . . positive self-attitude may have derived from these acts, rather than from normative experiences. In that case, we would expect to find little empirical association between self-esteem and deviant behavior" (Susan B. Crockenberg and Barbara Soby, "Self-Esteem and Teenage Pregnancy," in *The Social Importance of Self-Esteem*, ed. Neil J. Smelser, et al. [San Francisco: Univ. of California Press, 1989], 130).

3. *Toward a State of Self-Esteem*. The Final Report of the California Task Force to Promote Self-Esteem and Personal and Social Responsibility (January 1990).

4. Neil J. Smelser, "Self-Esteem and Social Problems: An Introduction," in Smelser, et al., *The Social Importance of Self-Esteem*, 10.

5. Richard L. Bednar, M. Gawain Wells, and Scott R. Peterson, eds., *Self-Esteem: Paradoxes and Innovations in Clinical Theory and Practice* (Washington, D.C.: American Psychological Association, 1989), 37–38.

6. Ibid., 111.

7. The Christian psychologist, Craig Ellison, offers a definition that includes the elements of self-concept and implies positive self-worth by suggesting that self-esteem results from a comparison between the perceived self and the ideal self. "The most commonly accepted analysis of self-esteem sees it as the result of comparisons between one's perceived self, which combines both the assessments of others and one's private perceptions, and the ideal self, which is both how one feels one would like to be and how one feels one ought to be" (Craig Ellison, *Your Better Self: Christianity, Psychology, and Self-Esteem* [New York: Harper and Row, 1983], 3).

8. Hart, *Unlocking the Mystery of Your Emotions*, 94. See also Hart, *Me, Myself and I — How Far Should We Go in Our Search for Self-Fulfillment?* 209ff.

9. Don Matzat, *Christ Esteem—Where the Search for Self-Esteem Ends* (Eugene, Ore.: Harvest House, 1990), 71–72. Emphasis in the original.

10. Meissner, *Life and Faith*, 140.

11. See Anderson, *On Being Human*, chap. 4.

12. Pedersen, *Israel: Its Life and Culture*, 310

13. Meissner, *Life and Faith*, 148–49.

14. See Richard J. Gelles and Claire Pedrick Cornell, *Intimate Violence in Families—Family Study Series #2*. (Newbury Park, Calif.: Sage. 1985).

15. For additional sources on domestic violence and spouse abuse, see: James Alsdurf and Phyllis Alsdurf, *Battered into Submission: The Tragedy of Wife Abuse in the Christian Home* (Downers Grove, Ill.: InterVarsity 1989); Joy M. Bussert, *Battered Women: From a Theology of Suffering to an Ethic of Empowerment* (New York: Division of Mission in North America. Lutheran Church in America, 1986); Lenore E. Walker, *The Battered Woman Syndrome* (New York: Spring, 1992); and Daniel J. Sonkin, *Learning to Live without Violence: A Handbook for Men* (Volcano, Calif.: Volcano Press, 1989).

16. Martin Bobgan and Diedre Bobgan, *Prophets of Psychoheresy II* (Santa Barbara, Calif.: Eastgate, 1990), 159–60.

17. Ibid., 188.

18. Ibid., 160.

19. Ibid., 157.

20. Matzat, *Christ Esteem*, 77.

21. Wolfhart Pannenberg, *Christian Spirituality and Sacramental Community* (London: Darton, Longman and Todd, 1983). 16–17.

22. Ibid., 20.

23. Robert Schuller, *Self-Esteem: The New Reformation* (Dallas: Word, 1982), 104.

24. Ibid., 65.

25. Jürgen Moltmann, *God and Creation* (New York: Harper and Row, 1985), 269.

26. Pannenberg, *Christian Spirituality*, 45.

Chapter 6: Abuse

1. Richard J. Gelles and Murray A. Straus, *Intimate Violence: The Causes and Consequences of Abuse in the American Family* (New York: Simon and Schuster/Touchstone, 1988), 18, 20–21.

2. Jill Smolowe, "What the Doctor Should Do," *Time*, 29 June 1992, 57.

3. Gelles and Straus, *Intimate Violence*, 51.

4. Ibid., 43. "Initially, the response to family violence was to assume that abusive family members were mentally ill. But over the past

two decades the tendency to diagnose the causes of violence as a psychological abnormality or mental illness has declined. We realize now that individual psychiatric care for violent family members is but one limited treatment for the problem. Since the roots of family violence lie in the structure of the family and society, we know that individual psychiatric treatment can be effective with only a small number of cases of violence and abuse" (Gelles and Straus, *Intimate Violence,* 128).

5. Gelles and Cornell distinguish between normal and abusive violence: "Normal violence is the commonplace pushes, shoves, and spankings that frequently are considered a normal or accepted part of raising children or interacting with a spouse. . . . The more dangerous acts of violence we shall refer to as 'abusive violence.' These acts are defined as acts that have the high potential for injuring the person being hit" (Gelles and Cornell, *Intimate Violence in Families,* 22–23). However, Gelles and Strauss, in a later book, appear to abandon this distinction: "Our view is that it is impossible to distinguish between force and violence. Rather, all violent acts — from pushing and shoving to shooting and stabbing — properly belong under a single definition of violence. . . . In reality, true insight into the nature of violence requires us to shed our stereotypes and blinders about routine spankings, normal pushings, and seemingly harmless grabbings, and to see these acts as part of the problem of intimate violence" (Gelles and Straus, *Intimate Violence,* 54–55).

6. Meissner, *Life and Faith,* 249, 252–53.

7. Gelles and Cornell, *Intimate Violence in Families,* 76.

8. Gelles and Straus, *Intimate Violence,* 32ff.

9. One of the most insightful and helpful treatments of recovery from traumatic and abusive experiences can be found in Judith Lewis Herman, M.D., *Trauma and Recovery: The Aftermath of Violence — From Domestic Abuse to Political Terror* (New York: HarperCollins/Basic Books, 1992). "Recovery," writes Herman, "can take place only in the context of relationships; it cannot occur in isolation. In her renewed connections with other people, the survivor re-creates the psychological faculties that were damaged or deformed by the traumatic experience. . . . Just as these capabilities are originally formed in relationships with other people, they must be reformed in such relationships" (p. 133).

10. Meissner, *Life and Faith,* 148–49.

11. Beverly Flanigan, *Forgiving the Unforgivable* (New York: Macmillan, 1992), 162.

12. Ibid., 168.

13. James Leehan, *Pastoral Care for Survivors of Family Abuse* (Louisville: Westminster/John Knox, 1989), 90.

14. Ibid., 97–98.

15. Cf. Erik Erikson, *Identity and the Life Cycle* (New York: International Universities Press, 1959); and *Childhood and Society* (reprint;

1950, New York: Norton, 1963). Kohlberg has ceveloped cognitive stages of moral development as a guide to individual and social behavior. See Lawrence Kohlberg, "Continuities and Discontinuities in Childhood and Adult Moral Development Revisited," in *Life-Span Development Psychology: Research and Theory*, ed. Paul B. Baltes and K. Warner Schaie (New York: Academic, 1973), 180–204.

16. Meissner, *Life and Faith*, 247.

17. "[The self] builds itself out of a matrix of value orientations from many sources, as well as providing a medium for the transformation of instinctual derivatives.... It is a process of creative self-synthesis that builds upon a uniquely autonomous and personal zed structure within the ego.... However, where the course of development allows for a more normal and adaptive integration of the superego and the internalization of parental images on which it rests, the quality of the child's introjections comes to be considerably less ambivalent, less laden with the residues of aggressive conflicts, and open to the emergence of meaningful identifications.... In proportion as the child internalises value systems because of constructive identifications rather than pathogenic and defensively based introjections, the role of the superego shifts from that of an aggressively, even pathologically punitive force in the psychic economy to that of a realistic and effectively integrated arbiter of ethical conduct" (Meissner, *Life and Faith*, 263–64).

Chapter 7: Shame

1. Karen, "Shame," 41.

2. John Bradshaw. *Bradshaw On: Healing the Shame That Binds You* (Deerfield Beach, Fla.: Health Communications, 1988), vii. Bradshaw notes, "Healthy shame keeps us grounded. It is a yellow light warning us that we are essentially limited. *Healthy shame is the basic metaphysical boundary for human beings.* It is the emotional energy which signals us that we are not God — that we have made and will make mistakes that we need help" (p. 4).

3. Lewis B. Smedes, *Shame and Grace: Healing the Shame We Don't Deserve* (San Francisco: HarperSan Francisco, 1993), 31.

4. Ibid., 42.

5. Ibid., 35.

6. Karen, "Shame," 40–70.

7. Ibid., 70.

8. See Stephen Arterburn and Jack Felton, *Toxic Faith: Faith That Hurts: Faith That Heals* (Nashville: Thomas Nelson, 1991); Ronald Enroth, *Recovering from Churches That Abuse* (Grand Rapids: Zondervan, 1994); and Ken Blue, *Healing Spiritual Abuse* (Downers Grove, Ill.: InterVarsity, 1993).

9. Bonhoeffer, *Letters and Papers from Prison,* 326–27.

10. Smedes, *Shame and Grace,* 116.

11. C. Norman Kraus, *Jesus Christ Our Lord: Christology from a Disciple's Perspective* (Scottdale, Pa.: Herald, 1987), 207.

12. Ibid., 211.

13. Karen, "Shame," 47.

14. Ibid., 42–43.

15. Ibid., 47.

16. Bradshaw, *Healing the Shame That Binds You,* 10.

17. See Walter Lowrie, *A Short Life of Kierkegaard* (Princeton: Princeton Univ. Press, 1951).

18. Søren Kierkegaard, *The Concept of Dread,* trans. Walter Lowrie (Princeton: Princeton Univ. Press, 1957).

19. Bradshaw, *Healing the Shame That Binds You,* 25.

20. Ibid., 26.

21. I have adapted these three concepts from Bradshaw, *Healing the Shame That Binds You,* 135, but have added my own commentary.

22. Insightful use of the Adam and Eve story as a metaphor for shame and recovery can be found in Curtis Levang, *The Adam and Eve Complex: Freedom from the Shame that Can Separate You from God, Others, and Yourself* (Minneapolis: SelfCare Books, 1992).

23. Smedes, *Shame and Grace,* 119. Smedes observes, "The effect of grace is not to eliminate healthy shame but to eliminate its threat. The threat is the possibility of being rejected. Once grace cancels that possibility, the pain of shame is easier to bear" (p. 154).

24. I have discussed the dynamics of this process of discovery, when transformation actually occurs through the motive power of love and the role of the counselor as mediator in *Christians Who Counsel: The Vocation of Wholistic Therapy,* 67ff.

25. As a case study in recovery from shame and self-condemnation, I wrote the book, *The Gospel According to Judas* (Colorado Springs: Helmers and Howard, 1991). For some suggested steps toward recovery, see pp. 151ff.

26. For practical help in stopping self-shaming habits and deflecting the shaming words and actions of others, I recommend the previously cited Levang, *The Adam and Eve Complex,* esp. 79–87.

Chapter 8: Betrayal

1. For further exploration of the dynamics of betrayal see my book, *The Gospel According to Judas* (Colorado Springs: Helmers and Howard Publishers, 1991).

2. Shaffer, *Equus,* 90–91.

3. A saying of Michael Polanyi, *The Tacit Dimension* (London: Routledge and Kegan Paul, 1967). Tacit knowledge is something that we know that we know, but cannot explain how we know it nor can we fully explain that knowledge to others.

4. Richard F. Vieth, *Holy Power, Human Pain* (Bloomington Ind.: Meyer-Stone Books, 1988), 106.

5. "For a family to be good-enough means that it is not perfect, and that perfection itself may be a standard which intrudes into the relationship between parent and child. . . . Through the good-enough family, the infant learns that life is both pleasant and unpleasant, that self and others are both strong and weak; and this is learned in a relational context which is able to incorporate both poles without fragmentation. . . . Without the good-enough environment, a defensive posture will be established which will make it impossible to work through to authentic personhood" (Cameron Lee "The Good Enough Family," *Journal of Psychology and Theology* 13, no. 3 [1985]: 89.

6. Craig Dykstra, "Family Promises: Faith and Families in the Context of the Church," in *Faith in Families*, ed. Lindell Sawyers (Philadelphia: Geneva, 1986), 143.

7. Anderson, *The Gospel According to Judas*, 14 –42.

8. Ibid, 125–26.

Chapter 9: Tragedy

1. Fyodor Dostoyevsky, *The Brothers Karamazov* (New York: Random House, 1950), 290

2. Ibid., 290–91.

3. See Moltmann, *The Crucified God*, previously cited. See also Jürgen Moltmann, *Experiences of God*, trans. Margaret Kohl (Philadelphia: Fortress, 1980). "Is God so absolute and sovereign that he reigns in heavenly glory, incapable of suffering and untouched by the death of his Son? And if God is essentially incapable of suffering, does this not mean that he is incapable of love as well? But if he is incapable of love, he is poorer than any man or woman who is able to love and suffer" (p. 15).

4. John Hick, *Evil and the God of Love* (London Macmillan, 1966), 15.

5. John Dart, "Process Theology: God's Power over Evil Questioned," Part 1, *The Los Angeles Times* 19 October 1982. The relentless logic of this view of God is drawn to a conclusion with a vengeance by Stephen Arnold Larson, Pastor of the Beverly Orthodox Presbyterian Church in Los Angeles: "As a Calvinist, I feel compelled to respond, both from practical and theoretical considerations. From a practical

standpoint, any view of God which denies that He controls all things and events makes God very quickly irrelevant. If God does not control all things, how can we be sure that we will even be around to enjoy the good things He has in store for us? . . . Process theology would answer that question by trying to redefine God in a more acceptable manner. People want a real God, or none. The real question is not 'Why does God allow suffering?' but rather, 'Why does God show mercy at all?' God loves some of us, and he doesn't love others in the same way, and that's why there is suffering for some, and salvation for others" (Letter to the Editor, *Los Angeles Times*, 23 October 1982).

6. Harold S. Kushner, *When Bad Things Happen to Good People* (New York: Avon, 1981), 134.

7. S. Paul Schilling, *God and Human Anguish* (Nashville: Abingdon, 1977), 10.

8. The foundational work for process thought is Alfred North Whitehead, *Process and Reality: An Essay in Cosmology* (New York: Macmillan, 1929). See also, Bernard Lee, S.M., *The Becoming of the Church: A Process Theology of the Structure of Christian Experience* (New York: Paulist, 1974); David Ray Griffin, *God, Power, and Evil: A Process Theodicy* (Philadelphia: Westminster, 1976); and Stephen T. David, ed., *Encountering Evil: Live Options in Theodicy* (Atlanta: John Knox, 1981).

9. Letter to the Editor, *Los Angeles Times*, 6 November 1982. See Dart, "Process Theology: God's Power over Evil Questioned."

10. For an insightful treatment of divine power and human suffering see Vieth, *Holy Power, Human Pain*, previously cited.

11. Graham Monteith, "Too Many Awkward Questions — Too Many Glib Answers," *New College Bulletin*, University of Edinburgh, September 1981, 10–13.

12. Ibid.

13. Bonhoeffer, *Letters and Papers from Prison*, 360–61.

14. Ibid., 348–49.

15. Ray S. Anderson, *The Love That God Is*, unpublished journal notes, August, 1963.

Chapter 10: Grief

1. Christopher Fry, *The Boy with a Cart* (New York: Oxford Univ. Press, 1939/1959), 6–7.

2. Douglas A. Puryear, *Helping People in Crisis* (San Francisco: Jossey-Bass, 1979), 10–11. Six types of crisis are described in David K. Switzer, *The Minister as Crisis Counselor* (Nashville: Abingdon, 1974): *Dispositional:* feelings of distress, anger, anxiety, hopelessness due to an external factor which can be removed or solved through immediate

treatment or action: *Anticipated Life Transition:* normal, life cycle types of transitions; *Sudden Traumatic Stress:* a rapid reaction of stress triggered by an external event which results in some degree of disequilibrium and breakdown in functioning; *Maturational/Developmental:* failure to make adjustments due to inadequate developmental growth and adaptation; *Psycho-pathological:* personal disorders and behavioral patterns approaching psychotic dimension due to severe pathology at emotional and mental level; and *Psychiatric Emergencies:* total loss of control resulting in need for hospitalization, restraint, or monitoring.

3. Ernest Becker, *The Denial of Death* (New York: Macmillan, 1973)

4. Anne Morrow Lindbergh, "Within the Wave," in *The Unicorn* (New York: Pantheon. 1956). 78.

5. Frederick Sontag, *The God of Evil* (San Francisco: Harper and Row, 1970), 95.

6. J. Christian Beker, *Suffering and Hope* (Philadelphia: Fortress, 1987), 21. For additional sources on suffering from a Christian perspective see: Randy Becton *Does God Care When We Suffer and Will He Do Anything about It?* (Grand Rapids: Baker, 1988); D.A. Carson, *How Long, O Lord? Reflections on Suffering and Evil* (Grand Rapids: Baker, 1990); Arthur C. McGill, *Suffering: A Test of Theological Method* (Philadelphia: Westminster, 1982); John Timmer, *God of Weakness* (Grand Rapids: Zondervan, 1988); W. Sibley Towner, *How God Deals with Evil* (Philadelphia: Westminster, 1976); and James Walsh and P.G. Walsh, *Divine Providence and Human Suffering: Message of the Fathers of the Church* (Wilmington, Del.: Michael Glazier, 1985).

7. The British school of object relations theory in the neo-Freudian tradition includes such names as W. Ronald Fairburn, H. Guntrip. D.W. Winnicott, and Melanie Klein. These theories sought to locate the source of psychological problems in birth trauma and/or in the few months immediately following birth, particularly in the infant's relation to the parent (mother) as an object of attachment. The infant struggles to internalize the mother object in a way that provides continuity through the stages of separation and perceived abandonment. Successful object internalization establishes an identity that can cope with change in the object to which one relates without suffering anxiety or panic. See also the work of Frank Lake, *Clinical Theology: A Theological and Psychological Basis to Clinical Pastoral Care* (New York: Crossroad, 1987).

8. C.S. Lewis, *A Grief Observed* (London: Faber and Faber, 1961), 44.

9. A reference to the book by Paul Tillich, *The Courage to Be* (London: Collins, 1962).

10. Lewis, *A Grief Observed*, 57.

11. Ibid., 46.

12. Arthur Miller, *After the Fall*, in *Arthur Miller's Collected Plays*, vol. 2 (New York: Viking, 1981), 190.

13. Anne Morrow Lindbergh, "Second Sowing," in *The Unicorn* (New York: Pantheon, 1956), 32.

Chapter 11: From Overcoming to Becoming

1. Leehan, *Pastoral Care for Survivors of Family Abuse*, 99–100.

2. Ibid., 114.

3. Heschel, *The Prophets*, 96–97.

4. Leehan, *Pastoral Care for Survivors of Family Abuse*, 101.

5. Walter Brueggemann, *Hope within History* (Atlanta: John Knox, 1987), 84.

6. Homeostasis may be defined as, "the coordinated physiological processes which maintain most of the steady states in the organism [which are] so complex and so peculiar to living beings. . . . The word does not imply something set and immobile, a stagnation. It means a condition—a condition which may vary, but which is relatively constant" (W.B. Cannon, *The Wisdom of the Body* [New York: W.W. Norton, 1939], 20, 24).

BIBLIOGRAPHY

A

Allport, Gordon W. *Becoming*. New Haven, Conn.: Yale Univ. Press, 1955.

Alsdurf, James, and Phyllis Alsdurf. *Battered into Submission: The Tragedy of Wife Abuse in the Christian Home*. Downers Grove, Ill.: InterVarsity, 1989.

Anderson, Ray S. *On Being Human: Essays in Theological Anthropology*. Grand Rapids: Eerdmans, 1982. Reprint. Pasadena: Fuller Seminary Press, 1991.

_____. *Christians Who Counsel: The Vocation of Wholistic Therapy*. Grand Rapids: Zondervan, 1990.

_____. *The Gospel According to Judas*. Colorado Springs: Helmers and Howard, 1991.

_____. "Self." In *New Dictionary of Christian Ethics and Pastoral Theology*. Leicester, England: Inter-Varsity, 1992.

Arterburn, Stephen, and Jack Felton. *Toxic Faith: Faith That Hurts, Faith That Heals.* Nashville: Thomas Nelson, 1991.

B

Balthasar, Hans Urs von. *A Theological Anthropology.* New York: Sheed and Ward, 1967.

Barth, Karl. *Church Dogmatics* 3/2. Edinburgh, Scotland: T & T Clark, 1960.

Becker, Ernest. *The Denial of Death.* New York: Macmillan/Free Press, 1973.

Becton, Randy. *Does God Care When We Suffer and Will He Do Anything about It?* Grand Rapids: Baker, 1988.

Bednar, Richard, Gawain M. Wells, and Scott R. Peterson, eds. *Self-Esteem: Paradoxes and Innovations in Clinical Theology and Practice.* Washington, D.C.: American Psychological Association, 1989.

Beker, J. Christian. *Suffering and Hope.* Philadelphia: Fortress, 1987.

Blue, Ken. *Healing Spiritual Abuse: How to Break Free from Bad Church Experiences.* Downers Grove, Ill.: InterVarsity, 1993.

Bobgan, Martin and Diedre. *Prophets of Psychoheresy II.* Santa Barbara, Calif.: Eastgate, 1990.

Bonhoeffer, Dietrich. *Letters and Papers from Prison.* New York: Macmillan, 1971.

Bradshaw, John. *Bradshaw On: Healing the Shame That Binds You.* Deerfield Beach, Fla.: Health Communications, 1988.

Brueggemann, Walter. *Hope within History.* Atlanta: John Knox, 1987.

Brunner, Emil. *Man in Revolt*. London: Lutterworth, 1939. Reprint. Philadelphia: Westminster, 1979.

Buber, Martin. *I and Thou*. Translated by Walter Kaufman. Edinburgh, Scotland: T & T Clark, 1979.

Bussert, Joy M. *Battered Women: From a Theology of Suffering to an Ethic of Empowerment*. New York: Division of Mission in North America, Lutheran Church in America, 1986.

C

Cannon, W.B. *The Wisdom of the Body*. New York: W.W. Norton, 1939.

Carson, D.A. *How Long, O Lord? Reflections on Suffering and Evil*. Grand Rapids: Baker, 1990.

Castell, A. *The Self in Philosophy*. New York: Macmillan, 1957.

Clark, David K. "Interpreting the Biblical Words for the Self." *Journal of Psychology and Theology* 18, no. 4 (1990): 309–17.

Crabb, Larry. *Inside Out*. Colorado Springs: NavPress, 1988.

Crockenberg, Susan B. and Barbara Soby, "Self-Esteem and Teenage Pregnancy." In *The Social Importance of Self-Esteem*, edited by Neil J. Smelser, et al. San Francisco: Univ. of California Press, 1989.

D

David, Stephen T., ed. *Encountering Evil: Live Options in Theodicy*. Atlanta: John Knox, 1981.

Dillard, Annie. *An American Childhood*. San Francisco: Harper and Row, 1987.

Dostoyevsky, Fyodor. *The Brothers Karamazov.* New York: Random House, 1950.

Dutton, Mary Ann. *Empowering and Healing the Battered Woman: A Model for Assesssment and Intervention.* New York: Spring, 1992.

Dykstra, Craig. "Family Promises: Faith and Families in the Context of the Church." In *Faith in Families,* edited by Lindell Sawyers. Philadelphia: Geneva, 1986.

E
Eichrodt, Walther. *Theology of the Old Testament.* Philadelphia: Westminster, 1975.

Ellison, Craig. *Your Better Self: Christianity, Psychology, and Self-Esteem.* New York: Harper and Row, 1983.

Enroth, Ronald. *Recovering from Churches That Abuse.* Grand Rapids: Zondervan, 1994.

Erikson, Erik. *Childhood and Society.* 1950. Reprint. New York: Norton, 1963.

_____. *Identity and the Life Cycle.* New York: International Universities Press, 1959.

_____. *Identity, Youth and Crisis.* New York: W.W. Norton, 1968.

_____. *The Life Cycle Completed: A Review.* New York: W.W. Norton, 1982.

Evans, C.S. "Self." In *Baker Encyclopedia of Psychology,* Edited by David G. Benner. Grand Rapids: Baker, 1985.

Evans, C. Stephen. *Wisdom and Humanness in Psychology: Prospects for a Christian Approach.* Grand Rapids: Baker, 1989.

F

Flanigan, Beverly. *Forgiving the Unforgivable*. New York Macmillan, 1992.

Fowler, James. *Stages of Faith*. San Francisco: Harper and Row, 1981.

Fry, Christopher. *The Boy with a Cart*. New York: Oxford Univ. Press, 1939.

G

Gelles, Richard J., and Claire Pedrick Cornell. *Intimate Violence in Families — Family Study Series, #2*. Newbury Park, Calif.: Sage, 1985.

Gelles, Richard J., and Murray A. Straus. *Intimate Violence: The Causes and Consequences of Abuse in the American Family*. New York: Simon and Schuster/Touchstone, 1988.

Gerkin, Charles V. *The Living Human Document: Revisioning Pastoral Counseling in a Hermeneutical Mode*. Nashville Abingdon, 1984.

Gilligan, Carol. *In a Different Voice: Psychological Theory and Women's Development*. Cambridge: Harvard Univ. Press, 1982

Gorman, M. "The Self." In *New Catholic Encyclopedia*. Vol. 13 San Francisco: Catholic Univ. of America, 1967.

Griffin, David Ray. *God, Power, and Evil: A Process Theodicy*. Philadelphia: Westminster, 1976.

Guntrip, H. *Psychoanalytic Theory, Therapy, and the Self*. New York: Basic Books, 1971.

H

Hart, Archibald. *Me, Myself and I: How Far Should We Go in Our Search for Self-Fulfillment?* Ann Arbor, Mich.: Servant, 1992.

_____. *Unlocking the Mystery of Your Emotions.* Dallas: Word, 1989.

Herman, Judith Lewis, M.D. *Trauma and Recovery: The Aftermath of Violence — From Domestic Abuse to Political Terror.* New York: Basic Books, 1992.

Heschel, Abraham J. *The Prophets.* Vol. 2. New York: Harper and Row, 1962.

Hick, John. *Evil and the God of Love.* London: Macmillan, 1966.

J

James, William. *Principles of Psychology.* Vol. 1. New York: Holt, 1890.

_____. *The Varieties of Religious Experience.* Cited in *Drawing on the Right Side of the Brain,* by Betty Edwards. Los Angeles: J.P. Tarcher, 1979.

K

Karen, Robert. "Shame." *The Atlantic Monthly,* February 1992, 40–70.

Kierkegaard, Sören. *The Concept of Dread.* Translated by Walter Lowrie. Princeton: Princeton Univ. Press, 1944.

_____. *Sickness Unto Death.* London: Oxford Univ. Press, 1941.

Kohlberg, Lawrence. "Continuities and Discontinuities in Childhood and Adult Moral Development Revisited." In *Life-Span Development Psychology: Research and Theory.* Edited by Paul B. Baltes and K. Warner Schaie. New York: Academic, 1973.

Kraus, C. Norman. *Jesus Christ Our Lord: Christology from a Disciple's Perspective.* Scottdale, Pa.: Herald, 1987.

Kushner, Harold S. *When Bad Things Happen to Good People.* New York: Avon, 1981.

L

Lake, Frank. *Clinical Theology: A Theological and Psychological Basis to Clinical Pastoral Care.* New York: Crossroads, 1987.

Lee, Benjamin, ed. *Psychological Theories of the Self.* New York and London: Plenum, 1982.

Lee, Bernard, S.M. *The Becoming of the Church: A Process Theology of the Structure of Christian Experience.* New York: Paulist, 1974.

Lee, Cameron. "The Good Enough Family." *Journal of Psychology and Theology* 13, no. 3 (1985): 182–89.

Leehan, James. *Pastoral Care for Survivors of Family Abuse.* Louisville: Westminster/John Knox, 1989.

Levang, Curtis. *The Adam and Eve Complex: Freedom from the Shame That Can Separate You from God, Others, and Yourself.* Minneapolis: SelfCare, 1992.

Lewis, C.S. *A Grief Observed.* London: Faber and Faber, 1961.

Lindbergh, Anne Morrow. *The Unicorn.* New York: Pantheon, 1956.

Lowrie, Walter. *A Short Life of Kierkegaard.* Princeton: Princeton Univ. Press, 1951.

M

Macmurray, John. *Persons in Relation.* London: Faber and Faber, 1961.

_____. *Reason and Emotion.* London: Faber and Faber, 1935.

_____. *The Self as Agent.* London: Faber and Faber, 1957.

Matzat, Donald. *Christ Esteem: Where the Search for Self-Esteem Ends.* Eugene, Ore.: Harvest House, 1990.

McFadyen, A.I. *The Call to Personhood: A Christian Theory of the Individual in Social Relationships.* Cambridge: Cambridge Univ. Press, 1990.

McGill, Arthur C. *Suffering: A Test of Theological Method.* Philadelphia: Westminster, 1982.

Meissner, William. *Life and Faith: Psychological Perspectives on Religious Experience.* Washington, D.C.: Georgetown Univ. Press, 1987.

Miller, Arthur. *After the Fall.* In *Arthur Miller's Collected Plays,* vol. 2. New York: Viking, 1987.

_____. *Death of a Salesman.* In *Arthur Miller's Collected Plays,* vol. 1. New York: Viking, 1987.

Moltmann, Jürgen. *The Crucified God: The Cross of Christ as the Foundation and Criticism of Christian Theology.* Translated by R.A. Wilson and John Bowden. New York: Harper and Row, 1974.

_____. *Experiences of God.* Translated by Margaret Kohl. Philadelphia: Fortress, 1980.

_____. *God and Creation.* San Francisco: Harper and Row, 1985.

Montieth, Graham. "Too Many Awkward Questions — Too Many Glib Answers." *New College Bulletin.* Edinburgh, Scotland: University of Edinburgh, 1981.

Moseley, Romney. *Becoming a Self: Critical Transformations before God.* Nashville: Abingdon, 1991.

O

Oden, Thomas. *The Living God: Systematic Theology, Vol. 1.* San Francisco: Harper and Row, 1987.

P

Pannenberg, Wolfhart. *Anthropology in Theological Perspective.* Philadelphia: Westminster, 1985.

_____. *Christian Spirituality and Sacramental Community.* London: Darton, Longman and Todd, 1983.

Pedersen, John. *Israel: Its Life and Culture.* Vol 1. London Oxford Univ. Press, 1973.

Piaget, Jean. *Six Psychological Studies.* New York: Random House/Vintage, 1967.

Polanyi, Michael. *The Tacit Dimension.* London: Routledge and Kegan Paul, 1967.

Puryear, Douglas A. *Helping People in Crisis.* San Francisco: Jossey-Bass, 1979.

R

Rogers, Carl. *On Becoming a Person.* Boston: Houghton Mifflin, 1961.

Ryan, Dale and Juanita. *Life Recovery Guides.* Downers Grove, Ill.: InterVarsity, 1990.

S

Schaffer, Peter. *Equus.* New York: Avon, 1974.

Schilling, S. Paul. *God and Human Anguish.* Nashville: Abingdon, 1977.

Schuller, Robert. *Self-Esteem: The New Reformation.* Dallas: Word, 1982.

Shibles, Warren. *Emotion: The Method of Philosophical Therapy.* Whitewater, Wis.: Language, 1974.

Skinner, B.F. *Science and Human Behavior.* New York: Macmillan, 1953.

Smedes, Lewis B. *Shame and Grace: Healing the Shame We Don't Deserve.* San Francisco: Harper San Francisco, 1993.

Smelser, Neil J. "Self-Esteem and Social Problems: An Introduction." In *The Social Importance of Self-Esteem,* edited by Neil J. Smelser et al. San Francisco: Univ. of California Press, 1989.

Smolowe, Jill. "What the Doctor Should Do." *Time,* 29 June 1992.

Sonkin, Daniel J. *Learning to Live without Violence: A Handbook for Men.* Volcano, Calif.: Volcano Press, 1989.

Sontag, Frederick. *The God of Evil.* San Francisco: Harper and Row, 1970.

Suls, Jerry M., ed. *Psychological Perspectives on the Self.* Vol. 1. Hillsdale, N.J.: Lawrence Erlbaum, 1982.

Switzer, David K. *The Minister as Crisis Counselor.* Nashville: Abingdon, 1974.

T

Thielicke, Helmut. *Theological Ethics.* Vol. 1. Grand Rapids: Eerdmans, 1984.

Tillich, Paul. *The Courage to Be.* London: Collins, 1962.

Timmer, John. *God of Weakness.* Grand Rapids: Zondervan, 1988.

Towner, W. Sibley. *How God Deals with Evil.* Philadelphia: Westminster, 1976.

V

Vander Goot, Mary. *Healthy Emotions: Helping Children Grow.* Grand Rapids: Baker, 1987.

Vieth, F. Richard. *Holy Power, Human Pain.* Bloomington, Ind.: Meyer-Stone, 1988.

W

Walker, Lenore E. *The Battered Woman Syndrome.* New York: Spring, 1992.

Walsh, P.G. *Divine Providence and Human Suffering: Message of the Fathers of the Church.* Wilmington, Del.: Michael Glazier, 1985.

Whitehead, Alfred North. *Process and Reality: An Essay in Cosmology.* New York: Macmillan, 1929.

Wolff, H.W. *Anthropology in the Old Testament.* Translated by Margaret Kohl. 1974. Reprint. Philadelphia: Fortress, 1981.

Y

Young, Peter M. "The Ontological Self in the Thinking of C. Stephen Evans and Ray S. Anderson: Towards an Integration of the Individual and Social Aspects of Personhood." Ph.D. diss., Fuller Theological Seminary, School of Psychology, 1992.

INDEX

healing of 84
Miller, Arthur 115, 217, 248, 256
Moltmann, Jürgen 46, 114, 189, 244, 249, 253
Monteith, Graham 193–94, 254
Moral outrage 124–25, 131, 135–36, 138, 154, 172
Moseley, Romney 29, 243
Moses 19–20
Motives 82–83, 89

N
Nathan 228
Nietzsche 112

O
Oden, Thomas 55, 243
Overcoming 223ff, 232–33

P
Pain 30–31, 52, 66–67, 135–36, 198, 211, 225
    emotional 232–33
    shared 178
Pannenberg, Wolfhart 56, 67, 73, 112–15, 244–45, 249
Pascal 86
Paul 19, 39, 41–43, 45, 49, 51, 74, 91, 99, 105–6, 109, 113, 136, 162, 193, 234–35, 238
Pedersen, John 71, 81, 83, 106, 245–47, 249
Peter 108
Peterson, Scott R. 248
Piaget, Jean 29, 242
Piety, penitential 112, 115
Polanyi, Michael 253

Power, spiritual 200–201
Primitive moral instinct 41, 126, 139, 172
Process theology 191–92
Promise, broken 173, 179, 209–10
    shared 178, 221
Puryear, Douglas A. 254

R
Reason, and emotion 71–72, 87–88
Rebecca 225
Recovery, phases of 214–15
Redemption 109
Regina, Ara 155–56
Repentance 91, 113, 172
Rogers, Carl 16, 241

S
Satan 170
Schaie, K. Warner 251
Schilling, S. Paul 254
Schuller, Robert 113, 249
Self, as agent 25, 81
    annihilation of 19, 111, 114
    assertion vs. submission 107ff
    biblical view of 17ff, 77
    center of 77
    concept of 15ff
    core self 32
    development of 29–30, 210
    ego self 30, 40
    essential self 24
    existential reality of 207–8
    functional self 24
    growth of 28–29, 235ff